ESSAYS IN THE ECONOMICS
OF RENEWABLE RESOURCES

CONTRIBUTIONS TO ECONOMIC ANALYSIS

143

Honorary Editor
J. TINBERGEN

Editors
D. W. JORGENSON
J. WAELBROECK

NORTH-HOLLAND PUBLISHING COMPANY
AMSTERDAM · NEW YORK · OXFORD

ESSAYS IN THE ECONOMICS
OF
RENEWABLE RESOURCES

Edited by

LEONARD J. MIRMAN
University of Illinois

and

DANIEL F. SPULBER
University of Southern California

1982

NORTH-HOLLAND PUBLISHING COMPANY
AMSTERDAM · NEW YORK · OXFORD

ISBN 0 444 86340 0

Publishers:

NORTH-HOLLAND PUBLISHING COMPANY
AMSTERDAM · NEW YORK · OXFORD

Sole distributors for the U.S.A. and Canada:

ELSEVIER SCIENCE PUBLISHING COMPANY, INC.
52 VANDERBILT AVENUE
NEW YORK, N.Y. 10017

Library of Congress Cataloging in Publication Data

Main entry under title:

Essays in the economics of renewable resources.

    (Contributions to economic analysis ; 143)
    Includes index.
    1. Fisheries--Economic aspects--Mathematical models. 2. Renewable natural resources--Economic aspects--Mathematical models. 3. Fishery management--Mathematical models. 4. Operations research. I. Mirman, Leonard J. II. Spulber, Daniel F. III. Series.
SH334.E8   333.95'6   81-22526
ISBN 0-444-86340-0 (U.S.)   AACR2

PRINTED IN THE NETHERLANDS

Introduction to the series

This series consists of a number of hitherto unpublished studies, which are introduced by the editors in the belief that they represent fresh contributions to economic science.

The term ''economic analysis'' as used in the title of the series has been adopted because it covers both the activities of the theoretical economist and the research worker.

Although the analytical methods used by the various contributors are not the same, they are nevertheless conditioned by the common origin of their studies, namely theoretical problems encountered in practical research. Since for this reason, business cycle research and national accounting, research work on behalf of economic policy, and problems of planning are the main sources of the subjects dealt with, they necessarily determine the manner of approach adopted by the authors. Their methods tend to be "practical" in the sense of not being too far remote from application to actual economic conditions. In addition they are quantitative rather than qualitative.

It is the hope of the editors that the publication of these studies will help to stimulate the exchange of scientific information and to reinforce international cooperation in the field of economics.

The Editors

To Barbara and Sue

Contents

Preface and acknowledgements

With the extension of national coastal boundaries and with international competition and negotiation regarding fishing rights, increased attention has focused upon the study of optimal use and management of fisheries resources. The many alternative uses of such renewable resources as ocean and fresh-water fish, whales, antarctic krill and game animals for food, commercial products, recreational harvesting, or as environmental amenities, has raised new questions regarding the allocation of these resources over time by competitive markets or by markets subject to government regulation. The importance of renewable resources as integral parts of complex ecosystems has been emphasized as a number of species have been threatened with extinction.

Increased interest in renewable resource management has been accompanied by important developments in the economics of renewable resources. This volume presents fifteen essays which explore and extend theoretical aspects of these developments. The volume begins with a selective survey of these developments and suggestions for future research. The modelling of renewable resource management within a capital-theoretic framework and the resulting optimal harvesting policies are then examined. Resource management in the presence of biological and technical nonconvexities and subject to environmental uncertainty is considered in detail. The problems of free and restricted access to renewable resource stocks are analyzed within the framework of industry structure, conduct and performance. Emphasis is also placed upon the question of strategic interfirm competition for resources within a game-theoretic framework. The volume concludes with an examination of alternative regulatory policies.

The book is intended for use by all those who are interested in renewable resources and in particular for students of fisheries economics whether they are fisheries managers, regulatory authorities, graduate students or researchers in the field. The volume could serve as an advanced introduction to fisheries economies or as an accompanying readings text which supplements and extends a textbook such as Colin Clark's excellent book, *Mathematical Bioeconomics: The Optimal Management of Renewable Resources*.

The volume is the outcome of a conference entitled ''The Economics of Renewable Resource Management'', presented at Brown University, 19 and

20 October 1979. The conference received the support of the National Science Foundation and Brown University. Most of the essays in the volume are papers presented at the conference and written for the volume. The final form of the essays reflects the lively and interesting discussion which took place at the conference. A number of essays, although not presented at the conference, were prepared especially for the volume. These are: ''A Selective Survey'' by Daniel Spulber, ''Optimal Use of Renewable Resources with Nonconvexities in Production'' by Tracy Lewis and Richard Schmalensee, and ''Dynamic Programming Models of Fishing: Monopoly'', by David Levhari, Ron Michener and Leonard Mirman.

Two papers have been previously published and are included here for completeness of treatment of particular topics. The paper by Colin Clark and Gordon Munro, ''The Economics of Fishing and Modern Capital Theory: A Simplified Approach'', is an extended version of a paper which appeared in the December 1975 issue of the *Journal of Environmental Economics and Management*. We thank that journal and the Academic Press for permission to print the paper. We also thank *The Bell Journal of Economics* for permission to reprint ''The Great Fish War'' by David Levhari and Leonard Mirman.

We wish to take this opportunity to thank the conference participants for their help in organizing a successful and stimulating conference. We also thank all of the contributors to the volume for their excellent papers and for making the difficult task of editing the volume into a pleasant and enjoyable experience. We also express our thanks to Professor Harl Ryder, Chairman of the Brown Economics Department and to Professor George Borts for their help and advice in the planning of the conference. Finally, we thank the Institute for Marine and Coastal Studies at the University of Southern California for help in preparing the conference volume.

The editors wish to thank the National Science Foundation for its support of the conference under grant number SES 79-14386, principal investigator Daniel Spulber. We are also grateful for the support of Brown University and for the use of the excellent facilities of the Brown University campus.

We would especially like to thank Marion Wathey for expert typing and valuable assistance in the preparation of the final manuscript of the conference volume. Marie Ferri deserves special thanks for her assistance in handling the administrative aspects involved in hosting the conference. Finally, we also thank John McLaughry, former Director of Brown Special Programs, for assistance in conference preparations.

List of contributors

Lee G. ANDERSON
College of Marine Studies
Department of Economics
University of Delaware

Colin W. CLARK
Department of Mathematics
University of British Columbia

John M. HARTWICK
Department of Economics
Queen's University

David LEVHARI
Department of Economics
The Hebrew University

Tracy R. LEWIS
Department of Economics
University of British Columbia

Mukul MAJUMDAR
Department of Economics
Cornell University

Kenneth E. McCONNELL
Department of Agricultural Economics
University of Maryland

Ron MICHENER
Department of Economics
University of Virginia

Leonard J. MIRMAN
Department of Economics
University of Illinois

Gordon R. MUNRO
Department of Economics
University of British Columbia

Philip NEHER
Department of Economics
University of British Columbia

Richard SCHMALENSEE
Sloan School of Management
Massachusetts Institute of Technology

Matthew J. SOBEL
College of Industrial Management
Georgia Institute of Technology

Daniel F. SPULBER
Department of Economics and
Institute for Marine and Coastal Studies
University of Southern California

Jon G. SUTINEN
Department of Resource Economics
University of Rhode Island

PART I

INTRODUCTION

CHAPTER 1

A selective survey

DANIEL F. SPULBER

1. Introduction

This volume presents essays on a number of significant theoretical developments in the economics of renewable resources. This introduction selectively surveys the background literature related to these developments and also discusses the contributions made by the papers in this volume. In addition, a number of important gaps in the existing literature are examined and suggestions for future research are outlined. The areas surveyed are (i) the relation between capital theory and optimal resource management, (ii) resource use in the presence of biological and technical nonconvexities, (iii) the optimal harvesting of renewable resources under uncertainty, (iv) industry structure and resource use, (v) game theory and interfirm competition for resources, and (vi) regulation of the fishery. The areas correspond to Parts II–VII in the volume.

The essays in the volume are intended to increase our understanding of the traditional questions of resource economics. Given consumer preferences, how are the services of the renewable resource stocks to be valued over time? Given the technology of resource extraction and the biological characteristics of the resources, how is production of the resource services to be carried on efficiently? Given the valuation of the resources over time and efficient production, what is the optimal economic allocation of the resources over time? How will the resource be harvested if it is freely accessible to competitive firms? How is access best controlled and how is harvesting best regulated? Finally, will a particular resource be viable under

Essays in the economics of renewable resources, edited by L.J. Mirman and D.F. Spulber
© *North-Holland Publishing Company, 1982*

optimal harvesting, under free access and under alternative regulatory policies?

The discussions of capital theory, nonconvexities and uncertainty as presented here address the problem of optimal harvesting over time. The discussions of industry structure and game theory address the problem of understanding firm behavior in free-access and regulated fisheries. These developments in renewable resource economics have implications for the design of public policy in renewable resource management.

In an area with as large a literature as resource economics, it is important to outline the limits of the scope of the volume. This volume concentrates upon theoretical fisheries models and does not consider the important empirical aspects of resource economics. The models are primarily of the lumped-parameter fishery. Age-structured population models, essential for some species of fish and for forestry problems, are not considered, although attention is paid to multi-species harvesting. An ecologist, Michael Goulding (1980) has examined interdependencies between over two hundred fish and tree species in the Amazon River basin, involving some species which are commercially harvested. The optimal harvesting of interdependent age-structured and lumped-parameter populations is certainly a topic for future research in renewable resource economics.

2. Capital theory, nonconvexities and resource management

2.1. Capital theory and renewable resources

The application of capital theory to the study of renewable resources, particularly to fisheries, has served to place fisheries economics in the proper dynamic context and has allowed the solution of complex models of harvest planning. The fisheries manager faces a tradeoff between the value of consumption of fish in the present and the discounted value of future consumption of the increase in the fish stock which will result from growth and reduced harvesting in the present period. In this sense, the fish stock is simply a special type of capital asset. The study of renewable resources, however, places very particular restrictions upon the capital theory model which distinguish the fish stock that is managed by a firm from various forms of plant and equipment which a firm may invest in. This section emphasizes these special restrictions and considers the different economic questions which may arise in renewable resource management.

For a decision-maker whose objective function is utility of a consumption stream over time, the renewable resource problem with zero harvesting costs is identical to the planner's problem in the literature on optimal economic growth. Indeed, renewable resources such as fish or game animals provide excellent examples of the composite commodity, which can be either consumed or invested, that is present in optimal growth models. When there are a number of renewable resources which interact, as in the multi-species fishery, the interconnected resource growth functions appear similar to a multi-sectoral growth model. The similarity of the biological resource growth function to an industry or aggregate production function should not be overemphasized, however. An important difference appears when nonresource inputs are present. For an ocean fishery, the biological growth function cannot be augmented or altered by the introduction of other inputs such as machines and labor. While a hatchery can affect fish growth by inputs of food, labor, energy and various types of equipment, this type of management is not possible for ocean and stream fish and game animals in their natural environment. Given the characteristics of the ecological niche, the maximum sustainable population or environmental carrying capacity are not subject to control by the decision-maker. In consequence, the investment good is the resource itself. Other inputs, such as labor and capital equipment, cannot be used to augment investment in the renewable resource. The investment or parent stock is constrained to be the escapement, that which is not harvested. A further consequence of the nature of a renewable resource is that unlike capital equipment, investment in the renewable resource stock can never be assumed to be irreversible since the stock itself must be directly consumed.

It is not necessarily correct to find differences in the objective functions in the capital and resource problem. The economic planner in a growth problem and in a resource problem both maximize a social welfare function. A firm planning capital investment and a firm managing a fishery both maximize the present discounted value of profits. The differences lie in the technological restrictions inherent in the resource problem. Some of these restrictions were mentioned above. The principal technological difference is that for a firm managing a renewable resource, inputs such as labor, boats, nets and fuel are devoted to the harvesting of the resource and not to its production. These technological assumptions will affect the reduced forms of the cost and production functions. This is significant since nonconvexities may be inherent in both the biological growth function and harvesting cost function. These will be discussed below.

In Chapter 2, "The Economics of Fishing and Modern Capital Theory: A Simplified Approach", Clark and Munro present an extended survey and synthesis of the capital-theoretic treatment of the problem of fisheries management. The analysis begins with a Cobb–Douglas yield–effect relation which is dependent upon the stock being harvested, a linear effort cost function and a strictly concave growth function. A competitive firm, assumed to be a sole owner, maximizes the present discounted value of rent from fishing. This implies that the objective function is linear in harvesting. The resulting linear optimal control problem allows an extensive analysis of the results obtained by applying capital theory to resource management. The model is used to obtain a modified golden-rule equilibrium at which the own rate of return to the resource equals the discount rate. The decision to deplete the stock below maximum sustainable yield is shown to depend on the relative size of the discount rate and the marginal stock effect. A pulse-fishing or "bank-bang" harvesting rule is obtained as a consequence of the linearity restrictions. The chapter then relaxes the assumptions of linearity and autonomy (stationarity) in turn. First, price and harvesting costs are assumed to be functions of time whose time paths are known. A nonliner, autonomous model is then considered where the fisheries manager maximizes utility of harvesting net of a nonlinear, stock-dependent harvesting cost function.

As noted above, the renewable resource problem imposes special restrictions which differ from those of capital theory. The questions posed in fisheries economics may also differ. The question of the potential exhaustion of a renewable resource becomes particularly significant if the resource stock itself provides a flow of benefits other than those obtained through its direct depletion. The depletion of a species of fish or an aquatic animal while possibly desirable from the point of view of the own rate of return from harvesting may be undesirable if there are extensive ecological impacts such as on the predators and prey of the species, if there is scientific interest in the species or simply if knowledge that the species exists yields utility as an environmental amenity. This is certainly true for whales. In Chapter 3, "Consistent and Revised Plans for Natural Resource Use", Lewis and Neher note that a forest may provide aesthetic and recreational benefits in addition to the value of the harvested wood. The objective function in fisheries management problems is frequently stock-dependent since yield–effort relations are usually affected by the size of the fish stock. Lewis and Neher include nondepleting services from the stock as part of the stock's total flow of net benefits and consider the renewable resource to be a public good which should be publicly managed. Lewis and Neher examine the allocation of resources over time which results from following a finite horizon but continuously revised harvesting plan. They then investigate whether an infinite horizon "phantom plan" exists which would result in the same intertemporal allocation. Lewis and Neher show that for a large class of renewable resource models the continuously revised plans can be replicated by a phantom plan through a manipulation of the rate of time discount and by a positive transform of the utility functional. The analysis of Lewis and Neher has a number of interesting policy implications regarding social planning for renewable resource management. The social planner following a continuously revised plan or an equivalent phantom plan is seen to be more "egalitarian" with respect to intergenerational equity.

The analysis of Lewis and Neher raises the important question of how to model social planning for renewable resource management. The general properties of finite-horizon rolling plans are analyzed by Easley and Spulber (1981) who demonstrate that rolling plans are ε-optimal for an appropriately chosen time horizon. The analysis allows uncertainty with regard to the reward function and the constraint correspondence. The general planning framework of Easley and Spulber could be applied to the problem of renewable resource planning under uncertainty. Of particular interest is the demonstration of convergence of shadow prices, as the planning horizon is lengthened, to the optimal infinite horizon shadow price. This suggests that shadow price rules which underlie regulatory instruments could be approximately optimal for a finite planning horizon. Finite horizon plans may be easier to calculate and may, therefore, be useful guides for renewable resource management.

2.2. Nonconvexities and renewable resources

The literature on the optimal management of a renewable resource when nonconvexities are present in the benefit, cost and production functions is surveyed and extended in two papers in this volume. Levhari, Michener and Mirman in "Nonconcave Dynamic Programming: An Example" focus primarily on nonconvexities in the biological growth function. These nonconvexities occur in the form of a convex growth relation for population levels below some critical size and a concave growth relation for populations above that critical size. The growth relation implies that the long-run population size (with and without harvesting) is dependent upon initial population size. The optimal population dynamics are examined in a discrete time framework and are shown to depend upon the discount factor and marginal growth rate when the utility function is linear.

Lewis and Schmalensee in "Optimal Use of Renewable Resources with Nonconvexities in Production", review and synthesize their previous work (Lewis and Schmalensee, 1975, 1977, 1979) as well as the contributions of Majumdar and Mitra (1980a,b) and present new results on chattering controls. Their analysis is carried out primarily in continuous time, although discrete time results are also discussed. They consider three types of nonconvexities. First, the biological growth relation may not be convex due to a positive minimum viable population size or due to increasing returns to reproduction at small population sizes. These possibilities are also examined by Levhari, Michener and Mirman. Secondly, the benefit function may exhibit nonconvexities due to positive fixed harvesting costs or due to nonconvexities in the yield–effort relation. Thirdly, a positive re-entry cost introduces nonconvexities and must be paid repeatedly if chattering controls are to be used. The types of nonconvexities which are present will determine the choice of an optimal policy from a wide range of policy types: depletion of the resource, chattering controls and continuous harvesting.

In Spulber's chapter in this volume nonconvexities in the form of fixed costs appear in a model with environmental uncertainty. The pulse-fishing property is seen to hold in a model with environmental randomness. Fixed costs are shown to drive a wedge between the optimal escapement level and the critical size needed for harvesting.

3. Uncertainty

Although fisheries face significant variability in stocks and yields, this aspect has often been neglected by fisheries economists. A 1975 survey article by Butlin finds that the development of stochastic models is "a major gap in the literature on the fishery" (p. 99). A number of more recent papers which introduce uncertainty into harvesting problems are surveyed here. The essays in this volume concerned with uncertainty are then briefly discussed. It is argued that they represent a number of advances over the existing literature.

The types of uncertainty relevant to renewable resource economics can be grouped under two broad categories: (a) uncertainty with regard to the *current state* of the system, and (b) uncertainty with regard to the *law of motion* of the system.

3.1. Uncertainty regarding the state

The complexity of the uncertainty with regard to the current state of the resource depends on the complexity of the description of the fish stock. There may be uncertainty concerning the total biomass, the location of the fish, and the age, weight and sex composition of the stock. These factors make it difficult to select the appropriate level of fishing effort and the optimal escapement level. This complicates the choices of the individual fisherman. Individual fishermen may face additional uncertainty regarding the form of the yield–effort relation as well as uncertainty regarding the catch of competing fishermen. From the point of view of a regulator, such choices as maximum catch levels are complicated by verifying the fish stock currently present within his jurisdiction.

Measurement of the current stock presents significant difficulties for ocean fisheries. Doubleday (1979) notes significant error in estimates from trawl surveys, cohort analysis and recruitment forecasts from young fish surveys. The chapter by Majumdar in this volume presents a general theoretical treatment of the difficult problem of learning and optimal decision-making when there is imperfect knowledge concerning the state of the system. This may be applied to renewable resource harvesting when imperfect signals are received in each period concerning the characteristics of the resource stock.

3.2. Uncertainty regarding the law of motion

Even if a complete description of the current stock may be obtained by sonar or by inference from data on catches and effort, a more fundamental uncertainty remains concerning tomorrow's stock. The uncertainty concerning tomorrow's stock may be classified according to whether it is due to (i) random environmental disturbances whose objective probabilities are known, or to (ii) lack of information concerning the form of the transition equation. In the second case, the decision-maker may hold subjective beliefs concerning the form of a probability distribution over alternative forms of the stock–recruitment relation. These two cases provide a convenient classification of the literature.

(i) Random environmental disturbances may be quite complex and involve variability in climate, currents, water temperature and available food supply. In addition, there is random interaction with predators and competing species. Finally, separating out the effects of several year classes may not be possible due to autocorrelation (Doubleday, 1979).

Most treatments of uncertainty have represented environmental disturbances by introducing a random parameter into a simple biomass dependent stock–recruitment relation. Simple pulse-fishing rules are obtained for discrete-time lumped-parameter models by Jaquette (1974, 1972a, b) and Reed (1974). Gleit (1978) examines a simple continuous-time stochastic control problem. Mann (1970) takes into account the number of members of each sex in the population for harvesting and population growth, and considers a vector of random growth parameters. Beddington and May (1977) posit a stochastic (logistic) growth function and examine the characteristic return time for the system to recover from a disturbance. Thompson et al. (1973) analyze uncertainty from the point of view of the individual firm in the case of the shrimp fishery. See May et al. (1978) for extensive reference to papers on uncertainty within the specialized fisheries literature. May et al. (1978) examine the effects of a maximum sustained yield policy for a number of alternative stochastic recruitment models. Finally, Mendelssohn (1978, 1980) examines optimal harvesting strategies for stochastic single-species, multi-age class models and for stochastic multi-species models.

While these papers have focused on optimal harvesting strategies, what is more interesting is the long-run equilibrium of the system. The paper of Spulber (this volume) presents the stochastic analogue to the deterministic optimal sustained yield. The long-run equilibrium of the system is the *time-invariant probability distribution on the harvest levels when the resource is harvested so as to maximize expected present discounted value*. This equilibrium distribution is characterized by means of an example which allows determination of the effects of environmental randomness and other parameters on the shape of the distribution. The analysis also yields a steady-state probability distribution on stock levels. The steady-state probability distribution on stock levels for *unharvested* natural populations has been examined extensively in the mathematical ecology literature. May (1974, p. 110) observes that, in randomly fluctuating natural environments, "[The] equilibrium probability distribution is to the stochastic environment as the stable equilibrium point is to the deterministic one." The concept of an equilibrium probability distribution on stock levels has appeared in the stochastic capital theory literature (see especially Mirman, 1972, 1973, and Brock and Mirman, 1972).

(ii) The decision-maker may not know the shape of the population growth function. The presence of environmental randomness complicates any attempt to estimate the unknown parameters of the growth function. A dynamic harvesting model must include a Bayesian mechanism for revision of expectations concerning the form of the population growth function. The size of the escapement will affect future information which will then affect future decisions. For this reason the dynamics of learning and population growth have a strong effect on current harvesting decisions. The analysis of dynamic decision-making with a partially observable state space by Majumdar can be used to analyze a problem where parameters of the growth function are part of the state space.

More research is needed on Bayesian learning and fishing with reference to biological growth functions. May et al. (1978) examine eight stock–recuitment relations for the effect of sustained yield harvesting on the natural populations. They suggest (p. 244) that "the designated harvesting strategy should possess features that allow for errors in parameter estimates... or for plain paucity of data". The models of fishing under uncertainty in this volume are an initial step in this direction.

4. Market structure

Owing to the depletable nature of fishery resources, the market structure of a particular fishery has a significant impact upon the conduct and performance of commercial fishing firms. The harvest rate and viability of the industry will depend upon the number and size of firms and entry possibilities as well as on the types of property rights to resources which are present. This section examines the effects of various types of industry structure beginning with the situation in which access to the fishery is not restricted. The case of sole ownership is considered when there is monopoly in the harvesting sector as well as when bilateral monopoly exists in both the harvesting and processing sectors. A generalization of firm conduct is made to the case of the multi-species fishery. Finally, the organization of the fishery is examined for the recreational fishery.

4.1. Free access and externalities

Competitive markets cannot achieve efficient allocation of scarce resources without the possibility of exclusion and clearly defined property rights. For many renewable resources, access is free resulting in stock externalities and other external diseconomies. The inefficient use of freely available but limited resources has a long history, from excessive hunting of North American mammals during the Pleistocene period (see Smith, 1975, 1969) to overgrazing of cattle on common pasture in post-medieval England (see Gonner, 1966; Slater, 1932, p. 117; and Coleman, 1977, p. 40). As Gonner notes (1966, p. 25): "As many beasts are put on the common as possible... with the result that the common is overstocked."

An early "congestion externality" seems to be observed by Coleman (1977, p. 40) who notes hardship resulting from "the pasturing on the commons of large numbers of cattle or sheep, by bigger farmers, thus making life more difficult for the smaller husbandman". Gordon (1954) in his classic paper notes the analogous possibilities for overexploitation of pasture land, ocean fisheries, hunting grounds and oil reserves when these resources are held in common, and where access is not controlled. Externalities related to exploration as well as stock effects are present in the extraction of petroleum and mineral resources. Finally, the process of excessive air and water pollution may result from free access to the environment.

The free-access problem, as it applies to commercial ocean fisheries, is best analyzed, I believe, within the *structure – conduct – performance* framework of industrial organization. This framework is useful for analyzing the economic literature on the free-access fishery and in addition raises a number of unanswered questions. The degree to which the ocean fishery is exploited depends crucially upon industry *structure*. Industry structure in commercial fishing refers to the number of fleets harvesting a particular species and the number and the size of the boats within each fleet. In addition, it must be determined whether the number of firms harvesting from the fishery is fixed or whether entry is instantaneous or whether lagged entry occurs due to various costs of adjustment and the existence of entry barriers. Since firms harvesting from independent fisheries may compete in the market place, the relevant concentration is also an important aspect of market structure for analyzing ocean fisheries. The number and size of firms operating within a fishery will depend primarily upon the cost structures for fleets and individual vessels, so that an analysis of firm costs is essential to a determination of the effects of free access.

The consequences of free access depend also upon firm *conduct*. With instantaneous entry, firm planning will be myopic. In lagged entry models, firms may make dynamic harvesting plans, although firm behavior is generally modelled as an ad hoc function of fishery rents. Finally, with a fixed number of firms, dynamic strategies may be followed. In a broader sense, firm conduct in ocean fisheries involves not only choosing the harvest size, but also the choice of the species to be harvested, the length of time of harvest, and the choice of mesh size and other actions affecting the age structure of the fish population. In addition, the level of firm investment in fishing equipment and vessels will affect harvest sizes.

Given industry structure, firm conduct and a description of the biological characteristics of the fish stock, we may predict and evaluate the *performance* of the fishing industry in terms of its dynamic allocative efficiency. Of particular interest are the questions of whether the fishery will be overharvested, and whether there can be an equilibrium in terms of the number of firms and annual harvest which does not exhaust the fish stock.

We turn now to a brief survey of the free-access literature within the structure–conduct–performance framework. The firm's costs in the free-access fishery may be classified into these categories: harvesting costs, costs resulting from congestion and other external effects, and entry costs. These costs are elements of market structure in the free-access fishery. Scott (1955, p. 120) was the first to introduce increasing costs to the fishery problem noting that "In the short run, fishermen do not expand their catch indefinitely because they *do* experience increasing costs in attempting to increase their landings." The possibility of a free-access equilibrium with a positive population is an important consequence of rising costs. This insight underlies Smith's (1968, p. 417) observation that "commercial production from a replenishable resource need not in time destroy the resource". Berck (1979) introduces fixed costs and obtains conditions for extinction based upon a comparison of minimum viable population size and the minimum population size at which exploitation is profitable. Using this analysis, Berck emphasizes that necessary conditions for extinction need not be stated in terms of returns to scale in fishing or biological growth rates. Hoel (1978) makes the point that increasing returns to scale is not a sufficient condition for extinction (contrary to Beddington, Watts and Wright, 1975).

Levhari, Michener and Mirman (1981) present the free-access problem in a discrete time framework, and obtain the potential output in each period from the condition that price equals marginal harvesting costs. Subtracting potential output from the biological growth function results in a description of the system's dynamics. When harvesting costs do not depend upon stock size, then, extinction occurs in finite time if potential output is larger than any sustainable output. If potential output is smaller than some sustainable output, then the occurrence of extinction depends upon whether or not the initial population is smaller than the minimum sustainable population level with free access. When harvesting costs are stock-dependent, an additional user cost externality is introduced.

The free-access fishery is beset by externalities beyond the important stock externality. In particular, there may be vessel or fishing gear congestion, and biological effects from choice of mesh size and other fishing practices (see Turvey, 1964; Smith, 1968, 1969; Quirk and Smith, 1970). As these authors note, the stock, congestion and mesh externalities affect firm decisions through the *cost function*. Smith (1968) argues that the increased costs from these external effects provide a "built-in mechanism" preventing excessive biological overfishing.

Underlying assumptions regarding the number of firms in the fishery and the entry of new firms are implicit assumptions about *entry costs*. Following Gordon (1954) the free-access fishery has been analyzed in a static setting where the instantaneous entry of firms drives rents to zero. The dissipation of rent must occur in a fishery without entry barriers or economies of scale. These assumptions underly analyses which assume that the number of firms exploiting the common property resource is finite (see Hoel 1978; Quirk and Smith, 1970; see also the discussion of game theory and the free-access fishery in section 6 below). For an interesting dynamic two-sector model with a fixed number of fishing firms, see Quirk and Smith (1970).

Between the extremes of instantaneous entry and a fixed number of firms is the possibility of lagged entry which must result from some type of set-up or adjustment costs. A lagged entry equation is employed in the dynamic analyses of Smith (1968, 1969), Fullenbaum, Carlson and Bell (1971), Beddington, Watts and Wright (1975), Leung and Wang (1976), Berck (1979), Hartwick (1980), and in the chapter by Hartwick in this volume. Hartwick goes beyond this literature by employing the lagged entry framework to investigate in detail the local *dynamic stability* of the free-access fishery. Conditions for stability and instability are obtained based upon the parameters of demand elasticity, environmental carrying capacity and the elasticity of the yield–effort relation.

The preceding discussion indicates that the free-access fishery has not been modelled for the case where increasing returns to scale limit the number of firms entering into the fishery, thus allowing strategic interaction. The endogenous determination of the number of fishing firms in a model with increasing returns would be more realistic. As Cheung notes, the observed number of fishermen is finite due to "economies of scale, in the minimum boat size, gear size and the distance of travel for operation" (1970, p. 105).

The question of the performance of the commercial fishing industry involves both static and intertemporal externalities. The chapter by Hartwick in this volume shows social welfare to be lowered by free access, even when the static stock externality is not present.

4.2. Monopoly

Although sole ownership is often prescribed as a way of internalizing both the static common property externality and the dynamic externality for a renewable resource, the presence of monopoly power may introduce distortions which cause the harvesting rate to depart from the social optimum. In view of the importance of sole ownership surprisingly little has been written about the monopoly case. The sole owner is generally modelled as a price-taking firm whose output is small relative to the total market supply of fish (see, for example, Smith, 1969; Clark 1976, pp. 37–38). The chapter by Levhari, Michener and Mirman in this volume introduces an analysis of the sole owner with market power. The harvesting level of the monopolist is compared to the competitive case with well-defined property rights. Elsewhere, Levhari, Michener and Mirman (1981) show that the optimal harvesting plan chosen by an economic planner maximizing consumers' surplus is identical to the market solution with futures markets and perfect foresight. The optimal path is compared here with the monopoly path for the cases where harvesting costs are and are not dependent upon the current stock of fish. With stock-dependent costs, they obtain the interesting result that the monopolist always invests in a larger stock of fish at the steady state than the planner (provided that the monopoly and planned solution both have a nonzero steady state). The comparison is not as clear-cut for the stock-independent cost function where a number of things are possible, including identical steady states with different harvesting rules away from the steady state. Further analysis of the difference between the monopoly and competitive cases needs to be performed for specific forms of the demand curve as Stiglitz (1976) has done for the exhaustible resource problem. The analysis of monopoly is performed in a partial equilibrium setting, suggesting the need for a general equilibrium framework with optimization by consumers and private ownership of the fishing monopoly.

Crutchfield and Pontecorvo (1969), Clark and Munro (1979) and others have noted that while the harvesting structure is generally competitive, the processing sector has strong monopsony power often through collusion, thus implying that the fishery may be optimally managed even if the harvesting and processing sectors are not integrated. This conclusion depends crucially on two assumptions. First, it must be assumed that the processing sector is a price-taker in the market for processed fish. If it has monopoly power in the processed fish market, then the analysis of monopoly discussed above implies that there may be divergence from the optimal outcome. Secondly, the harvesting sector must be assumed to remain competitive. Clark and Munro (1979) suggest that "it seems far more likely that fishermen will react by establishing a local raw-fish monopoly". The chapter by Munro in this volume presents an analysis of bilateral monopoly in which the harvesting and processing sectors engage in a two-person cooperative bargaining game (see Nash, 1953). Munro analyzes the *potential* agreement reached by the two partners which is maximization of a weighted sum of the net returns of the fishery to the respective partners. The discount rates of the harvesting and processing sectors are allowed to differ. This is seen to significantly affect the outcome of the cooperative game. The bilateral monopoly problem yields interesting policy implications. Munro finds that while corrective taxes may be applied successfully when a competitive harvesting sector faces a monopsonistic processing sector, this policy may not work in the bilateral monopoly case. Given the political difficulty of limiting controls to the harvesting sector, Munro argues that the bilateral monopoly option deserves further study.

4.3. The multi-species fishery

The structure of the industry is affected by the available species which can be harvested and the harvesting technology. Anderson's chapter in this volume examines the multi-purpose fleet and its allocation of effort between two *independent* species. Two variants of the model are examined: the first constrains total fishing time which can be devoted to harvesting either species, the second individually constrains the time available for each species (as occurs when the species are harvested during different times of the year). The analysis of Anderson, which is static, extends the model of Huppert (1979) which assumes quota constraints and a constant catch per unit of effort. Anderson examines vessel and fleet behavior with free access and compares the results to the social optimum.

The multi-species fishery presents a number of important problems for future research. First, the model must be extended to a dynamic setting. The allocation of effort to independent species is reminiscent of the dynamic portfolio problem of capital theory since varying growth rates for the two species will yield differing returns to conservation.

Secondly, the market demands for the two species will in general be interdependent. The independence assumption made by Anderson is generally made in multi-species models (see, for example, Clark, 1976, ch. 9). A perfect foresight model will take into account the cross elasticities of demand. In addition, the effects of imperfect competition on the multi-species fishery need to be examined. A monopolist harvesting the two species will take advantage of the market interdependence, since the marginal revenue for each species will be affected by the supply of the other.

Thirdly, restricting access to a muti-species fishery introduces strategic aspects to the multi-purpose fleet problem. Sobel's chapter in this volume (discussed in the next section) introduces multiple species into a stochastic game model of the fishery. The imperfect competition framework could benefit from explicit attention to the multiple species problem and constraints such as the time limits on fishing days.

Fourthly, the assumption of biological independence of species needs to be relaxed. Harvested species may be predator and prey, directly competitive or related through more distant connections in the trophic web. May et al. (1979) discuss the management of multi-species fisheries and the effects of maximum sustained yield policies for very complicated ecosystems, including, for example, harvesting at the top and bottom of a three-level trophic ladder of prey–predator–top predator form. The optimal harvesting of multi-species fisheries is examined by Quirk and Smith (1970), Clark (1976, ch. 9), Anderson (1975) and Silvert and Smith (1977). The time constraints discussed by Anderson (and other technical constraints such as the yield–effort relation and limits on the degree to which species may be harvested separately) raise questions about the applicability of complex optimal harvesting for the multi-species fishery. What needs to be investigated is the optimal dynamic behavior of the multi-purpose fleet harvesting interrelated species under a time constraint. Given the large number of fisheries of this type (see May et al., 1979) the implications for fishery regulation will be of significance.

4.4. The recreational fishery

As is well known, there is a significant demand for the use of certain fisheries for sport and recreational purposes. The chapter by McConnell and Sutinen in this volume presents an economic model of a recreational fishery in which fishermen may vary their catch rate and the number of fishing trips taken. The model of McConnell and Sutinen notes that a central management authority would maximize the flow of net benefits from the recreational harvest. The sport fisheries model raises a number of interesting questions concerning the types of externalities which will occur and their effect on a recreational fishery. Specifically, are the stock externalities, mesh externalities and crowding externalities which are discussed by Smith (1969) for commercial fishing present in the recreational fishery? If so, how should the management authority organize a limited access program to correct for these external diseconomies? A related question is the competition for scarce resources between commercial and recreational fisheries. This problem was first discussed by McConnell and Sutinen (1979) who examined the optimal allocation between commercial and recreational use. They showed that recreational fishing with open access may result in overfishing, and they calculated the steady-state marginal value of the fish stock when it is optimally managed. In their present chapter McConnell and Sutinen show that the estimation of the marginal value of the fish stock is still tractable when a household production function is incorporated in the recreational fisherman's decision problem. Since the Fishery Conservation and Management Act precludes user fees as a means of limiting access to recreational fisheries, this marginal value of the fish stock must be considered in further work on the incentive properties of alternative management schemes. May et al. (1979) raise the interesting and complex problem of competition between sports fishermen and commercial fisheries through different species which are nonetheless ecologically interdependent. In a case considered by May et al. (1979) commercial harvesting of the California anchovy population may affect the food supply of certain sport fishes. This is certainly an interesting externality which bears further examination.

5. Game theory

Many fisheries are exploited by a few firms or agents who are aware of each other's harvesting levels, and who may choose their harvesting in a strategic manner. A small number of firms may be present in either the restricted-access or open-access fishery. Ever since the first model of the open-access fishery was set forth by Gordon (1954), the focus of economic analysis of this problem has been upon the "dissipation of economic rent" through entry. Entry occurs until profits are competed to zero which may or may not result in extinction of the species, but surely results in nonoptimal harvesting levels. However, some open-access fisheries may have only a few large harvesting groups. This is particularly true in some small coastal fisheries. This implies that the fishing firms may be aware of the actions of the other firms and may seek to behave strategically. The interaction of a few participants in a fishery is particularly evident if competition by the fleets of countries for ocean fisheries is examined. When fisheries establish limited entry programs, strategic interaction by producers is even more likely to occur.

Using the Nash N-person differential game, Clark (1979b) examines the strategic effort choices when N producers exploit a restricted access fishery. As Clark notes, the literature on fisheries economics has focused upon the extremes of sole ownership and open access thus avoiding the problem of competition by a few producers. A Nash equilibrium is shown to occur in which inefficient producers are progressively eliminated as the fish stock is reduced, with overfishing taking place. These strategic considerations enter into Clark's chapter in this volume "Models of Fishery Regulation", which is discussed in a later section. The chapter by Levhari and Mirman in this volume, "The Great Fish War", studies an international fishery game and provides an explicit solution of a Cournot–Nash equilibrium in which each country chooses catch levels to maximize the sum of discounted utilities, and obtains closed form expressions for the Cournot–Nash policies. These papers focus on strategic interaction with regard to the commonly held resource, without the market interaction originally described by Cournot. Mirman (1979) introduces a duopoly model in which the two firms interact strategically through the market as well as through the stock externality.

Finally, the chapter by Sobel provides the most general strategic interaction framework using a sequential stochastic game. Sobel considers a set of relevant species allowing predator–prey interaction and competing species. In addition, the dynamics of the fishery involve Markovian uncertainty. Sobel demonstrates the existence of a myopic equilibrium point whose repetition over an infinite time horizon is an equilibrium of the dynamic game. The general result of Sobel bears further analysis for special cases of particular biological growth functions and explicit forms of uncertainty. An interesting extension would involve an examination of the effects of uncertainty within a duopoly model admitting closed form harvesting policies for the participants.

As was discussed in the previous section, Munro's chapter in this volume, "Bilateral Monopoly in Fisheries and Optimal Management Policy", introduces a Nash cooperative game in which the participants are monopolists in the harvesting and processing sectors. The possibility of cooperation and bargaining between fishing firms considered by Munro raises the question of whether other forms of cooperation may obtain in fisheries. In particular, competing firms harvesting a particular fishery may coordinate their harvesting through implicit agreements or through trade associations. Countries negotiating fishing policies involving reciprocal access arrangements may bargain in a way that may be described by a Nash cooperative game. The coordination problems of countries managing transboundary resources have been examined elsewhere by Munro (1979).

6. Regulation and resource use

The many types of externalities present in fisheries suggest the need for regulation by governments or other central authorities, such as trade associations. The problem lies in the selection of regulatory instruments with the appropriate incentive properties. As is often the case with attempts at external control, optimization by firms may reinforce certain policy instruments while eliminating welfare gains from other instruments. Regulation may have undesired effects upon input or output mixes or upon entry decisions. Evaluating the effects of a policy on market structure and firm conduct is essential to determining the resulting dynamic performance of the fishing industry.

In the free-access fishery, a classification of externalities is needed to examine alternative policy instruments. As already pointed out, the primary externality is the stock externality. Unrestricted access to a renewable resource stock leads to the problem of *static* allocation of a fixed stock as well as the problem of dynamic allocation of harvesting over time since the returns to conservation are not appropriable. The second type of externality may be labelled a production externality, and includes interfirm effects due to choice of fishing gear or mesh size and interspecies harvesting effects. The third type of externality, related to the second, results from crowding or congestion of vessels. To these types of market failure due to external effects, one must add market failure which may occur due to imperfect competition in the sale of the resource. Promoting competition in the resource market may conflict with other efficiency goals.

The selection of a regulatory instrument is complicated by the existence of quantity or price duals for each instrument which generally perform equally well. As is well known (see, for example, Weitzman 1974b), these planning instruments generally have the same informational requirements whether they are in the form of quantity constraints or price incentives.

Consider first the problem of static allocation of a fixed stock to which there is free access. The correct solution is a shadow price imposed upon the resource itself which is zero if the resource is not fully utilized and positive otherwise. This resource price will ensure both the correct entry of firms and the proper scale for each firm. The shadow price can be administered through either a tax or royalty per unit of the resource which is extracted or through quantity-restricted licenses which may be sold. For the fishery, the current stock must not only be allocated among firms in the current period but it must also be allocated over time. The single shadow price, whether administered through a landings tax or marketable licenses, will serve to correctly allocate the resource over time and will also lead to the correct number of firms exploiting the fishery, each operating at an optimal scale. This depends, however, upon an adjustment of the shadow price in every period.

Unless a firm's choice variable can be uniquely associated with its harvesting level, other policies may be expected to fail to achieve dynamic allocative efficiency. Thus, regulation of vessel size (length, horsepower, tonnage), fishing gear, time and place of fishing, and species harvested will often cause unexpected distortions as individual firms attempt to avoid the intended impact of the regulation. For example, regulation of vessel size may result in longer fishing periods or more vessels, while regulation of the fishing season may result in longer hours per day during the season, better fish detection equipment or larger vessels. When effort is uniquely associated with catch size, and vessels or firms are identical, uniform effort taxes are possible (if indeed effort can be observed at all). However, if effort involves a number of inputs, regulation of any of these inputs will cause distortions in the firm's input mix without the intended effects on effort or catch size. Restriction of entry will not prevent overfishing by these firms within the fishery, whether entry is restricted by an entry fee, vessel licenses or by direct restrictions on the total number of firms. The firms allowed into the fishery will compensate for limited entry by increasing fishing effort, vessel size, fishing time, etc. For each of the regulations which do not directly price the resource, the possibilities of substitution of nontaxed activities appears almost limitless. Combinations involving more than one regulatory instrument complicate the regulator's and the firm's decision problems without necessarily eliminating the opportunities for avoiding the regulatory impact. Regulation of the individual firm's total catch through a quota system where an optimal catch limit is set individually for each firm is sufficient for the control of an individual firm's harvest levels, yet the industry will respond with excessive entry, leading to overfishing. Restrictions on catch per firm must therefore be combined with entry restrictions, and the number of quotas must be restricted and adjusted each fishing season. The proper tailoring of optimal quotas to each vessel presents information problems which go far beyond the requirements needed for a landings tax or marketable permit schemes. The shadow price on the fish stock involves knowing only the types of firms and the number of firms of each type. This is general information about the size or type distribution of firms. The individual firm quota involves identification of the costs and characteristics of *each* individual firm.

The presence of production externalities and congestion may prevent the attainment of dynamic allocative efficiency, even with a correctly set landings tax. An additional tax of the externality producing activity or an entry fee in the congestion case must supplement the landings tax. As in the case of harveting regulation, attempts to control selected inputs to the activities which create the externalities may also cause unwanted distortions.

An extensive literature on fisheries management has developed which has primarily centered on policy considerations. Anderson (1979) and Clark (1979a) discuss license schemes, landings taxes, effort taxes, effort quotas, vessel licenses and actually employed regulations regarding gears, fishing seasons, restricted areas and catch quotas. See also Anderson (1977a, b), Munro (1977) and Crutchfield (1979). Anderson (1979) considers a number of aspects of regulation which go beyond economic efficiency, in particular management operations (flexibility, implementation, intrafishery conflicts, multi-purpose fleet conflicts), biological effectiveness and socioeconomic effects.

In the final chapter of this volume, "Models of Fishery Regulation", Clark considers the effects of four regulatory policies: total catch quotas, restricted access, allocated vessel quotas and taxes and compares these policies to the welfare-optimizing outcome and to the outcome which occurs in the absence of regulation. The model disaggregates fishing to the level of individual vessels, and allows continuous harvesting during each fishing season. The analysis produces the interesting result that the optimal landings tax must decrease over the fishing season as well as varying from one season to the next. The time-dependent tax serves to optimize effort, vessel numbers and the stock of fish. Restricted access is shown to be sub-optimal due to excessive fishing effort by those vessels with access to the fishery. If catch per unit of effort does not vary over the fishing season, vessel quotas are seen to have the same efficiency results as a landings tax if the quotas are correctly allocated.

7. Conclusion

The issues raised in this volume have implications for future study of regulation of the fishery. The impacts of alternative regulatory instruments have been studied in models which assume competitive firms with convex cost functions, concave biological growth functions and perfect information. The conclusions of these models need to be re-examined when these assumptions are relaxed. The presence of nonconvexities in either the biological growth function or in the firm's cost function may cause pulse-fishing to occur. How is the fishery best regulated when individual firms find pulse-fishing optimal? If fishing firms are subject to start-up costs every time they recommence fishing, how will they respond to the various regulatory instruments?

When environmental randomness is present, such as perturbations of the biological growth function, the way that the landings tax is calculated will be altered. The impacts of nonoptimal policies such as vessel size or gear restrictions may be worsened by the effects of uncertainty. Policies involving quotas may not be sufficiently flexible to avoid distortions when yield–effort relations are variable.

When imperfect competition exists in the fisheries market, the results of output regulation will be second-best solutions. Alternative regulatory instruments have not been examined in the presence of imperfect competition. The strategic interaction of fishing firms when small numbers of firms are present in a fishery, poses additional problems for the selection of regulatory instruments. The study of nonconvexities, uncertainty, imperfect competition and strategic interaction of fishing firms should lead to a better understanding of how regulatory instruments are to be selected and applied in the management of actual fisheries.

References

Anderson, L.G. (1979) "A Comparison of Limited Entry Fisheries Management Schemes", F.A.O. Fisheries Report No. 236, *Report of the ACMRR Working Party on the Scientific Basis of Determining Management Measures*, December, pp. 47–74.

Anderson, L.G. (1975) "Analysis of Commercial Exploitation and Maximum Economic Yield in Biologically and Technologically Interdependent Fisheries", *Journal of the Fisheries Research Board of Canada*, 32, November, 1825–1942.

Anderson, L.G. (Ed.) (1977a) *Economic Impacts of Extended Fisheries Jurisdiction* (Ann Arbor, Science).

Anderson, L.G. (1977b) *The Economics of Fisheries Management* (Johns Hopkins University Press, Baltimore).

Beddington, J.R. and R.M. May (1977) "Harvesting Natural Populations in a Randomly Fluctuating Environment", *Science*, 197, 29 July, 463–465.

Beddington, J.R., C.M.K. Watts and W.D.C. Wright (1975) "Optimal Cropping of Self-Reproducible Natural Resources", *Econometrica*, 43, 4, July, 789–802.

Berck, P. (1979) "Open Access and Extinction", *Econometrica*, 47, 4, July, 877–882.

Brock, W.A. and L.J. Mirman (1972) "Optimal Economic Growth and Uncertainty", *Journal of Economic Theory*, 4, June, 479–513.
Butlin, J. (1975) "Optimal Depletion of a Replenishable Resource: An Evaluation of Recent Contributions to Fisheries Economics", in: Pearce, D.W. and J. Rose, eds. *The Economics of Natural Resource Depletion* Wiley, New York, pp. 85–114.
Cheung, S.N.S. (1970) "Contractual Arrangements and Resource Allocation in Marine Fisheries," in: A.D. Scott, ed., *Economics of Fisheries Management: A Symposium*, (Institute of Animal Resource Ecology, The University of British Columbia, Vancouver) pp. 97–108.
Christy, F.T., Jr. and A.D. Scott (1965) *The Common Wealth in Ocean Fisheries* (Johns Hopkins Press, Baltimore).
Clark, C.W. (1976) *Mathematical Bioeconomics: The Optimal Management of Renewable Resources* (John Wiley and Sons, New York).
Clark, C.W. (1979a) "Fishery Management and Fishing Rights", F.A.O. Fisheries Report No. 236, *Report of the ACMRR Working Party on the Scientific Basis of Determining Management Measures*, December, pp. 101–113.
Clark, C.W. (1979b) "Restricted Entry to Common-Property Fishery Resources: A Game-Theoretic Analysis", in: P.-T. Liu, ed., *Dynamic Optimization and Mathematical Economics*, (Plenum, New York).
Clark, C.W. and G.R. Munro (1979) "Fisheries and the Processing Sector: Some Implications for Management Policy", University of British Columbia, Departments of Mathematics and Economics, Resources Paper No. 34, February.
Coleman, D.C. (1977) *The Economy of England, 1450–1750* (Oxford University Press).
Crutchfield, J.A. and G. Pontecorvo (1969) *The Pacific Salmon Fisheries: A Study of Irrational Conservation* (The Johns Hopkins University Press, Baltimore).
Crutchfield, J.A. (1979) "Economic and Social Implications of the Main Policy Alternatives for Controlling Fishing Effort", *Journal of the Fisheries Resources Board of Canada*, 36, 7, 742–752.
Crutchfield, J.A. and A. Zellner (1962) "Economic Aspects of the Pacific Halibut Fishery", *Fishery Industrial Research*, 1, 1, U.S. Department of the Interior, Washington, D.C.
Doubleday, W.G. (1979) "Coping with Variability in Fisheries", Food and Agriculture Organization of the United Nations Fisheries Report No. 236, ACMRR Working Party on the Scientific Basis of Determining Management Measures, Hong Kong, December, pp. 131–139.
Easley, D. and Daniel F. Spulber (1981) "Stochastic Equilibrium and Optimality with Rolling Plans", *International Economic Review*, 22, 1, February, 79–103.
Fullenbaum, R.F., E.W. Carlson and F.W. Bell (1971) "Economics of Production from Natural Resources: Comment", *American Economic Review*, 61, 483–487.
Gleit, A. (1978) "Optimal Harvesting in Continuous Time with Stochastic Growth", *Mathematical Biosciences*, 41, 111–123.
Gonner, E.C.K. (1966) *Common Land and Inclosure* (1912), reprinted 1966 (Kelly, New York).
Gordon, H.S. (1954) "Economic Theory of a Common-Property Resource: The Fishery", *Journal of Political Economy*, 62, April, 124–142.
Gould, J.R. (1972) "Extinction of a Fishery by Commercial Exploitation: A Note", *Journal of Political Economy*, 80, 1031–1038.
Goulding, M. (1980) *The Fishes and the Forest* (University of California Press).
Hartwick, J.M. (1980) "The Intertemporal Externality in the Dynamic Common Property Renewable Resource Problem", *Economics Letters*, 5, 275–280.
Hoel, M. (1978) "Extermination of Self-Reproducible Natural Resources Under Competitive Conditions", *Econometrica*, 46, 1, January, 219–224.
Huppert, D.D. (1979) "Implications for Multipurpose Fleets and Mixed Stocks for Control Policies", *Journal of the Fisheries Research Board of Canada*, 36, July, 845–854.
Jaquette, L. (1972a) "Mathematical Models for the Control of Growing Biological Populations: A Survey", *Operations Research*, 20, 1142–1151.
Jaquette, L. (1972b) "A Discrete-Time Population-Control Model", *Mathematical Biosciences*, 15, 231–252.

Jaquette, L. (1974) "A Discrete-Time Population Control Model with Setup Cost", *Operations Research*, 22, 298–303.

Leung, A. and A.-Y. Wang (1976) "Analysis of Models for Commercial Fishing: Mathematical and Economic Aspects", *Econometrica*, 44, 2, March, 295–303.

Levhari, D., R. Michener and L.J. Mirman (1981) "Dynamic Programming Models of Fishing: Competition", *American Economic Review*, 71, September, 649–661.

Lewis, T.R. and R. Schmalensee (1975) "Nonconvexities and the Theory of Renewable Resource Management", Discussion Paper 75-16, Department of Economics, University of California, San Diego.

Lewis, T.R. and R. Schmalensee (1977) "Nonconvexity and Optimal Exhaustion of Renewable Resources", *International Economic Review*, 18, 535–552.

Lewis, T.R. and R. Schmalensee (1979) "Nonconvexity and Optimal Harvesting Strategies for Renewable Resources", *Canadian Journal of Economics*, 12, 677–691.

Majumdar, M. and T. Mitra (1980a) "On Optimal Exploitation of a Renewable Resource in a Non-Convex Environment and the Minimum Safe Standard of Conservation", Working Paper 223, Department of Economics, Cornell University.

Majumdar, M. and T. Mitra (1980b) "Intertemporal Allocation with a Non-Convex Technology: The Aggregative Framework", Working Paper 221, Department of Economics, Cornell University.

Mann, Stuart, H. (1970) "A Mathematical Theory for the Harvest of Natural Animal Populations When Birth Rates are Dependent on Total Population Sizes", *Mathematical Biosciences*, 7, 97–110.

May, R.M. (1974) *Stability and Complexity in Model Ecosystems*, 2nd edn. (Princeton University Press, Princeton, 1974).

May, R.M., J.R. Beddington, C.W. Clark, S.J. Holt and R.M. Laws (1979) "Management of Multispecies Fisheries", *Science*, 20, July, 267–277.

May, R.M., J.R. Beddington, J.W. Horwood and J.G. Shepherd (1978) "Exploiting Natural Populations in an Uncertain World", *Mathematical Biosciences*, 42, 219–252.

McConnell, K.E. and J.G. Sutinen (1979) "Bioeconomic Models of Marine Recreational Fishing", *Journal of Environment Economic Management*, 6, 127–139.

Mendelssohn, R. (1978) "Optimal Harvesting Strategies for Stochastic Single-Species, Multiage Class Models", *Mathematical Biosciences*, 41, 159–174.

Mendelssohn, R. (1980) "Managing Stochastic Multispecies Models", *Mathematical Biosciences*, 49, 249–261.

Mirman, L.J. (1972) "On the Existence of Steady-State Measures for One Sector Growth Models with Uncertain Technology", *International Economic Review*, 13, June, 271–286.

Mirman, L.J. (1973) "The Steady-State Behavior of a Class of One Sector Growth Models with Uncertain Technology", *Journal of Economic Theory*, 6, June, 219–242.

Mirman, L.J. (1979) "Dynamic Models of Fishing: A Heuristic Approach", in: P.-T. Liu and J.G. Sutinen, eds. *Control Theory in Mathematical Economics* (Marcel Dekker, New York) pp. 39–73.

Munro, G.R. (1977) "Canada and Fisheries Management with Extended Jurisdiction: A Preliminary View", in: L.G. Anderson, ed., *Economic Aspects of Extended Fisheries Jurisdiction* (Ann Arbor, Ann Arbor Science) pp. 29–50.

Munro, G.R. (1979) "The Optimal Management of Transboundary Renewable Resources", *Canadian Journal of Economics*, XII, 3, August.

Nash, J.F. (1953) "Two-Person Cooperative Games", *Econometrica*, 21, January, 128–140.

Peterson, F.M. and A.C. Fisher (1977) "The Exploitation of Extractive Resources: A Survey", *The Economic Journal*, 87, December, 681–721.

Quirk, J.P. and V.L. Smith (1970) "Dynamic Economic Models of Fishing", in: A.D. Scott, ed., *Economics of Fisheries Management: A Symposium* (Institute of Animal Resource Ecology, The University of British Columbia, Vancouver) pp. 3–32.

Reed, W.J. (1974) "A Stochastic Model of the Economic Management of a Renewable Animal Resource", *Mathematical Biosciences*, 22, 313–337.

Scott, A.D. (1955) "The Fishery: The Objectives of Sole Ownership", *Journal of Political Economy*, 63, 4, April, 116–124.

Silvert, W. and W.R. Smith (1977) "Optimal Exploitation of a Multi-Species Community", *Mathematical Biosciences*, 33, 121.

Slater, G. (1932) *The Growth of Modern England* (Houghton-Mifflin).

Smith, V.L. (1968) "Economics of Production From Natural Resources", *American Economic Review*, 58, 409–431.

Smith, V.L. (1969) "On Models of Commercial Fishing", *Journal of Political Economy*, 77, 181–198.

Smith, V.L. (1975) "The Primitive Hunter Culture, Pleistocene Extinction, and the Rise of Agriculture", *Journal of Political Economy*, 83, 727–755.

Stiglitz, J.E. (1976) "Monopoly and the Rate of Extraction of Exhaustible Resources", *American Economic Review*, 66, 4, 655–661.

Thompson, R.G., M.D. George, R.J. Callen and L.C. Walken (1973) "A Stochastic Investment Model for a Survival Conscious Firm Applied to Shrimp Fishing", *Applied Economics*, V, 2.

Turvey, R. (1964) "Optimization and Suboptimization in Fishery Regulation", *American Economic Review*, 54, March, 64–76.

Weitzman, M.L. (1974a) "Free Access vs. Private Ownership as Alternative Systems for Managing Common Property", *Journal of Economic Theory*, 8, June, 225–234.

Weitzman, M.L. (1974b) "Prices vs. Quantities", *Review of Economic Studies*, XLI (4), no. 128, October, 477–492.

PART II

CAPITAL THEORY AND RESOURCE MANAGEMENT

Introduction to Part II

It has been known for many years among resource economists that capital-theoretic models are the best vehicles for studying the exploitation of natural resources. However, the mere recognition that the allocation of the natural resource over time is a capital-theoretic problem does not automatically lead to the solution of many of the issues raised in the resource literature. The problem involved in treating a natural resource as a capital stock is that each generation must decide how large a legacy to leave to future generations. There are many aspects to the problem of allocating these resources over time which go beyond the recognition that the theory of natural resources can incorporate the ideas of capital theory. One of the significant problems in natural resource economics is to design a mechanism so that a decentralized society can maintain an optimal "centralized" plan. Also important is the question of how an optimal plan can be made consistent with the tastes of future generations so that "optimal" plans do not become obsolete. The papers of this part, although very different in nature, deal with the adaptation of the ideas and techniques of capital theory to the economics of natural resources as well as with the adaptation of some of the capital-theoretic concepts to the specific questions arising in the economics of fishing.

Two differences between growth theory and resource management bear special emphasis. In the growth literature, the utility or benefit function is usually assumed to be strictly concave. However, the benefit function used to study exploitation of natural resources by firms is a nonstrictly concave profit function. This slight change in the model has a pronounced effect on the optimal dynamics. A second difference is that in the field of natural resources the question of the possible depletion of the resource plays an important role whereas the question does not arise in the study of capital theory. The importance of depletion is due to the common-property nature of many fisheries and other natural resources.

In Chapter 2, "The Economics of Fishing and Modern Capital Theory: A Simplified Approach", Clark and Munro use the techniques of optimal control theory to study the "optimal" exploitation of the stock of fish. They use a very simple fishery model which has been widely used in the fishing

29

literature. Particular emphasis is put on the steady-state solution for the dynamic behavior of the fish stock under the influence of an optimal policy. Their basic model consists of three aspects. First, the biological growth curve is a nonlinear (concave) function. The demand for fish is infinitely elastic, which implies a linear objective function. Finally, the cost of catching fish depends upon the stock of fish. This is also an assumption quite common and natural to the economics of fishing. The last assumption implies that, in the steady state, fish are not a free good. This assumption is particularly interesting since in the usual capital-theoretic models the stock does not enter the objective function. Having the stock in the objective function is analogous to having a wealth effect in capital theory. However, in the economics of fishing having the stock in the objective function is a very important consideration, while in capital theory the wealth effect is much less important.

Clark and Munro discuss a number of issues relating to the depletion of the fish stock. Among the issues considered are the effects of technological improvements on the eventual depletion of the stock, and the question of a tax policy which allows a decentralized and competitive industry to approximate the optimal centralized plan. Also discussed is the possibility of a tax system which maintains an optimal steady state. It is shown that the tax should be set equal to the "marginal users cost" to bring long-run equilibrium to the market.

Chapter 3, "Consistent and Revised Plans for Natural Resource Use", by Lewis and Neher, deals with an important question originally raised by capital theorists. In deciding the "optimal" allocation of resources over time each generation is assigned some weight. These weights determine how well off any particular generation will be. It is possible that some future generations will decide not to stick to the plan of a previous generation. In this case the optimal plan would be inconsistent.

Lewis and Neher study finite horizon plans (consistent with the present generation's preferences) which would be revised from time to time and compare these plans to the optimal plan which is, in fact, consistent. They show that in general it is not too difficult to manipulate these finite horizon plans (with revision) to be optimal plans. This question is particularly relevant to the decision regarding the allocation of natural resources where markets and central planning combine to determine the amount of fish to be consumed at each point in time.

CHAPTER 2

The economics of fishing and modern capital theory: A simplified approach

COLIN W. CLARK and GORDON R. MUNRO*

1. Introduction

It has been recognized, virtually from the time of its inception, that fisheries economics, like other aspects of resource economics, should ideally be cast in capital-theoretic terms. The fish population, or biomass, can be viewed as a capital stock in that, like "conventional" or man-made capital, it is capable of yielding a sustainable consumption flow through time. As with "conventional" capital, today's consumption decision will, by its impact upon the stock level, have implications for future consumption options. The resource management problem thus becomes one of selecting an optimal consumption flow through time, which in turn implies selecting an optimal stock level as a function of time.

   In a pioneering and much cited paper, Scott (1955) attempted to cast the problem of the management of a fishery resource as a problem in capital theory. The attempt was followed by Crutchfield and Zellner's (1962) formulation of the problem in terms of a dynamic mathematical model. In spite of these works, however, the received theory of fisheries economics, founded by Gordon (1954), continued to be formulated largely in static terms.[1] Indeed, one finds the static analysis being employed right up to the present day.[2] Reasons for the retreat to nondynamic analysis are not

*The authors wish to express their gratitude to Professors A.D. Scott and H.F. Campbell for their helpful criticisms of and comments on earlier drafts of this article.
[1]See, for example, Christy and Scott (1965), Anderson (1973), Bell (1972), Bradley (1970), Copes (1970, 1972), Mohring (n.d.), Smith (1968), Turvey (1964).
[2]See Christy (1973).

Essays in the economics of renewable resources, edited by L.J. Mirman and D.F. Spulber
© *North-Holland Publishing Company, 1982*

difficult to discover. While being warned that explicit consideration of time ought properly to be brought into the analysis, the reader was also advised that this could be an extraordinarily complex, if not impossible, undertaking.[3] It is perhaps reasonable to argue that the problem lay not with the attempt to apply capital theory to fisheries economics, but rather with capital theory itself which, as Dorfman (1969) has argued, suffered from an inadequacy of mathematical instruments.

Since the work of Ramsey (1928), it has been clearly recognized that capital theory is in essence a problem in the calculus of variations. It was also recognized, however, that, in its classical formulation, the techniques provided by calculus of variations were inadequate to the task (Dorfman, 1969). The extensions of calculus of variations provided by optimal control theory (Bellman, 1957; Pontrjagin et al., 1962) eliminated the inadequacies of the classical techniques to a large extent. Economists were quick to appreciate the implications for capital theory; indeed Dorfman goes so far as to argue that modern capital theory traces its origins to the development of optimal control theory.[4] It seemed only a matter of time before the techniques of optimal control theory would be brought to bear upon fisheries economics.

Several attempts in this direction have by now been made.[5] This chapter, with the aid of a simple linear model, summarizes most of the major results achieved so far, but does so in a manner such that the links with capital theory are made transparent. The chapter then explores two sets of problems which have yet to be properly dealt with in the fisheries economics literature. The first concerns the optimal approach to the equilibrium stock, i.e. the optimal "investment" policy. The second set of problems arises from the relaxation of the highly restrictive assumption of autonomy (i.e. the assumption that the parameters are independent of time). The chapter then concludes with an examination of the complexities that can arise when the assumption of linearity is relaxed.

2. The basic model

We commence with a simple dynamic model used widely in fisheries economics (e.g. Crutchfield and Zellner, 1962; Plourde, 1970; Clark, 1973),

---

[3]See Crutchfield and Zellner (1962, appendix I). Turvey (1964, p. 75), on the other hand, argued rather curiously (and incorrectly in our belief), that even if one did make the analysis dynamic, no new interesting results would be forthcoming.

[4]See Dorfman (1969, p. 817).

[5]See Brown (1974), Clark (1973a,b), Cummings and Burt (1969), Neher (1974), Plourde (1970, 1971), Quirk and Smith (1970), Spence (1973).

which is usually associated with the name of Schaefer (1957). The model rests upon the Pearl–Verhulst or logistic equation of population dynamics.

Let $x = x(t)$ represent the biomass at time t. Corresponding to each level of biomass, there exists (according to Schaefer) a certain natural rate of increase, $F(x)$:

$$\frac{dx}{dt} = F(x). \tag{1}$$

Eq. (1) can be viewed as the net recruitment function or as the "natural" production function.[6] It is assumed that.[7]

$$F(x) > 0 \quad \text{for } 0 < x < K;$$
$$F(0) = F(K) = 0; \qquad F''(x) < 0, \tag{2}$$

where K denotes the carrying capacity of the environment, i.e. $\lim_{t \to \infty} x(t) = K$.

When harvesting is introduced, eq. (1) is altered to

$$\frac{dx}{dt} = F(x) - h(t), \tag{3}$$

where $h(t) \geq 0$ represents the harvest rate, assumed to be equal to the consumption rate, and where dx/dt can be interpreted as the rate of investment (positive or negative[8]) to the stock (biomass).

Society's basic resource-management problem is that of determining the optimal consumption/harvest time path with the object of maximizing social utility (welfare). From eq. (3) it is clear that this is the equivalent of determining the optimal stock-level time path.

There is, of course, the complication to be faced that fish do not harvest themselves, that scarce labor and man-made or conventional capital must be allocated to the harvesting process. In addition to the biological constraint (3), then, there is a harvesting-cost constraint. The harvesting-cost function is dependent upon an effort (labor plus conventional capital applied to fishing) cost function and a "harvest" production function

$$C_E = g(E), \tag{4}$$

---

[6] The "natural" production function can also be expressed as $\dot{x} = G(x, z)$, where z denotes the input of the aquatic environment. The input z is normally assumed to be constant, thus $\dot{x} = G(x, z)$ can be reduced to $\dot{x} = F(x)$. The fixity of z, of course, explains the diminishing returns to which x is assumed to be subject [$F''(x) < 0$]; cf. Schaefer (1957).

[7] The conditions (2) are automatically satisfied for the case $F(x) = rx(1 - x/K)$, which is the standard Pearl–Verhulst logistic model. Virtually all of our analysis is valid, however, under the less restrictive hypothesis (2).

[8] It may be worth stressing that in contrast to the standard or typical model in capital theory, disinvestment is not only allowed for in the fisheries model, but plays a critical role.

where E is effort and C_E total effort cost; and

$$h(t) = h(E, x). \tag{5}$$

We shall assume, in keeping with many standard fisheries models (e.g. Crutchfield and Zellner, 1962) that

$$C_E = aE, \tag{6}$$

where a is a constant[9] and that

$$h(t) = bE^\alpha x^\beta, \tag{7}$$

where b, α and β are constants. It is assumed further that α is equal to 1.[10] From (6) and (7) a harvesting-cost function can easily be derived:

$$C_h = \frac{ch(t)}{x^\beta}, \tag{8}$$

where C_h denotes total harvesting costs and $c = a/b$. Harvesting costs are thus linear in harvesting and are a decreasing function of the biomass (so long as $\beta > 0$).[11]

Given these assumptions, the complication introduced by positive harvesting costs does not alter the basic nature of society's optimization problem. It remains in essence the selection of an optimal consumption-flow/stock-level time path. Indeed, it will be demonstrated that for most of the cases encountered in this paper, the one major consequence of positive harvesting costs will be to introduce an effect directly analogous to the "wealth effect" encountered in modern capital theory.

In addition to the above assumptions, we abstract from all second-best considerations, and assume that the price of fish adequately measures the marginal social benefit (gross) derived from the consumption of the fish, and also that the demand for fish is infinitely elastic.[12] The problem can thus be viewed in terms of rent maximization, as in the received theory.[13]

---

[9] That is, the supply function of effort is infinitely elastic.

[10] We do not assume that β is constrainted to equal 1, but only that $\beta \geq 0$.

[11] The assumption that harvesting costs are a decreasing function of the biomass is almost universal in the literature – although exceptions to this rule can be found in the literature (see, for example, Smith, 1968). The assumption that costs are, or can be, linear in harvesting is employed by Schaefer and by those who have used his model. This assumption implies that $\partial h/\partial E$ is independent of E, an assumption which seems very restrictive, but one which is widely used by fisheries biologists. The reader is referred to Gordon (1954, pp. 138–140), who gives a strong defence of the use of the assumption.

[12] Although this assumption appears to be highly restrictive, it is reasonable when applied to fisheries where the harvested fish are sold in large markets supplied by many other fisheries.

[13] The theory as expounded by Gordon (1954), Christy and Scott (1965), and many others.

In the model the fundamental differential equation or state equation is (3):

$$\frac{\mathrm{d}x}{\mathrm{d}t} = F(x) - h(t); \qquad x(0) = x_0;$$

the variable $x = x(t)$ is the state variable and $h = h(t)$ is the control variable. The initial population $x(0)$ is assumed to be known. The control $h(t)$ is assumed subject to the constraints

$$0 \leqslant h(t) \leqslant h_{max}, \tag{9}$$

where h_{max} may in general be a given function, $h_{max} = h_{max}(t; x(t))$.[14]

The object is to maximize the present value of rent derived from fishing. Given the assumptions of constant price and costs linear in harvesting, the objective functional can be expressed as

$$P.V. = \int_0^\infty e^{-\delta t} \{ p - c(x(t)) \} h(t) \, \mathrm{d}t, \tag{10}$$

where δ is the instantaneous social rate of discount, p the price and $c(x)$ the unit cost of harvesting.

Given that the objective functional is linear in the control variable, $h(t)$, we face a linear optimal control problem. The problem is to determine the optimal control $h(t) = h^*(t)$, $t \geqslant 0$, and the corresponding optimal population $x(t) = x^*(t)$, $t \geqslant 0$, subject to the state equation (3) and the control constraints (9), such that the objective functional (10) assumes a maximum value. The problem is straightforward and easily solved via the maximum principle.

The Hamiltonian of our problem is

$$H = e^{-\delta t} \big[\{ p - c(x) \} h(t) + \psi(t) \{ F(x) - h(t) \} \big]$$
$$= \sigma(t) h(t) + e^{-\delta t} \psi(t) F(x), \tag{11}$$

where $\sigma(t)$, the switching function, is given by

$$\sigma(t) = e^{-\delta t} [p - c(x) - \psi(t)], \tag{12}$$

and where $\psi(t)$ is the adjoint or costate variable.

The standard procedure for solving linear optimal control problems proceeds as follows (see the appendix). First one determines the so-called

---

[14] The mathematical implications of the upper control constraint, h_{max}, will be described further in the appendix.

"singular" solution, which arises when

$$\sigma(t) \equiv 0. \tag{13}$$

It is easily verified, via the maximum principle (see appendix) that for our model, eq. (13) implies that

$$\frac{1}{\delta}\left[\frac{d}{dx}\{(p - c(x))F(x)\}\right] = p - c(x). \tag{14}$$

Eq. (14) does not involve the time t explicitly, but is merely an implicit equation for x, which consequently determines a finite number of equilibrium solutions $x = x^* = \text{constant}.$[15]

If one employs specifically the Schaefer model, for which $F(x) = rx(1 - x/K)$ and $C(x) = cx^{-1}$, it then becomes possible to solve eq. (14) explicitly for $x = x^*$:

$$x^* = \frac{K}{4}\left\{1 + \frac{c}{pK} - \frac{\delta}{r} + \sqrt{\left[\left(1 + \frac{c}{pK} - \frac{\delta}{r}\right)^2 + \frac{8c}{pK}\frac{\delta}{r}\right]}\right\}$$

(cf. Crutchfield and Zellner, 1962, p. 117). Thus, for the case of the Schaefer model we always obtain a unique and computable optimal equilibrium stock level $x^* > 0.$[16]

It is easy to show, however, that for more general models, eq. (14) may possess multiple solutions – or no solutions at all (Clark, 1973). In such cases, the determination of an optimum optimorum is more difficult, and will generally depend upon the initial conditions.

Henceforth we shall suppose, unless stated to the contrary, that eq. (14) determines a unique equilibrium solution $x = x^*$. The question of the optimal approach to this equilibrium will be discussed at a later point.

Equation (14) can be interpreted without difficulty. The L.H.S. is the present value of the marginal sustainable rent, $d\{(p - c(x^*))F(x^*)\}/dx^*$, afforded by the marginal increment to the stock. The R.H.S. is the marginal rent enjoyed from *current* harvesting. On the one hand, the L.H.S. of (14) can be interpreted as an expression of marginal user cost (Scott, 1953, 1955), in that it shows the cost of capturing today the marginal increment of

---

[15] Eq. (14) is in fact the Euler equation for the integral (10), with h replaced by $F(x) - \dot{x}$. In this linear model the Euler equation thus provides only a discrete family (possibly empty) of singular extremals, namely the equilibrium solutions $x = x^*$. Nevertheless, as explained below, these singular extremals normally form the main components of our desired optimal solution.

[16] If $p < c/K$, it can be seen that $x^* > K$, which merely supports our intuition: when harvesting costs exceed price at all levels of population up to $x = K$, then no feasible nonzero harvest policy is optimal.

fish, a cost which has to be weighed against the marginal gain from current capture. On the other hand, the L.H.S. and R.H.S. of the equation can be viewed as the imputed demand price and the supply price of the capital "asset" at the time t, respectively.[17]

Equation (14) is, of course, an implicit equation in x^*. Once x^* is known, the optimal harvest rate is automatically determined by virtue of the fact that x^* is constant, i.e. $h^*(t) = F(x^*)$. The optimal rate of *effort* accompanying x^* and $F(x^*)$ can readily be determined from the model.[18] From eq. (7), effort can be expressed as

$$E = \frac{h(t)}{bx^\beta},\qquad(15)$$

given that $\alpha = 1$. Thus, the optimal effort rate, E^*, can be expressed as

$$E^* = \frac{F(x^*)}{b \cdot (x^*)^\beta}.$$

A more transparent form of (14) is obtained by carrying out the differentiation on the L.H.S. and then multiplying through by $\delta/(p - c(x^*))$:

$$F'(x^*) - \frac{c'(x^*)F(x^*)}{p - c(x^*)} = \delta.\qquad(16)$$

This equation is recognizable from capital theory as a modified golden-rule equilibrium equation, being modified both by the discount rate and by what we shall refer to as the marginal stock effect. The L.H.S. of (16) is the "own rate of interest", i.e. the instantaneous marginal sustainable rent divided by the supply price of the asset. Thus, (16) states simply that the optimal stock is the one at which the own rate of interest of the stock is equal to the social

---

[17]It is usual in the literature to refer to the adjoint variable as the imputed price, or, more properly, the imputed demand price of capital (Shell, 1962). The L.H.S. of (14) is identical to the adjoint variable along the singular path. We know that achieving the optimal capital stock involves maximizing the Hamiltonian with respect to the control variable, i.e. $\partial H/\partial h = \sigma = 0$. This implies that $\psi(t) = p - c(x)$. We know that along the singular path

$$p - c(x) = \frac{1}{\delta}\{[p - c(x)]F'(x) - c'(x)F(x)\}.$$

Thus, the L.H.S. of (14) can be seen as the adjoint variable along the singular path.

In using the term "supply price" here we are using an essentially Marshallian/Keynesian definition: namely, the amount that must be paid to obtain the additional increment to the stock. In the context of this model the amount that must be "paid" is the current rent forgone at the margin (Keynes, 1936, p. 135).

[18]We could in fact have chosen to use $E(t)$ as the control variable. This was not done because the notation would have become considerably more cumbersome.

rate of discount. The own rate of interest consists of two components: $F'(x^*)$, the instantaneous marginal physical product of the capital, and $c'(x^*)F(x^*)/(p - c(x^*))$, the marginal stock effect.

The marginal stock effect is analogous to the "wealth effect" to be found in modern capital theory. Kurz (1968, p. 352) defines wealth effects to mean that "in addition to the consumption stream the utility function is also sensitive to the capital stock...". While the utility (gross) derived from the consumption of fish is not itself sensitive to the biomass, the *net economic benefit* derived from fish consumption clearly is sensitive, by virtue of the fact that harvesting costs are a function of the biomass. The term "wealth effect" is inappropriate in this context, and so is replaced by "stock effect". As expressed in (16), the marginal stock effect is the partial derivative of total harvesting costs with respect to the biomass divided by the supply price of capital. As such it makes transparent the fact that in the linear model harvesting costs influence the choice of x only by virtue of their sensitivity to the biomass. If harvesting costs are insensitive to the size of x, harvesting costs – and the price of fish for that matter – become irrelevant to the optimization process (given that $p > c(K)$).

The modified golden-rule equilibrium condition, as expressed in (16), permits us to deal easily with a troublesome issue; namely, whether or not the rational sole owner or social manager would opt to "deplete" the stock. In the literature "depletion", or its equivalent, "biological overfishing", is deemed to have occurred if fishing effort is raised to a level such that the sustainable yield falls below the maximum (Christy, 1973), implying in turn that the stock level has been reduced below that associated with maximum sustained yield – x_{MSY}. The problem is essentially whether the short-run benefits of depleting the stock (or the short-run costs of building up an already depleted stock) will be such as to cause x^* to be less than x_{MSY}. The issue revolves around the magnitude of the social discount rate, the relationship of harvesting costs to the size of the biomass and the supply price of the capital stock.

Crutchfield and Zellner (1962, p. 117) in developing their dynamic model argued that the *minimum* possible optimal stock level is x_{MSY} – regardless of the size of the discount rate.[19] Plourde in his 1970 article indicated that $x^* < x_{MSY}$ was indeed a possible outcome, but then muddied the waters

---

[19]Crutchfield and Zellner are quite emphatic on this point at several places in their discussion: "It should be clear that the... biological overfishing case, in which effort is pushed to the point where physical yields actually decline could not arise under private ownership of the resource." And, "Such a condition makes even less sense in economic terms than in biological" (1962, pp. 19 and 26).

somewhat in a 1971 article (Plourde, 1971, p. 262) by implying that his results did not really conflict with those of Crutchfield and Zellner. In a recent paper, Cooper (1974) allows for the possibility that $x^* < x_{MSY}$, but implies that such an outcome is likely only if the level of the discount rate is in some sense "high", i.e. higher than real rates of interest currently experienced in practice. Brown (1974) provides the clearest exposition of all on the matter, but unfortunately is unable to locate the optimal stock in population space, except in extreme cases. As we shall see, these problems can now easily be resolved.

Return now to eq. (16). It has already been demonstrated that given the existence of a unique solution, it is possible to locate x^* in population space without difficulty. Secondly, note that if the discount rate and the marginal stock effect are both equal to zero, then $x^* = x_{MSY}$, i.e. $F'(x^*) = 0$. This makes it obvious that whether x^* is greater than, equal to, or less than x_{MSY} depends upon the relative strength of the two correctives, δ and the marginal stock effect. Indeed, we can postulate a simple rule. Let

$$R = - \frac{c'(x_{MSY})F(x_{MSY})}{p - c(x_{MSY})} \, .$$

Then

$$x^* \begin{cases} < x_{MSY}, & \text{if } \delta > R, \\ = x_{MSY}, & \text{if } \delta = R, \\ > x_{MSY}, & \text{if } \delta < R. \end{cases} \tag{17}$$

Thus, clearly, the rational social manager can opt for a "depleted" stock. Indeed, he could conceivably opt to deplete the stock to the point of extinction.[20]

It should also be clear from (17) that one cannot comfortably assume that x^* will never be less than x_{MSY} unless δ is "large" (however one defines "large"). There is no a priori reason for assuming that R for any given stock level will be, in some meaningful sense, "large". Indeed, if harvesting costs were insensitive to the biomass, R would vanish. Yet even if one refuses to admit to the possibility that $c'(x)$ could equal zero, one must note that R is dependent, not only upon the sensitivity of harvesting costs to the stock size at $x = x_{MSY}$, but also upon the supply price of the capital stock at x_{MSY}, a point that will be emphasized further in a following paragraph.[21]

---

[20] See Clark (1973a,b); Beddington et al. (1975).
[21] In the case of the Antarctic whale populations, for example, Clark (1981) has argued that depletion might be optimal at discount rates as low as 1 percent per annum.

One practical consequence of all of this is that evidence of "depletion" as defined above cannot be accepted, ipso facto, as evidence of economic waste. Thus, in a recent commentary on waste of resources in fishing an example is given of the harvesting of demersal fish on the Georges Bank in the Northwest Atlantic. According to a report cited, fishing effort applied in 1971 was 31 percent in excess of the amount required to achieve MSY.[22] Yet this information *by itself* tells us nothing about the actual amount of waste (if any) involved in these operations.

It has been recognized by Turvey (1964), Christy and Scott (1965), Copes (1970, 1972) and others that successive exogenous increases in the price of fish or technological improvements in fishing techniques would, under conditions of an unregulated competitive fishery, lead eventually to a decline in sustainable yields, i.e. depletion, this being cited as one of the perversities of the common-property nature of many fisheries. Yet it is quite possible that price increases or cost decreases could also lead to depletion under optimal social management, in terms of the present model. This arises from the fact that the marginal stock effect is a decreasing function of the supply price of capital. It can be seen in eq. (17) that if p rises sufficiently high, or if costs shift downwards sufficiently far, R will prove to be less than δ, given that $\delta \neq 0$. One need only observe that

$$\lim_{p \to \infty} \left(\frac{c'(x)F(x)}{p - c(x)} \right) = 0; \qquad \lim_{c(x) \to 0} \left(\frac{c'(x)F(x)}{p - c(x)} \right) = 0. \tag{18}$$

We have as yet not attempted to relate the model presented here with the static or received theory. The objective of the sole owner in terms of the static theory is to maximize the sustainable rent, i.e. $[p - c(x)]F(x)$. Therefore the optimal stock (in the linear case) will be given by the equation[23]

$$\frac{\mathrm{d}}{\mathrm{d}x^*} \{ [p - c(x^*)] F(x^*) \} = 0. \tag{19}$$

From (16) this can be seen as the equivalent of setting the discount rate equal to zero. Thus, the static model predicts the correct optimal stock level

---

[22] See Christy (1973, p. 17).

[23] This is with reference to the version of the received theory based upon the Schaefer model. The alternative biological model often cited, the Beverton–Holt (1957) model, is not discussed in this paper. The reason for this is that the complexities introduced by making the growth rate of the fish and the age structure of the fishery explicit are immense and have yet to be properly explored. Certainly, they cannot be adequately dealt with by making references to eumetric yield curves or by introducing a simple mesh-size variable to an economic model, which in turn rest upon a biological model totally different from the Beverton–Holt model.

For an insight into some of the problems the Beverton–Holt model poses for the economist, see Clark, Edwards and Friedlaender (1974).

only under the extreme assumption that $\delta = 0$. The common-property outcome, it might be noted in passing, is the equivalent of setting $\delta = \infty$. Finally, from (19) it can be seen why the static model predicts that the rational sole owner will never "deplete" the stock. With $\delta = 0$, the temporary gains (costs) derived from reducing (restoring) a stock become trivial, so that one always obtains $x^* \geqslant x_{MSY}$.

Brown (1974) and others have made the point that, if the fishery remains decentralized and competitive and is to be regulated by means of a tax programme, the correct per-unit harvest tax is, barring crowding externalities, one equal to the adjoint or costate variable. This taxation policy is indeed correct once equilibrium has been reached at x^*. A tax equal to what we have termed in our model the marginal user cost (which is identically equal to the adjoint variable along the singular path)[24] would produce a *perceived* zero-rent situation for the industry, i.e. every vessel owner would find his total revenue equal to his total costs inclusive of the tax. Thus, once the stock level x^* has been reached the taxation policy will assure that the industry harvest rate will equal $F(x^*)$.

All of this, however, says nothing about what the optimal tax rate is *before* x^* is reached. It is not at all clear that setting the tax rate equal to the adjoint variable is optimal when $x(t) \neq x^*(t)$. To see why this is so, suppose that in fact $x(0) \neq x^*(0)$. The first problem becomes that of determining the optimal approach path to x^*, in other words to determine the optimal investment policy vis-à-vis the biomass. With the linear model the problem has an easy solution, for the linearity of the model assures that there are no penalties to approaching the optimal stock level rapidly. The optimal approach is the so-called "bang-bang" approach:

$$h^*(t) = \begin{cases} h_{max}, & \text{whenever } x(t) > x^*, \\ 0, & \text{whenever } x(t) < x^*. \end{cases} \tag{20}$$

In terms of investment policy, eq. (20) states that, if one commences at a point such as A in fig. 2.1, the appropriate policy is to set the rate of investment, $(F(x) - h(t))$, equal to the maximum, which in turn implies setting $h(t) = 0$. Conversely, if one commences at a point such as B, the appropriate policy is to disinvest as rapidly as possible, i.e. set $h(t) = h_{max}$. Once stated, the rule becomes obvious, if not downright banal.[25]

---

[24] See footnote 17 above.
[25] While the rule may seem obvious intuitively, the mathematical justification may be less transparent. This question is discussed in the Appendix.

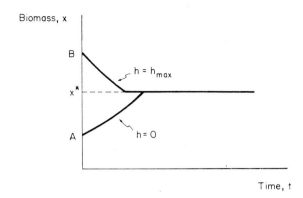

Figure 2.1

What is important to note, however, is the fact that we cannot know what the appropriate tax rates are until we are provided with more information on how the industry will respond to various tax rates, until, that is, a reaction function for the industry has been specified (cf. Smith, 1969). Certainly there is no necessary reason to suppose that the correct policy would be to set the tax equal to the adjoint variable. Suppose, for example, that we commenced at A (fig. 2.1). What is called for is an abrupt cessation of fishing activity until the stock has grown to x^*. Indeed, one might well want to abandon (temporarily) taxation as a method of control altogether and impose an outright ban on fishing (i.e. quantitative controls) until the stock level had risen to x^*.

3. Nonautonomous models

The model in the previous section rested upon highly restrictive assumptions of linearity and autonomy. The model can, however, quite easily be extended to make it either nonautonomous or nonlinear. In this section we make the model nonautonomous while retaining the linearity assumptions. Nonlinearity assumptions are introduced in the following section.

The model is made nonautonomous by introducing continuous parameter shifts through time. In effect certain parameters are now transformed into exogenous variables. We shall confine the analysis to price and harvesting-cost shifts, but the analysis could easily be applied to continuous shifts in other parameters such as the discount rate.

While revenue and harvesting costs continue to be assumed linear in harvesting, it will now be assumed that both price and the harvesting-cost function will be subject to known continuous shifts over the time range $t=0$ to $t=\infty$, i.e. the future time paths of price and costs are fully known. Price can now be expressed as $p(t)$. Unit costs of harvesting $c(x, t)$ will now be expressed as

$$c(x,t)=\phi(t)c(x(t)),\tag{21}$$

where $\phi(t)\geqslant 0$ is a variable coefficient which permits us to account for shifts in the cost function.

The objective functional can now be expressed as

$$P.V.=\int_{0}^{\infty}e^{-\delta t}[p(t)-\phi(t)c(x(t))]h(t)\,dt.\tag{22}$$

The present value of rent is to be maximized subject to the usual conditions. A routine calculation as before (see the appendix) leads easily to the following equation for the singular solution, $x(t)=x^{*}(t)$:

$$F'(x^{*})-\frac{\phi(t)c'(x^{*})F(x^{*})}{p(t)-\phi(t)c(x^{*})}=\delta-\frac{\dot{p}(t)-\dot{\phi}(t)c(x^{*})}{p(t)-\phi(t)c(x^{*})}.\tag{23}$$

If we can assume that there exists an unique solution x^{*} at each point t, then $x^{*}(t)$ can be seen as tracing out an optimal time path for the stock or biomass level.

The effect of incorporating continuous shifts in price and the harvesting-cost function is to introduce an additional corrective to the modified golden-rule equation (16), a corrective which can be interpreted as the instantaneous percentage change in the supply price of capital. The effect of the new corrective upon the process of stock-level optimization can be seen as follows. Let it be supposed that the supply price of capital is expected to increase, the expected increase being due either to an expected increase in the price of fish or to an expected exogenous decrease in harvesting costs or to both. In the previous section it was observed that upward shifts in the supply price of capital lead to lower optimal stock levels. The effect of *anticipation* of the immediate increase in supply price, however, will be to increase the optimal stock level at time t. The rationale is obvious enough. Anticipation of greater benefits from fishing tomorrow will cause a reduction in harvesting today.

The new modified golden rule (23) is "myopic" (Arrow, 1964, 1968) in the sense that the decision rule is independent of both the past and the future, except to the extent that one must anticipate the immediate change in the capital supply price. Thus, the information demands imposed by the rule are extremely limited. In spite of the fact that prices and costs may be fluctuating steadily over time, the only information required for determining the optimal stock, $x^*(t)$, is the marginal product of x at time t, the price of fish and harvesting costs at time t plus the instantaneous rates of change of $p(t)$ and $c(x, t)$.

In section 2 an optimal tax for a decentralized competitive fishery could be specified to keep the fishery operating at the optimal stock level once the singular path had been reached. The tax was found to be equal to the marginal user cost. It is tempting to suggest in the nonautonomous case that, once the singular path has been reached, the optimal tax at any time t would be one equal to the marginal user cost adjusted for rates of change in p and $c(x)$. We can express the adjusted marginal user cost as

$$\frac{1}{\delta}\left(p(t) - \phi(t)c(x^*)F'(x^*) - \phi(t)c'(x^*)F(x^*) + \dot{p}(t) - \dot{\phi}(t)c(x^*) \right).$$

$$(24)$$

Unfortunately, the temptation must be resisted, because even though the adjustments in stock levels and hence effort levels may be small, we are still plagued by the absence of an industry reaction function. Linking the optimal tax to the adjoint variable or marginal user cost is valid then only if one is actually on the singular path (which in turn supposes that the linear model is valid) and if one can safely assume that harvesting costs and the price of fish are not subject to exogenous shifts through time.

The myopic rule and the optimal tax policy stemming from it hold so long as the constraints upon the control variable do not become binding, meaning by this that the adjustments in x^* demanded by supply price changes are not so great as to drive $h(t)$ to $h = 0$ or to $h = h_{max}$. If in fact the constraints do become binding, then the stock level $x(t)$ is temporarily forced off the singular path $x^*(t)$. We are then faced with what Arrow (1968) refers to as a "blocked interval." The myopic rule must consequently be modified and the optimization problem becomes more difficult, but not insoluble.

Consider, for example, the effect of a large discrete increase in the supply price of the capital occurring at time T. The supply price is assumed to be constant before T and after T (figure 2.2). The singular path follows the

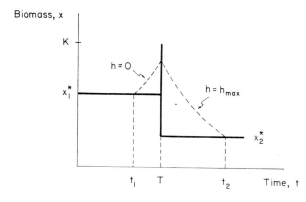

Figure 2.2

solid line.[26] Ideally x should be increased to the biological maximum, $x = K$, the instant before T (as $d/dt(p - \phi c(x))$) goes to infinity) and then should be immediately reduced to x_2^* at time T. This is clearly impossible since h cannot be reduced below $h = 0$ nor increased above $h = h_{max}$. In other words, the constraints upon the control variable become binding. If $x(T)$ is to be larger than x_1^*, then at some point of time $t_1 < T$, harvesting must be reduced in order to permit the stock level to increase. The time period $t_1 \leqslant t \leqslant T$, then, is a blocked interval in the sense that we are forced temporarily off the singular path. At time T, the stock cannot be instantaneously reduced to x_2^*. The best that can be done is to harvest at the maximum rate until x_2^* is reached at some time $t_2 > T$. The time period $T \leqslant t \leqslant t_2$ then constitutes a second blocked interval.

The problem then is to select the optimal value of t_1, i.e. the point in time at which harvesting is reduced to permit x to rise above x_1^*. Once t_1 is selected, $x(T)$ is automatically determined, as is t_2. It is a consequence of the maximum principle (see appendix) that the optimal harvest rates during the blocked intervals are $h(t) = 0$ and $h(t) = h_{max}$, respectively.

Conceptually the nature of this optimization problem is straightforward. The later t_1 is, the shorter will be the period of sacrifice during which society forgoes harvesting, e.g. if $t_1 = T$ there will be no period of sacrifice. On the other hand, the later t_1, the smaller will be $x(T)$, and the smaller will be the benefit enjoyed from harvesting at the higher supply price.

---

[26] Note that the singular path has a "spike" at $t = T$; this corresponds to the occurrence of the term $\dot{p}(T) = +\infty$ in eq. (23), resulting from the discrete jump in $p(t)$ at that point.

Let the present value to be enjoyed from harvesting the fish now be expressed as

$$P.V. = \int_0^{t_1} e^{-\delta t}(p_1 - \phi_1 c(x_1^*))F(x_1^*)\,dt$$

$$+ \int_T^{t_2} e^{-\delta t}(p_2 - \phi_2 c(x, t))h_{max}\,dt$$

$$+ \int_{t_2}^{\infty} e^{-\delta t}(p_2 - \phi_2 c(x_2^*))F(x_2^*)\,dt. \tag{25}$$

Differentiating $P.V.$ with respect to t_1 and setting $\partial P.V./\partial t_1 = 0$, we have

$$e^{-\delta t_1}[p_1 - \phi_1 c(x_1^*)]F(x_1^*) = \{e^{-\delta t_2}[p_2 - \phi_2 c(x_2^*)](F(x_2^*) - h_{max})\}\frac{dt_2}{dt_1}$$

$$+ \int_T^{t_2} e^{-\delta t}\frac{\partial \phi_2 c[x(t, t_1)]h_{max}}{\partial t_1}\,dt. \tag{26}$$

This apparently complex equation can be interpreted simply as stating that the optimal t_1 will be that at which the marginal benefit derived from extending t_1 (L.H.S.), is equal to the marginal cost from so doing (R.H.S.).

Finally, it should be clear that when faced with blocked intervals the information demands could become extensive. The supply price change occurring at T will have to be anticipated in advance of T, possibly far in advance.

4. Nonlinear models

We turn now to a consideration of nonlinear models, while at the same time restoring the assumption of autonomy. Nonlinearity is introduced first by relaxing the assumption that the demand function for fish has a price elasticity equal to infinity, and secondly by permitting effort costs to be nonlinear in effort, which in turn implies that harvesting costs are nonlinear in harvesting. It shall be assumed that $\partial^2 C_E/\partial E^2 > 0$, thus implying that $\partial^2 C_h/\partial h^2 > 0$, where C_E and C_h denote total effort costs and total harvesting costs, respectively.

Several authors, Copes (1970) and Anderson (1973) among them, have made the point that once one relaxes the assumption that the demand function is infinitely elastic, the object of social utility maximization can no longer be expressed in terms of rent maximization.[27] Hence, the objective functional must now be expressed as

$$P.V. = \int_0^\infty e^{-\delta t}[U(h) - c(x, h)h]\,dt, \qquad (27)$$

where $U(h)$ is total utility derived from the consumption of fish and where $c(x, h)$ denotes unit harvesting costs as a function of x and h. We assume that $U'(h) > 0$ and $U''(h) < 0$. Given the other underlying assumptions, we have $U'(h) = p(h)$. Since the objective functional (27) is a nonlinear function of the control variable, h, the model itself is now nonlinear.

The Hamiltonian of the above nonlinear optimal control problem is

$$H = e^{-\delta t}\{U(h) - c(x, h)h + \psi(t)(F(x) - h)\}. \qquad (28)$$

From the maximum principle in the nonlinear case (see appendix),[28] we obtain the following equation for equilibrium solutions (i.e. with $h = F(x^*)$):

$$F'(x^*) - \frac{\dfrac{\partial c(x^*, F(x^*))}{\partial x^*} \cdot F(x^*)}{p(F(x^*)) - \left[c(x^*, F(x^*)) + \dfrac{\partial c(x^*, F(x^*))}{\partial h} \cdot F(x^*)\right]} = \delta.$$

$$(29)$$

The marginal stock-effect term now looks somewhat formidable, but can be interpreted in the same way as before. The numerator is the partial derivative of total harvesting costs with respect to the biomass, while the denominator is a more complex version of the supply price of capital. The expression $[c(x^*, F(x^*)) + \partial c(x^*, F(x^*))/\partial h \cdot F(x^*)]$ is the partial derivative of total harvesting costs with respect to the harvest rate.

An interesting feature of eq. (29) is that it may give rise to multiple equilibria. It has long been recognized that multiple equilibria could emerge

---

[27]This statement is not entirely accurate. One can think of exceptions. Suppose that the social manager was a *national* social manager, that the harvest was sold entirely to foreigners, and that the foreign demand function had a price elasticity less than infinity. Then the manager should act like a private sole manager and maximize the present value of rent from the fishery. The objective functional would be simply

$$P.V. = \int_0^\infty e^{-\delta t}[p(h) - c(x, h)]h\,dt.$$

[28]Our assumptions imply that the integrand in eq. (27) is a concave function of the control variable, h, so that the maximum principle is relevant.

in the case of competitive, unregulated fisheries when the demand function had a price elasticity less than infinity.[29] It appeared, however, that one could confidently assume there would be a unique optimal solution for the socially managed fishery.[30] Eq. (29) indicates that, in the context of a dynamic model, the confidence is unwarranted.

If there are three equilibria,[31] i.e. an unstable equilibrium bounded by two stable equilibria, no serious problem exists, so long as the initial position is given (Clark, 1974). Suppose that the equilibrium stocks are x_1^*, x_2^* and x_3^*, where $x_1^* < x_2^* < x_3^*$. The stock level x_2^*, the unstable equilibrium, constitutes a "watershed"[32] in the sense that if $x(0) < x_2^*$, the optimal equilibrium stock will be x_1^*, whereas if $x(0) > x_2^*$ the optimal equilibrium stock will be x_3^*. It is conceivable, however, that one might encounter more than three equilibria in which case selecting an optimum optimorum could prove to be extremely difficult, if not impossible.

Next we observe that in the nonlinear model, the optimal approach to equilibrium (even where a unique equilibrium exists) will differ from that encountered in the linear model. The "bang-bang" approach of the linear case will be replaced by an asymptotic approach. The decision rule to be applied along the approach path can be expressed as

$$F'(x) - \frac{[\partial c(x,h)/\partial x] \cdot h}{p(h) - [c(x,h) + (\partial c(x,h)/\partial h) \cdot h]} + \frac{\dot{\psi}}{\psi} = \delta, \tag{30}$$

where ψ, it will be recalled, is the demand price of the resource. As one approaches the equilibrium stock level, ψ will be subject to continuous change. Thus, capital gains (losses) will be continuously generated, which must be accounted for in the decision rule. When the equilibrium stock, x^*, is reached, $\dot{\psi}$ will equal zero and eq. (30) reduces to eq. (29).

After having discussed nonautonomous and nonlinear models individually, it would seem advisable to discuss models which are both nonautonomous and nonlinear. However, we shall not do so because such models present complexities which would carry us far beyond the scope of this paper. Further comments on nonautonomous, nonlinear models and the difficulties they pose will be found in the appendix.

---

[29]See, for example, Christy and Scott (1965), Copes (1970), Anderson (1973).

[30]See Anderson (1973).

[31]Cases can arise in which eq. (29) possesses an even number of solutions, but except under pathological circumstances $x = 0$ will then also become a stable equilibrium, so that the number of equilibria remains odd. For example, if (29) has no solutions, then $x = 0$ becomes a stable equilibrium, and optimal harvesting may lead to the extinction of the fishery. Cf. footnote 20 above.

[32]See Leviatan and Samuelson (1969).

5. Conclusion

As has been recognized from its inception, the economics of fishing, like other branches of natural resource economics, should ideally be cast in capital-theoretic terms. The fact that what we have termed the received theory was cast in nondynamic terms was as much as anything a reflection on the inadequacies of capital theory. With the advent of optimal control theory, capital theory became transformed into a powerful and flexible tool of analysis. This in turn has led to various attempts to reformulate the economic theory of fishing in dynamic terms. The purpose of this chapter has been to attempt to explore the relationships between the economics of fishing and modern capital theory in a systematic and rigorous manner, but to do so in such a way that the reader does not lose sight of the economics by becoming enmeshed in unnecessarily complex mathematical formulations.

The study commences with a simple linear autonomous model of optimal fishery management. Here the results are particularly straightforward. An optimal stationary equilibrium exists, determined by a generalized "modified golden rule". The optimal management policy which emerges is that of following the "bang-bang" feedback law: adjust the stock level towards the stationary equilibrium as rapidly as possible.

The model is then extended in two directions by relaxing in turn the assumptions of autonomy and linearity. While the basic results obtained can be readily interpreted, the simplicity of the linear autonomous theory is soon lost with the advent of such complications as blocked intervals and multiple equilibria. However, the presence of such difficulties should evoke no surprise. The complexities arising from nonautonomous and nonlinear models are, after all, major sources of uncertainty and controversy in present-day capital theory.

The models developed in this chapter have been confined entirely to fishing. It should, however, be clear that the analysis could, mutatis mutandis, be extended to other areas of renewable resource management.[33]

Appendix

As linear optimal control problems arise only infrequently in economics, it may be of some benefit to the reader to have the techniques of the linear

---

[33] See Clark and De Pree (1979).

theory outlined and contrasted with the more familiar techniques of nonlinear optimal control theory. Further details can be found in the work of Bryson and Ho (1969). The discussion is based upon the Pontrjagin maximum principle (Pontrjagin et al., 1962).

In the general case (linear or nonlinear) we begin with a state equation,

$$\frac{dx}{dt} = F(x, t; u), \qquad 0 \leqslant t \leqslant T, \tag{A.1}$$

and an objective functional,

$$J = \int_0^T G(x, t; u) \, dt, \tag{A.2}$$

which is to be maximized by appropriate choice of the control $u(t)$, subject to (A.1). The maximum principle is formulated in terms of the Hamiltonian expression[34]

$$H(x, t; u, \lambda) = G(x, t; u) + \lambda(t) F(x, t; u), \tag{A.3}$$

where $\lambda(t)$, the adjoint variable, is to be determined.

In the nonlinear (classical) case, the maximum principle asserts the following two equations (plus appropriate transversality conditions) as necessary conditions for optimality:

$$\frac{\partial H}{\partial u} = 0 \tag{A.4}$$

and

$$\frac{\partial H}{\partial x} = -\frac{d\lambda}{dt}. \tag{A.5}$$

Since H is nonlinear in u, eq. (A.4) can be solved in principle (by virtue of the implicit function theorem) for u in terms of x and λ. Substituting this solution into (A.1) and (A.5) then yields a coupled system of two differential equations, determining the optimal trajectories $(x(t), \lambda(t))$. If the original problem (A.1), (A.2) is autonomous, the same will be true of the differential equation (A.5), so that the well-developed theory of plane autonomous systems can be utilized. The typical problem in capital theory possesses a unique solution (x^*, λ^*) which turns out to be a saddle point. Hence, optimal trajectories can be seen to possess the "catenary turnpike" property (in finite time-horizon problems) – fig. 2.3.

---

[34] This formulation assumes "normality" of the given optimal control problem; cf. Bryson and Ho (1969).

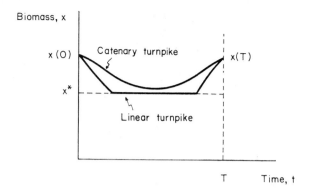

Figure 2.3

Next consider the linear case, in which

$$F(x, t, u) = F_1(x, t)u + F_2(x, t)$$

and

$$G(x, t, u) = G_1(x, t)u + G_2(x, t).$$

Thus, the Hamiltonian is also linear:

$$H(x, t; u, \lambda) = (G_1 + \lambda F_1)u + (G_2 + \lambda F_2). \tag{A.6}$$

Let $\sigma(t)$ denote the coefficient of u in this expression:

$$\sigma(t) = G_1(x(t), t) + \lambda(t)F_1(x(t), t). \tag{A.7}$$

Since $\partial H/\partial u$ does not contain u, the approach used in the nonlinear case is unsuccessful. Rather, one requires the generalized (Pontrjagin) version of (A.4), namely

$$u(t) \text{ maximizes } H(x(t), t; u; \lambda(t)), \quad \text{for all } t, \tag{A.8}$$

where the maximization is taken over u belonging to a predetermined control set, e.g.

$$a \leqslant u \leqslant b. \tag{A.9}$$

Here a and b may depend explicitly on t and $x(t)$.

Clearly, at any time t we must have either $u(t) = a$ or b ("bang-bang control") or else $\sigma(t) = 0$. Of particular interest is the case, called "singular control", in which

$$\sigma(t) \equiv 0 \tag{A.10}$$

over an open time interval (t_1, t_2). A standard algorithm for solving linear problems now proceeds as follows.

First we determine the singular solution, using (A.10) and its derived form:

$$\frac{d\sigma}{dt} = \left\{ \frac{\partial G_1}{\partial x} + \frac{\partial F_1}{\partial x} \right\} \frac{dx}{dt} + \frac{\partial G_1}{\partial t} + \lambda \frac{\partial F_1}{\partial t} + F_1 \frac{d\lambda}{dt} \equiv 0. \tag{A.11}$$

Substituting from eqs. (A.1) and (A.5) we then obtain a single equation for the singular path $x(t) = x^*(t)$, since $u(t)$ drops out at this stage. We assume that $x^*(t)$ is uniquely determined (the contrary case is interesting but difficult to handle).

Next, if $x^*(0) \neq x_0$, the given initial value, then we must utilize a bang-bang adjustment control to drive the state variable $x(t)$ to the singular path.[35] A similar terminal adjustment phase may also be required. The resulting optimal path is illustrated in fig. 2.3. Finally, it may happen that the control constraints (A.9) prevent $x(t)$ from following the singular path $x^*(t)$; giving rise to a so-called "blocked interval", as encountered in section 3 above.

In this paper we have made use of the fact that nonautonomous linear control problems can often be solved quite easily by using the above algorithm. On the other hand, nonautonomous nonlinear control problems are generally much more difficult, for the good reason that nonautonomous nonlinear differential equations are difficult. Specialized methods, usually based on numerical computation, are required for each particular type of problem. Many additional complexities can arise.

References

Anderson, L.G. (1973) "Optimum Economic Yield of a Fishery Given a Variable Price of Output", *Journal of the Fisheries Research Board of Canada*, 30, 4, 509–518.

Arrow, K.J. (1964) "Optimal Capital Policy, The Cost of Capital, and Myopic Decision Rules", *Annals of the Institute of Statistical Mathematics*, 16, 21–30.

Arrow, K.J. (1968) "Optimal Capital Policy with Irreversible Investment", in: J.N. Wolfe, ed., *Value Capital and Growth*, Papers in Honour of Sir John Hicks (Edinburgh University Press) pp. 1–20.

[35] For the sake of uniformity in handling both linear and nonlinear control problems, we have chosen to discuss both on the basis of the mathematically profound maximum principle, omitting numerous technical details. It happens, however, that the linear case (in one state dimension) can be treated rigorously on a much more elementary level: a single application of Green's theorem in the plane immediately establishes optimality of the bang-bang-singular solution described here.

Beddington, J.R., C.M.K. Watts and W.D.C. Wright (1975) "Optimal cropping of self-reproducible natural resources", *Econometrica*, 43, 789–802.

Bell, F.W. (1972) "Technological Externalities and Common-Property Resources: An Empirical Study of the U.S. Northern Lobster Fishery", *Journal of Political-Economy*, 80, 148–158.

Bellman, R. (1957) *Dynamic Programming* (Princeton University Press, Princeton).

Beverton, R.J.H. and S.J. Holt (1957) "On the Dynamics of Exploited Fish Populations", Ministry of Agriculture, Fisheries and Food, Fisheries Invest. Ser. 2, no. 19 (London).

Bradley, P.G. (1970) "Seasonal Models of the Fishing Industry", in: A.D. Scott, ed., *Economics of Fisheries Management: A Symposium* (University of British Columbia, Institute of Animal Resource Ecology, Vancouver).

Brown, G. (1974) "An Optimal Program for Managing Common Property Resources with Congestion Externalities", *Journal of Political Economy*, 82, 163–174.

Bryson, A.E. and Y.C. Ho (1969) *Applied Optimal Control* (Blaisdell, Waltham, Mass.).

Christy, F.T. (1973) "Alternative Arrangements for Marine Fisheries: An Overview", *Resources for the Future* (Washington, D.C.).

Christy, F.T. and A.D. Scott (1965) *The Common Wealth in Ocean Fisheries* (John Hopkins Press, Baltimore, Md.).

Clark, C.W. (1973a) "The Economics of Overexploitation", *Science*, 181, 630–634.

Clark, C.W. (1973b) "Profit Maximization and the Extinction of Animal Species", *Journal of Political Economy*, 81, 950–961.

Clark, C.W. (1974) *Supply and Demand Relationships in Fisheries Economics*, Proc. IRIA Symposium on Control Theory (Paris).

Clark, C.W. (1981) "The Economics of Whaling: A Two-Species Model", *Simulation*.

Clark, C.W. and J. de Pree (1979) "A Simple Linear Model for the Optimal Exploitation of Renewable Resources", *Applied Mathematics and Optimization*, 5, 181–196.

Clark, C.W., G. Edwards and M. Friedlaender (1974) "Beverton–Holt Model of a Commercial Fishery: Optimal Dynamics", *Journal of the Fisheries Research Board of Canada*, 30, 1629–1640.

Cooper, R.N. (1974) "An Economist's View of the Oceans", in: *Proc. Conference on Conflict and Order in Ocean Relations*.

Copes, P. (1970) "The Backwards-Bending Supply Curve of the Fishing Industry", *Scottish Journal of Political Economy*, 17, 69–77.

Copes, P. (1972) "Factor Rents, Sole Ownership and the Optimum Level of Fisheries Exploitation", *The Manchester School of Economics and Social Studies*, 40, 145–164.

Crutchfield, J.A. and A. Zellner (1962) "Economic Aspects of the Pacific Halibut Fishery", *Fishery Industrial Research*, vol. 1, no. 1 (U.S. Department of the Interior, Washington, D.C.).

Cummings, R.G. and O.R. Burt (1969) "The Economics of Production from Natural Resources. A Note", *American Economic Review*, 59, 985–990.

Dorfman, R. (1969) "An Economic Interpretation of Optimal Control Theory", *American Economic Review*, 59, 817–831.

Gordon, H. (1954) "The Economic Theory of a Common-Property Resource: The Fishery", *Journal of Political Economy*, 62, 124–142.

Keynes, J.M. (1936) *The General Theory of Employment, Interest and Money* (Harcourt and Brace, New York).

Kurz, M. (1968) "Optimal Economic Growth and Wealth Effects", *International Economic Review*, 9, 348–357.

Leviatan, N. and P.A. Samuelson (1969) "Notes on Turnpikes: Stable and Unstable", *Journal of Economic Theory*, 1, 454–475.

Mohring, H.S. (n.d.) The Costs of Inefficient Fishery Regulation: A Partial Study of the Pacific Coast Halibut Industry, Unpublished.

Neher, P.A. (1974) "Notes on the Volterra-Quadratic Fishery", *Journal of Economic Theory*, 6, 39–49.

Plourde, C.G. (1970) "A Simple Model of Replenishable Natural Resource Exploitation, *American Economic Review*, 60, 518–522.

Plourde, C.G. (1971) "Exploitation of Common-Property Replenishable Resources", *Western Economic Journal*, 9, 256–266.

Pontrjagin, L.S., V.S. Boltjanskii, R.V. Gamkrelidze and E.F. Mishchenko (1962) *The Mathematical Theory of Optimal Processes* (Wiley, New York).

Quirk, J.P. and V.L. Smith (1970) "Dynamic Economic Models of Fishing", in A.d. Scott, ed., *Economics of Fisheries Management: A Symposium* (University of British Columbia, Institute of Animal Resource, Ecology Vancouver) pp. 1–32.

Ramsey, F.P. (1928) "Mathematical Theory of Saving", *Economic Journal*, 38, 543–559.

Schaefer, M.B. (1957) "Some Considerations of Population Dynamics and Economics in Relation to the Management of Marine Fisheries", *Journal of the Fisheries Research Board of Canada*, 14, 5, 669–681.

Scott, A.D. (1953) "Notes on User Cost", *Economic Journal*, 63, 368–384.

Scott, A.D. (1955) "The Fishery: The Objectives of Sole Ownership, *Journal of Political Economy*, 63, 116–124.

Shell, K. (1962) "Applications of Pontrjagin's Maximum Principle to Economics, in: H.W. Kuhn and G.P. Szego, eds., *Mathematical Systems Theory in Economics I*, Lecture Notes in Operations Research and Mathematical Economics, vol. 2, (Springer-Verlag, Berlin) pp. 241–292.

Smith, V.L. (1968) "Economics of Production from Natural Resources", *American Economic Review*, 58, 409–431.

Smith, V.L. (1969) "On Models of Commercial Fishing, *Journal of Political Economy*, 77, 181–198.

Spence, M. (1973) *Blue Whales and Applied Control Theory*, Technical Report no. 108, (Stanford University, Institute for Mathematical Studies in the Social Sciences).

Turvey, R. (1964) "Optimization and Suboptimization in Fishery Regulation", *American Economic Review*, 54, 64–76.

CHAPTER 3

Consistent and revised plans for natural resource use

TRACY R. LEWIS and PHILIP NEHER*

1. Introduction

Many natural resources are allocated to the public domain and the exploitation of them is generally viewed as a matter of social concern. There are important exceptions, of course, but even in the United States and Canada, where a predisposition in favor of private property is deeply embedded, ownership or control of territorial endowments has been recognized as a public responsibility. The ocean fishery has never been alienated and newly extended national jurisdictions over the fishery and enlarged economic zones are taken to be extensions of the public, not the private, domain.

How should these resources be allocated over time? A common view is represented in Frank Ramsey's seminal article (Ramsey, 1928) and related works that follow. The state appears as an indefinitely long-lived institution representing an on-going society. Each citizen's well-being is accounted for in the calculation of the optimal allocation plan. Since potential as well as extant citizens have already been counted, Ramsey type plans are *consistent* (Strotz, 1956). There can be no reason for regrets and revision as time goes on.

It is well known that Ramsey allocation paths can entail substantial sacrifices or bonuses for some citizens compared with others, even if all

*We are grateful to David Donaldson, Stu Burness, Keizo Nagatani and Harl Ryder for consultations. The paper was read at the Economics of Renewable Resource Management Conference at Brown University (October 1979). We thank Len Mirman, Dan Spulber and other conferees for their comments, and the Canada Council and National Science Foundation for their support.

Essays in the economics of renewable resources, edited by L.J. Mirman and D.F. Spulber
© *North-Holland Publishing Company, 1982*

generations are weighted equally, depending on when the person happens to exist relative to the course of the plan. In particular, if a Ramsey plan requires accumulation of capital in the early years, citizens alive then will be asked to sacrifice their own consumptions for the sake of future persons. If these sacrifices are not congenial to living persons, they may seek to overturn the plan by whatever means. Put another way, it may not be possible to implement a Ramsey plan if currently alive citizens generally do not embrace the intertemporal ethic embodied in it.

Another approach would seek to have the allocation over time of public resources more closely approximate the preferences of citizens who are alive at any one time. If these people have a lesser concern for future persons than they have for themselves, they will want the allocating authority to take a shorter view: a view more consistent with their own consumption and imperfectly altruistic bequest motives.

If this were done, the social plan would reflect the selfishness and myopia of people, arising from the fact of their mortality, as compared with the even-handed farsightedness of an immortal state. Plans would have finite horizons and would be *revised* from time to time so that any current plan in force would be congenial to the currently alive population.

Finitely lived, revised plans have been studied by Goldman (1968) and Neher (1976) and this research builds on these studies. The next section concentrates on a particularly simple resource problem where the natural growth of the resource is geometric and the elasticity of the marginal utility of consumption is a constant. The motivation for such simplification is to clearly expose differences between Ramsey and revised plans. But we are also interested in similarities. In particular, could it be that a society of selfish mortals would choose the same intertemporal allocation of resources as would be chosen by an immortal state which, however, is motivated by another criterion functional? And could it be that this functional is related in a simple and direct way to the one advocated by Ramsey? If such a plan can be found, we shall call it a *Phantom Plan*. It represents the solution to an inverse optimal problem. It is an indefinitely long-lived plan which replicates the intertemporal allocation yielded by a succession of continuously revised, finitely lived, plans.

It turns out that Phantom Plans can be shown to exist in these particularly simple cases.

Encouraged by these results, we go on to investigate some properties of revised plans in a larger class of renewable resource models where utility depends on the flow of consumption and the current resource stock. This exercise lays the foundation for demonstrating the existence of Phantom

Plans in this more general context, and for deriving some of their properties. In particular, we show how a sequence of finitely lived, continuously revised plans can be replicated by an indefinitely long-lived Phantom Plan through manipulation of a single parameter, the uniform rate of time discount, and by a positive transform of the utility functional.

We conclude with some conjectures on the significance of our results for the role of the state in the intertemporal distribution of income.

2. A worked example

2.1. The primitive problem

Revised planning procedures link together a sequence of self-contained, finitely lived, plans. Each one of these we take to be optimal with respect to a utilitarian criterion functional. For illustration, we have chosen a particularly simple and tractable representation of momentary utility (u) for each citizen as it depends upon his consumption. The number of citizens is unchanging:

$$u = u(c); \quad u' > 0, \quad u'' < 0,$$
$$u'' \cdot c / u' = \varepsilon \text{ a constant.}$$

The problem is to

$$\max_{\{c\}} \cdot J = \int_0^T u(c) e^{-rt} dt, \tag{1}$$

where r is an appropriate discount rate, possibly equal to zero.

The natural technology is chosen to be equally simple. The basic resource ($A \geqslant 0$) grows at a constant rate ($g \geqslant 0$) but is diminished by consumption ($c \geqslant 0$). Thus, (1) is maximized subject to

$$\dot{A} = g \cdot A - c,$$
$$\dot{A} = dA / dt. \tag{2}$$

A solution to the problem posed by (1) and (2) with $T < +\infty$ is the first step toward the construction of a sequence of revised plans. The solution for $T = +\infty$ is the solution for infinitely lived plans used for comparison.

The necessary conditions for an interior maximum to this problem are

$$u'(c) = \rho, \tag{3}$$
$$\dot{\rho} = \rho[r - g]. \tag{4}$$

The marginal utility of consumption should rise at a rate equal to the difference between the rate of discount and the natural growth rate of the economy. We shall assume that $r > g$. Moreover, since ε is a constant,

$$\dot{c} = -\frac{1}{\varepsilon} \cdot [r - g] \cdot c. \tag{5}$$

This, taken along with (2),

$$\dot{A} = g \cdot A - c,$$

is all we need to obtain closed-form solutions for c and A.

Integrating,

$$c = j \cdot \frac{r - (1 - \varepsilon) \cdot g}{\varepsilon} \cdot \exp\left(\frac{g - r}{\varepsilon} t\right), \tag{6}$$

$$A = A_0 e^{gt} - j \cdot \left[e^{gt} - \exp\left(\frac{g - r}{\varepsilon} t\right) \right], \tag{7}$$

$$j = \frac{A_0 e^{gT} - A(T)}{e^{gT} - \exp\left(\frac{g - r}{\varepsilon} T\right)},$$

where T and $A(T)$ are yet to be assigned.

2.2. Revised plans

A sequence of revised plans is obtained by linking the *initial* state of the subsequent plan. To see how this is done, it is convenient to adopt a proportional (by α) bequest rule. For each plan, $A(T) = \alpha \cdot A(0)$. This is a generalization of Solow's (1974) "keep the capital intact" rule. In this case, it is easy to see from (6) and (7) that *each plan begins by consuming a given fraction of the endowment.* From (6), and for any $T < +\infty$,

$$c(0) = k \cdot A(0),$$

$$k = \frac{(1 - \alpha) e^{gT}}{e^{gT} - \exp\left(\frac{g - r}{\varepsilon} T\right)} \cdot \frac{r - (1 - \varepsilon) g}{\varepsilon}. \tag{8}$$

Hence, for a sequence of revised plans,

$$c = k \cdot A. \tag{9}$$

There is a certain irony here. Even if it were the case that every person who ever lives consumes according to social plans which provide no bequests ($\alpha = 0$), it is apparent that social bequests are always made.

Taking (9) along with the dynamic constraint (2) we have

$$\dot{c} = -k \cdot (k-g) \cdot A, \tag{10}$$

$$A = -(k-g)A, \qquad A = A_0 e^{-(k-g)t}, \tag{11}$$

which describe the motions of c and A during a revised planning sequence. Note that the slope of the $c - A$ relationship is a constant, with c and A approaching zero as time goes on.[1]

2.3. *Infinitely lived plans*

For this case, set $T = +\infty$ in (6) and (7):

$$c = \frac{r-(1-\varepsilon)\cdot g}{\varepsilon} \cdot A(0) \exp\left(\frac{r-g}{\varepsilon}t\right), \tag{12}$$

$$A = A(0) \exp\left(\frac{r-g}{\varepsilon}t\right). \tag{13}$$

Apparently, like the sequence of revised plans, the corresponding infinitely lived plan also has consumption as a constant fraction of the asset:

$$c = \ell \cdot A,$$

$$\ell = \frac{r-(1-\varepsilon)\cdot g}{\varepsilon}. \tag{14}$$

And both c and A approach zero as time goes on.

2.4. *The correspondence*

We now seek to describe a sequence of revised plans with a single, indefinitely long-lived plan. If we can find such a plan, we shall call it a Phantom Plan. We use this term to convey the notion that although such a plan would not be consciously implemented by a society which is revising its plans, such a society could be described as behaving as if it were pursuing such a plan.

We have already noted that for a α sufficiently small, the revised and infinitely lived plans show the property of an asymptotic, proportional approach toward the origin (extinction). Specifically, the two planning

---

[1] Of course we are assuming α is sufficiently small so that $k - g > 0$.

procedures yield identical plans if $k = \ell$ or

$$\frac{\delta - (1-\varepsilon)\cdot g}{\varepsilon} = \frac{r - (1-\varepsilon)\cdot g}{\varepsilon} \cdot \frac{(1-\alpha)\cdot e^{gT}}{e^{gT} - \exp\left(\frac{g-r}{\varepsilon}T\right)}. \tag{15}$$

Here, we have introduced a new parameter, δ. It is the Phantom discount rate imputed to the Phantom Plan. The discount rate used to compute individual revised plans remains r and, other things equal, it will fall short of δ. However, if we experimentally let the revised planning period get larger and larger $(T \to +\infty)$ we find that δ declines and approaches r.

2.5. Cake eating

Suppose that the natural growth rate of the economy is zero ($g = 0$), that each plan of the revised sequence incorporates a zero bequest ($\alpha = 0$), and that sequential plans discount utilities not at all ($r = 0$). Then it can be shown that

$$\delta = \varepsilon / T. \tag{16}$$

This result (Burness–Lewis, 1977) is appealing because it provides a particularly tractable example of how a sequence of short plans with no discounting could appear to be a long plan with positive discounting.

The correspondence is illustrated in fig. 3.1.

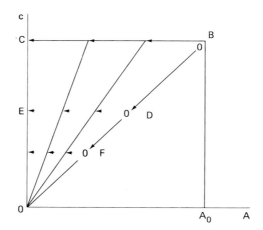

Figure 3.1

Beginning at $t=0$, and with $g=\alpha=r=0$, the first momentary plan will look forward to steady average consumption ($c=C$) as the initial stock (A_0) is consumed over the life (T) of the plan ($C=A_0/T$). However, no sooner does the economy start down the road from B to C than the plan is revised. The new plan will also require a flat consumption path from, say D to E. But it must start with less A than the initial plan because a "bit" of cake was eaten during the "moment" of revision. Successive plans will be flat as well, but the sequence of starting points $B \to D \to F \to \cdots \to 0$ will be on a declining path with c and A falling at the rate ε/T.[2] For example, if $T=40$ years for each of a sequence of revised plans, and if $\varepsilon=1$, then the apparent phantom rate of discount will be 2.5 percent.

3. Revised planning procedures

3.1. The basic model

This section considers a more general class of renewable resource models. The resource, for example a forest, is valued both as a source of primary inputs like wood and for its aesthetic beauty, and recreational benefits. The flow of net benefits or income Y generated from the resource is given by

$$Y=c+\phi(A); \qquad \phi'>0, \quad \phi''<0, \tag{17}$$

where c is the rate of resource harvesting, and $\phi(A)$ measures the benefit flow accruing to society from having a stock A of the resource in place. Here, the stock itself is a public good which argues for public resource management.

The utility of income enjoyed by society is represented by the strictly increasing and concave utility function $u(Y)$. The elasticity of marginal utility, previously constant, now generally depends on the level of consumption. In addition, we will assume that $-u'(Y)/u''(Y)=\gamma(Y)$ is nonincreasing in Y. For simplicity we assume that the rate of change in the resource stock is still given by eq. (2). The problem of optimal resource

---

[2] The $B \to D \to F \to \cdots \to 0$ sequence might be called a "modified Rawlsian Plan". Equality of consumption is preserved in each plan. However, nonaugmentability of the resource imposes declining consumption over time.

allocation is to

$$\text{maximize}_{\{c(t)\}} \int_0^T e^{-rt} u(Y) \, dt \tag{18}$$

subject to $A(T) = A_T$ and eq. (2). The necessary conditions for the solution to (18) are characterized by (assuming an interior solution)

$$u'(Y) = \rho \tag{19}$$

and

$$\dot{\rho} = -\rho[\phi'(A) + (g - r)]. \tag{20}$$

Differentiating eq. (19) with respect to time and substituting for $\dot{\rho}$ from eq. (20) we obtain:

$$\dot{Y} = \gamma(Y)[\phi'(A) + (g - r)]; \qquad \gamma(Y) = -u'(Y)/u''(Y). \tag{21}$$

Rewriting eq. (2) in terms of Y yields

$$\dot{A} = g \cdot A + \phi(A) - Y. \tag{22}$$

Together eqs. (21) and (22) characterize the movements of A and Y along an optimal consumption path. Assuming the rate of discount, r, exceeds the intrinsic growth rate, g, we have two possible phase diagram configurations in fig. 3.2(a and b). Side constraints and the planning horizon, T, are needed to select *the* trajectory that solves the problem in eq. (18).

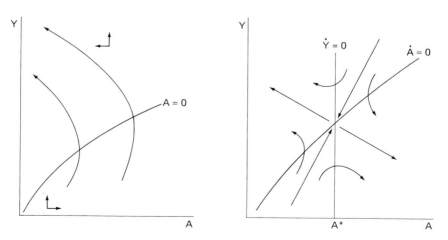

Figure 3.2

In fig. 3.2(a) the discount rate is so high that society may choose to eventually exhaust the resource. In this case, society's desire to conserve the resource for its public goods value is swamped by the economy's impatience to consume it. A particular example of this with $\phi(A)=0$ appeared in sections 1 and 2.

This section treats the case depicted in fig. 3.2(b). A society planning over an infinite time horizon will move along the stable arms leading to the steady state at A^*. At the steady state $\phi'(A)+g=r$; the marginal return from not consuming an extra unit of the resource, reflected by increased public good benefits and more rapid natural resource growth, is equal to society's time rate of discount. Thus, the equilibrium stock varies directly with society's marginal evaluation of the public good and inversely with its impatience to consume the resource.

3.2. Revised plans

Consider the following revised planning procedure. Society selects a time horizon T and terminal state A_T; the choice procedure is outlined below. The plan maximizing discounted utility through time T with $A(T)=A_T$ is adopted. Society starts out following this plan, but only for an instant, because a revised plan with terminal date T and stock A_T is chosen at the next instant and so on.

Any finite plan forming part of a revised planning sequence must be consistent with the chosen time horizon (T) and terminal state (A_T). It is natural to think of T being determined in a democracy by the median expected length of life contemplated by the citizens (Neher, 1976). In a stochastic context, T might be endogenous to a system where probability distributions over future states of the world were known.

The axiom of selfishness requires that $A_T=0$. But people do not seem well disposed to plans which contemplate extinction in finite time. So we want to allow for plans having $A_T>0$. In specifying the terminal stock A_T two possibilities are investigated: the bequest is some exogenously imposed amount, and the bequest is equal to the initial endowment.

3.2.1. Fixed bequests

Given T, A_T and the initial stock $A(0)$, the differential equations (21) and (22) can be solved for the time paths of $A(t)$ and $Y(t)$. In fig. 3.3 the path

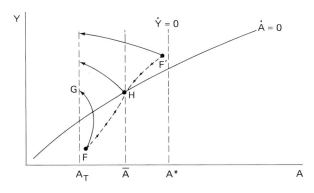

Figure 3.3

beginning at F is uniquely projected to G where $A = A_T$ in T years. Hence, if we fix the bequest at A_T, then a path beginning with an endowment of A_0 is uniquely determined. A revised path is traced out by a sequence of points like F, H and F'. These points each begin a T year plan terminating at $A(T) = A_T$. Specifically, the beginnings are represented by $Y(0) = Y(A_0/T, A_T)$ or, in short, $Y = Y(A/T, A_T)$, where it is understood that Y and A are functions of time along the revised paths satisfying eq. (22).

The following properties of revised plans are formally derived in the appendices. Along a revised path, like FHF' in fig. 3.3, Y is an increasing function of A. In general c may either be increasing or decreasing in A. However, there is a unique steady-state stock size, $\bar{A}$, such that $\dot{A} > 0$ (<0) for $A < \bar{A}$ $(A > \bar{A})$ along the revised path. In particular, $\bar{A} < A^*(\bar{A} \geqslant A^*)$ for $A_T < A^*(A_T \geqslant A^*)$.

Figure 3.4 illustrates how the revised path $Y(A/A_T, T)$ is conditioned on A_T and T. Fig. 3.4(a) demonstrates how $Y(0)$ varies with the targeted A_T given A_0 and T. There we find that $\partial Y/\partial A_T < 0$.[3] In fig. 3.4(b) we see how $Y(0)$ varies with T, given A_0 and A_T. There we find,[4]

$$\frac{\partial Y}{\partial T} < 0, \quad \text{if } A_0 > A_T,$$

and

$$\frac{\partial Y}{\partial T} > 0, \quad \text{if } A_0 < A_T.$$

---

[3] We are assuming that Y is a differentiable function of A_T and T.
[4] The case where $A_T = A_0$ is covered in the next section.

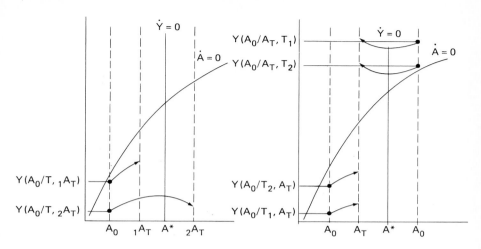

Figure 3.4

3.2.2. Keep the stock intact

Now we consider an alternative bequest rule requiring $A_T = A(0)$. This is consistent with the "keep the capital intact" rules which are commonly observed: "leave it the way you found it" is a familiar imperative; entailment of estates was not exceptional in Britain prior to the reforms of 1925. More formally, Phelps' (1966) "Golden Rule of Saving", Rawls' (1971) "Justice as Fairness", and Solow (1974) and Hartwick (1978) norms of maintaining productive power have appeared in the economic literature and have in common the notion that one should bequeath as one is endowed.

Suppose that each momentary generation adopts this rule. Then our revised path for Y can be written as

$$Y(0) = Y(A_0/T, A_T)$$
$$= Y(A_0/T, A_0)$$
$$= Y(A_0/T),$$

where it is understood that $A_T = A_0$. Revised plans corresponding to a keep the stock intact plan have a number of interesting properties. First, Y is strictly increasing with A_0 (this is demonstrated in appendix C). Secondly, along the revised path (indicated by the dotted line in fig. 3.5(a)), the stock is driven to a steady state at A^*.

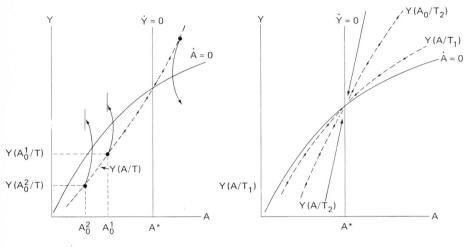

Figure 3.5

A continually revised plan that adheres to a keep the stock intact rule drives the economy toward the same state that an economy following an infinite horizon plan tends toward. Of course the approach to equilibrium is different; the revised plan path is flatter and takes more time to reach A^* than the approach along the stable arms. Notice that $Y(A/T)$ paths become flatter with shorter time horizons, T (see fig. 3.5(b)). This result is developed further in the next section with regard to its implications for the intergenerational distribution of income and wealth.

3.2.3. *The correspondence*

The stable arms depicted in fig. 3.2(b) show how an on-going society would plan its consumption over time. We might imagine that these plans would be devised by societies composed of immortal persons or those who believe themselves subject to instant reincarnation. In both cases, no person can escape the consequence of selfishness or generosity by dying.

Notice that Y is an increasing function of A along the stable arms. Furthermore, movement along the stable arms drives the economy to a unique steady state at A^*. It is also apparent that continuous revision of short plans yields paths which "look like" infinitely lived plans. Both classes of plans provide for income to increase at larger stocks and both types of plans are subject to nature's own budget constraint, so that all plans of both classes ultimately terminate on the $\dot{A} = 0$ line. Is it possible to describe a sequence of revised plans with a single infinitely long-lived plan? If we can find such a plan, we shall call it a Phantom Plan.

To construct a Phantom Plan we find a discount rate δ and a utility indicator (Y) which when used in the calculation of eq. (18) produces an infinite horizon plan that replicates the revised plan given by $Y(A/A_T, T)$. We define the phantom rate of discount by the equilibrium condition for infinite horizon plans.

$$\delta = g + \phi'(\overline{A}), \tag{23}$$

where $\overline{A}$ is the steady-state stock for the revised plan. Eq. (23) defines δ as a function of $\overline{A}$ with $d\delta/d\overline{A} < 0$. For the case of fixed bequest revised plans, larger $\overline{A}$'s are associated with plans that are generous to future generations (A_T large). Thus, it is to be expected that the more egalitarian revised plans are associated with more even-handed phantom plans where δ is small.

To specify the phantom utility function, $v(Y)$, we require $Y(A/A_T, T)$ or, in short, $Y(A)$ to coincide with the stable arm path which implies by eq. (19)

$$v'(Y(A)) = \rho(A).$$

Differentiating with respect to A, we obtain the condition

$$v''Y'(A) = \rho'(A) = \dot{\rho}/\dot{A} = -v'[\phi' + g - r]/\dot{A},$$

which can be rearranged to obtain

$$-\frac{v'(Y)}{v''(Y)} = \frac{Y'(A(Y)) \cdot \dot{A}(A(Y))}{[\phi'(A(Y)) + g - \delta]}. \tag{24}$$

Note that since $Y(A)$ is monotonically increasing, we can write A as a function of Y as we have done in eq. (24). Define $\lambda(Y) \equiv -v'(Y)/v''(Y)$. Knowledge of $\lambda(Y)$ is sufficient to determine $v(Y)$ up to a positive linear transformation where

$$v(Y) = \int_{\hat{Y}}^{Y} \exp\left(\int_{\hat{Y}}^{z} (1/\lambda(X)) \, dx \right) dz, \tag{25}$$

where $\hat{Y}$ is an arbitrary constant of integration.

Equation (25) defines our phantom utility function. Differentiating eq. (25) with respect to Y, one can show that $v(Y)$ is strictly increasing and concave. Furthermore, it is straightforward to verify that the revised path $Y(A/A_T, T)$ is also the path that maximizes (18) given δ and $v(Y)$.

This is a remarkable result. It tells us that under general conditions, the consumption path resulting from a sequence of revised plans coincides with the consumption path for a consistent infinite horizon plan, assuming the planner uses the discount rate and utility indicator defined in eqs. (23) and (25) respectively. This suggests a revealed preference approach to analyzing society's behavior in consuming a natural resource over time. Each revised path $Y(A/A_T, T)$ coincides with a consistent infinite horizon path for some phantom discount rate and utility function. In following a revised plan, a society is *acting as though* it was following a long-range plan to maximize a chosen stream of discount utility.

What do the phantom discount rate and utility function suggest about how egalitarian revised plans are? For fixed bequest plans, there is a relationship between the discount rate δ and the parameter A_T, of the revised plans. As defined by eq. (23), δ is a decreasing function of $\bar{A}$, the revised steady-state stock. Larger $\bar{A}$ are associated with plans that are more generous to future generations (A_T large). Thus, the more egalitarian revised plans are associated with more even-handed Phantom Plans, where δ is small.

For the keep the stock intact plans, $\bar{A} = A^*$ so that eq. (23) implies that $\delta = r$. Looking at fig. 3.6, which displays a keep the stock intact path, we can establish a relationship between the phantom utility function $v(Y)$ and society's utility indicator $u(Y)$. Consider the trajectory through F, a point on the revised path, which leads to G, where $A = A_0$ at time T. Points like F' that lie on or to the left of the trajectory through F and G must be situated above $Y(A_0/T)$ since it takes less than T periods to travel from F' to G'. Consequently, the slope of $Y(A_0/T)$ is less than the slope of the trajectory

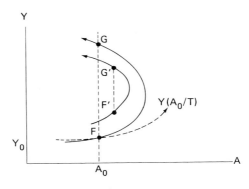

Figure 3.6

through F, or

$$Y'(A/T)<dY/dA,$$

where dY/dA is the trajectory slope. It is easy to see that this relationship holds for all points on $Y(A_0/T)$. Rewriting eq. (21) slightly we have

$$\gamma(Y) = -\frac{u'(Y)}{u''(Y)} = \frac{dY/dA}{[\phi'+g-r]\dot{A}}.$$

Comparing this with our equation for $\lambda(Y)$,

$$\alpha(Y) = -\frac{v'(Y)}{v''(Y)} = \frac{Y'(A/T)}{[\phi'+g-r]\dot{A}}$$

implies that

$$\lambda(Y)>\lambda(Y) \tag{26}$$

Suppose we can write v as a differentiable function of u such that

$$v = f(u(Y)). \tag{27}$$

Repeated differentiation of eq. (27) with respect to Y yields

$$v' = f'u'; \qquad v'' = f'u'' + f''u'$$

and

$$\lambda(Y) = -\frac{v'}{v''} = \frac{f'u'}{f''u'' + f'u''}. \tag{28}$$

Rearranging eq. (28) we find that

$$\lambda(Y) = \frac{f'\gamma(Y)}{f''\gamma(Y)+f'}.$$

But this implies that $\lambda(Y)<\gamma(Y)$ if and only if $f''<0$. Thus, $v(Y)$ must be a positive concave transformation of $u(Y)$.

What is the significance of this result? Define $\bar{Y}_1$ and $\bar{Y}_2$ by

$$u(\bar{Y}_1) = \int_0^T u(Y(t))\,dt/T \tag{29a}$$

and

$$v(\bar{Y}_2) = \int_0^T v(Y(t))\,dt/T, \tag{29b}$$

where $\bar{Y}_1$ and $\bar{Y}_2$ are the constant income levels that yield the same average utility as the nonconstant income stream $\{Y(t)\}$ given $u(Y)$ and $v(Y)$, respectively. Since $v(Y) = fu(Y)$, we have from eq. (29b)

$$f\big(u(\overline{Y}_2)\big) = \int_0^T f(u(Y(t))) \frac{1}{T}\, dt < f\big(u(\overline{Y}_1)\big), \tag{30}$$

where the inequality follows from f being strictly concave. Consequently, $\overline{Y}_2 < \overline{Y}_1$. The utility function $v(Y)$ is said to display more *aversion to inequality* than $u(Y)$. A society with a utility function $v(Y)$ would accept a lower constant income stream in order to avoid inequality in income across different generations.

4. The question of the relevant constituency

If economics is the science of choice, a welfare economist must know for whom choices are being made. Starting with Ramsey, economists have focused on centrally managed or dictatorial schemes for resource allocation in which the interests of all current and future generations are accounted for in an on-going never-ending plan. With such plans, the welfare of future generations is typically discounted, presumably to reflect society's impatience for consumption. (For an exception see Ramsey.)

Are such infinitely lived plans to be taken seriously? Who is to engineer these plans and who is to enforce them?

In this paper we have explored an alternative allocation scheme that allows only extant persons to make intertemporal allocations decisions. Natural mortality and imperfect altruism can give rise to continuously revised plans that can be replicated by Phantom Plans, having the same structure and characteristics as Ramsey plans.

The existence of Phantom Plans allows us to evaluate the egalitarian properties of revised plans by looking at the discount rate, δ, and the utility function, $v(Y)$, that are implied. A complete or satisfying treatment of comparative equality cannot be attempted here. But we can illustrate how one might proceed by looking at the properties of the "keep the resource intact" revised plans. Here we find that the Phantom Plan gives rise to more intergenerational equality; the Phantom Planner is more altruistic than his Ramsey counterpart.

Figure 3.7 illustrates the revised path $Y(A_0/T)$ (the dotted line from F to H) along with the Ramsey path (the solid line from J to H). The first momentary plan along the revised path anticipates travelling from F to G,

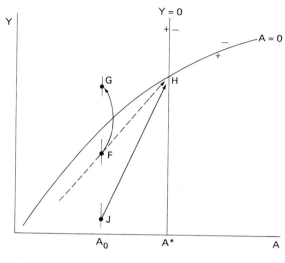

Figure 3.7

inheriting A_0, and bequeathing the same amount of A after T years. The equations of motion require that F is above the stable arm. The revised path is composed of a sequence of points like F. Hence, the revised path lies everywhere above the stable arm, except in the limit where both paths converge on the point H. Meanwhile, consumption has been rising on both paths.

Initially, the revised path yields more consumption. However, the Ramsey path reaches a neighborhood of "bliss" (at H) more quickly. In short, the revised path begins with more consumption, but after "awhile" it yields less. It is more egalitarian.

In terms of the Phantom Plan giving rise to the FH path, the transformation of the utility functional required to obtain that path was derived by imparting more concavity to the phantom momentary utility function. That is to say, at every point in time the Phantom Planner would be induced by the transformation to perceive a higher marginal cost of forgone current consumption compared with the benefits of more future consumption. As a consequence, he would be more cautious than a Ramsey planner in extracting utility sacrifices from currently extant persons for the benefit of the unborn: he is more inequality adverse. This is consistent with the notion that a Phantom Planner looks after extant people as he would look after himself.

How is one to choose between the Ramsey and the Phantom plans? Who should count and how much? Who qualifies to attend the constitutional conference behind the veil of Rawlsian ignorance? We can recommend no answers. But any judgement is better informed if the consequences of that judgement for intertemporal equality are better understood.

Appendix A: Proof that $Y'(A/A_T, T) > 0$

Let $V(A/A_T, T)$ represent the value of the optimal program described by eq. (18). Assume V is twice differentiable; then it is easy to show that $\rho(A) = V'$. Since $Y' = \rho'/V''$, by eq. (19), we must demonstrate that V is strictly concave for our proof.

Consider two different initial stocks, $A_1(0)$ and $A_2(0)$, and define

$$A_w(0) \equiv wA_1(0) + (1-w)A_2(0); \qquad 0 < w < 1.$$

Let $Y_1(t)$ and $Y_2(t)$ be the income flows and $A_1(t)$ and $A_2(t)$ be the stock sizes at time t resulting from the optimal program starting with $A_1(0)$ and $A_2(0)$, respectively. Define

$$Y_w(t) \equiv wY_1(t) + (1-w)Y_2(t).$$

Since $\dot{A} = g \cdot A + \phi(A) - Y$, where ϕ is concave, it is easy to show that $A_w(t)$, the stock at time t for a program that chooses income to be $Y_w(t)$, satisfies

$$A_w(t) \geq wA_1 + (1-w)A_2(t).$$

In particular, $A_w(T) \geq A_T$, so that a program with incomes flow $Y_w(t)$ is feasible. We then have the following string of inequalities:

$$
\begin{aligned}
V(A_w(0)/A_T, T) &= \max_{\{Y(t)\}} \int_0^T u(Y(t)e^{-rt}\mathrm{d}t \\
&\geq \int_0^T u(Y_w(t))e^{-rt}\mathrm{d}t \\
&> \int_0^T \left(wu(Y_1(t)) + (1-w)u(Y_2(t)) \right)e^{-rt}\mathrm{d}t \\
&= wV(A_1(0)/A_T, T) + (1-w)V(A_2(0)/A_T, T).
\end{aligned}
$$

The first inequality is deduced from the fact that $Y_w(t)$ is not necessarily optimal; the second one follows from u being strictly concave. We have shown V to be strictly concave, thus completing our proof.

Appendix B: Proof that $Y(A/A_T, T)$ intersects the $\dot{A}=0$ curve at one spot

Consider the case $A_T < A^*$, where A^*, depicted in fig. 3.3, is the stock where the $\dot{Y}=0$ and $\dot{A}=0$ curves intersect (the case $A_T \geqslant A^*$ is handled similarly and thus is omitted). If $Y(A/A_T, T)$ intersects the $\dot{A}=0$ line, it must be between the stocks A_T and A^*, since paths starting elsewhere on the $\dot{A}=0$ line never reach A_T. Clearly, if we start at $A = A_T$ ($A = A^*$) on the $\dot{A}=0$ line, the time necessary to reach A_T is zero (infinity). It is easy to show that the solution to the differential equations (21) and (22) are uniformly continuous in $A(0)$, $Y(0)$ and t. Thus, there exists at least one stock, call it A_0, such that the path starting at A_0 on the $\dot{A}=0$ curve terminates at A_T at time T.

We want to show that this is the only point of intersection. Differentiating (21) with respect to time yields

$$\ddot{A} = (g+\phi')\dot{A} - \dot{Y}$$
$$= (g+\phi')\dot{A} + \gamma(Y)[g+\phi'-r].$$

There are a collection of $\dot{A}=m\leqslant 0$ curves in the phase plane that are parallel to the $\dot{A}=0$ curve. To the left of the $\dot{Y}=0$ line, along each of these paths, $\ddot{A}<0$ and is decreasing in absolute value as we move left to right down these curves. This follows from the fact that ϕ' is decreasing in A, and $\gamma(Y)$ is nonincreasing in Y. That is, the rate at which A goes to zero decreases as we move in the south-west direction. Thus, along the $\dot{A}=0$ curve the time necessary to arrive at A_T decreases monotonically from infinity to zero as we move from the intersection of the $\dot{Y}=0$ and $\dot{A}=0$ curves to the point A_T on the $\dot{A}=0$ curve. Thus, for $T\in[0,\infty]$ there exists a unique point on the $\dot{A}=0$ curve such that the time until exhaustion along the optimal path starting from that point is equal to T. But $Y(A/A_T, T)$ is the locus of starting points $A(0)$ where $A(T)=A_T$.

Appendix C: Proof that $Y(A_0^1/T) > Y(A_0^2/T)$ for $A_0^1 > A_0^2$

First suppose $A^* > A_0^1 > A_0^2$, as in fig. 3.5, and that $Y(A_0^1) \leqslant Y(A_0^2)$. Then initially, $\dot{A}(A_0^1) > \dot{A}(A_0^2)$ and the gap between $A^1(t)$ and $A^2(t)$ (the time path of stocks given $A^1(0)=A_0^1$ and $A^2(0)=A_0^2$) widens. But since $\dot{Y}$ is increasing in Y, it follows that $Y(A^1(t)) < Y(A^2(t))$ for all t. But this implies that $\dot{A}(A^1(t)) > \dot{A}(A^2(t))$ which is not possible. Thus, $Y(A_0^1) > Y(A_0^2)$ whenever $A^* > A_0^1 > A_0^2$. A similar argument establishes the same inequality when $A_0^1 > A_0^2 > A^*$.

References

Burness, H.S. and T.R. Lewis (1977) "Democratic Exploitation of a Non-Replenishable Resource", Social Science Working Paper 161, California Institute of Technology.

Goldman, S. (1968) "Optimal Growth and Continual Planning Revision", *Review of Economic Studies*, 35, 2, April, 145–154.

Hartwick, J.M. (1978) "Substitution Among Exhaustible Resources and Intergenerational Equity", *Review of Economic Studies*, 45, 347–354.

Neher, P.A. (1976) "Democratic Exploitation of a Replenishable Resource", *Journal of Public Economics*, 5, 361–371.

Page, R.T. (1977) *Conservation and Economic Efficiency* (Johns Hopkins University Press for Resources for the Future, Baltimore).

Phelps, E.A. (1966) *Golden Rules of Economic Growth* (W.W. Norton, New York).

Ramsey, Frank (1928) "A Mathematical Theory of Saving", *Economic Journal*, 28 December, 543–559.

Rawls, J. (1971) *A Theory of Justice* (Belknap Press, Cambridge, Mass.).

Sen, A. (1973) *On Economic Inequality* (The Clarendon Press, Oxford).

Solow, R.M. (1974) "Intergenerational Equity and Exhaustable Resources", *Review of Economic Studies*, Symposium on the Economics of Exhaustable Resources.

Strotz, R.H. (1956) "Myopia and Inconsistency in Dynamic Utility Maximization", *Review of Economic Studies*, 23, 165–180.

PART III

NONCONVEXITIES AND OPTIMAL RESOURCE USE

Introduction to Part III

Part II analyzed the application of dynamic models of optimal resource harvesting which are analogous to models used in capital and growth theory. Part III studies an important difference between the assumptions of capital theory and those of natural resources. In the literature on growth and capital theory it is assumed that both the objective function and the dynamics are characterized by concave functions. However, recently there has been activity, especially in the resources literature, loosening these concavity assumptions. For example, Koopmans, in "Proof for a Case Where Discounting Advances the Doomsday", studies the effect of a nonconcavity of the utility function on the optimal policy. The possibility of nonconcavity has also been recognized, although implicitly, in the early literature on natural resources. Smith, in his famous seminal article, implicitly assumed a nonconcave population growth function since in his model the time derivative of the stock is zero if the level of the stock is zero; however, this time derivative is assumed to be negative when the stock level is small.

For natural resources these two types of nonconcavities arise very naturally. The first type of nonconcavity arises in the biological growth curve. For many species increasing returns for small values of the stock seems to be the usual case since, for example, it is more difficult to find a mate and reproduce when the stock is small. When the stock is large, predators find it easy to hunt and consume their prey. The second type of nonconcavity arises in the benefit function. For example, there may be fixed or set-up costs in each period or a minimum utility level needed for survival or guaranteed by government policy. In most of these cases the benefit function is constant until a given point after which it is an increasing concave function.

The chapter by Levhari, Michener and Mirman, "Nonconcave Dynamic Programming: An example", illustrates the relationship between nonconcavities in the population dynamics and nonconcavities in the objective function and considers the effect of these nonconcavities on optimal harvesting over time.

77

The Lewis and Schmalensee chapter on "Optimal Use of Renewable Resources with Nonconvexities in Production" discusses pulse-fishing strategies, i.e. where harvesting occurs only after the stock reaches a sufficiently large size and then is rapidly drawn down and not harvested until it is replenished. They also study "chattering controls" which act to convexify the objective function by rapid switching between policies. Chattering controls are only possible in continuous time analysis since discrete time does not allow rapid switching. These oscillations are observed in practical situations quite frequently and the presence of nonconcavities provides an explanation of observed pulse-fishing behavior.

CHAPTER 4

Nonconcave dynamic programming: An example

DAVID LEVHARI, RON MICHENER and LEONARD J. MIRMAN*

1. Introduction

The purpose of this chapter is to present an example of a nonconcave programming problem. This example explores the effects of a specific type of nonconcavity in the dynamics. We show that the analysis is also applicable to an important type of nonconcavity in the utility function. Other sorts of nonconcavities have been studied in the literature. These studies have some bearing on the implications of our results; hence, before presenting our example we briefly discuss some of the previous literature.

The usual analysis of the optimal exploitation of renewable resources is based on the assumption that the natural biological growth curve is concave – this will be referred to as the classical case. Recently, several authors have studied resource problems with a growth curve having a convex segment followed by a concave segment – this will be referred to as the nonclassical case. In both cases it is assumed that the objective is to maximize the discounted utility of consumption where utility is a strictly increasing, concave function $u(x)$, with $u(0) = 0$. Also, the natural biological growth curve, $f(x)$, has the property that $f(0) = 0$. The discount rate is given by δ, $0 < \delta < 1$.

The first case which we shall discuss has been studied by Majumdar and Mitra (1980a) and Clark (1971). The utility function is assumed to be linear, i.e. $u(x) = x$, and the biological growth function has the property that

*Partial support for this research by the NSF through Grant 79-05900 and the U.S.–Israel BSF Grant 1828-79 is gratefully acknowledged.

Essays in the economics of renewable resources, edited by L.J. Mirman and D.F. Spulber
© *North-Holland Publishing Company, 1982*

$f'(0) \geqslant 1$ (note, it is possible, under this assumption, that $\delta f'(0) < 1$). First consider the classical case, assuming that $\delta f'(0) > 1$. Since $u'(x) = 1$, the first-order condition for maximizing the sum of discounted utilities is

$$1 = \delta f'(x). \tag{1}$$

Since $f'(x)$ is decreasing, there exists an $\bar{x}$ such that this condition is satisfied. Hence, the optimal policy, letting $y = f(x)$, is

$$c(y) = y - \bar{x}, \quad \text{if } 1 > \delta f'(x),$$

and

$$c(y) = 0, \quad \text{if } 1 \leqslant \delta f'(x).$$

If the initial stock y is such that $y > \bar{x}$, then $c(y) = y - \bar{x}$ so that (1) is satisfied. If $y < \bar{x}$, then $c(y) = 0$ and pure accumulation is the optimal policy until $\bar{x}$ is reached (cf. fig. 4.1), i.e.

$$y_{t+1} = f(y_t), \quad \text{if } y_t < \bar{x},$$

and

$$y_{t+1} = f(\bar{x}), \quad \text{if } y_t \geqslant \bar{x}.$$

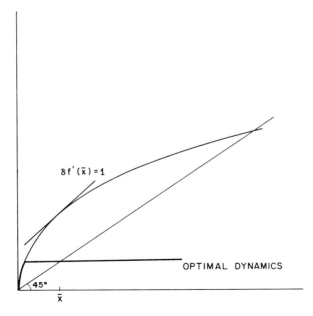

Figure 4.1

When $\delta f'(0) \leqslant 1, c(y) = y$, for all x, i.e. everything is consumed immediately.

Next consider the nonclassical case. We shall split the discussion into several parts. First, if $\delta f'(0) \geqslant 1$, the dynamics are similar to the case in which the growth curve is concave. In fact, there exists a unique $\bar{x}$ such that $\delta f'(\bar{x}) = 1$. The optimal policy is $c(y) = y - \bar{x}$, if $y \geqslant \bar{x}$ and $c(y) = 0$ otherwise. Hence, if $y < \bar{x}$, the pure accumulation program is optimal since $\delta f'(y) > 1$. This case is similar (except for the addition of an initial convex segment) to the case depicted in fig. 4.1. If $\delta f'(x) < 1$, *for all x*, then, as in the nonclassical case, the optimal policy is to consume everything immediately.

An interesting special case is when $\delta f'(\bar{x}) = 1$ at the point of inflection. Here $\bar{x}$ is the unique such x. When $f''(\bar{x}) = 0$, then $\delta f'(x) < 1$, for all $x \neq \bar{x}$, hence $c(y) = y$. In fact this case is the essence of the effect of the nonconcavity. To see this, consider fig. 4.2. Let x_M have the property that the "average slope", i.e. $f(x)/x$, and $f'(x)$, coincide. The average slope at x_M is the maximum average slope of f. Thus, since $\delta f'(x_M) < 1$, the discounted average slope at this point is also less than one. Moreover, since

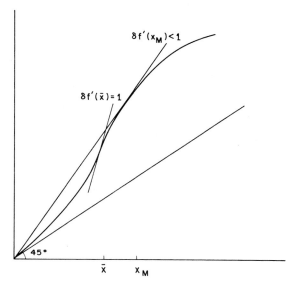

Figure 4.2

the average discounted return is less than one everywhere, the discounted value of the stock in the next period is always less than in the present. The fact that the utility function is linear means that spreading consumption over time does not increase utility as it does with a concave utility function. Hence, the optimal policy for any initial stock is to consume everything immediately.

In order for the stock to be sustained over time under an optimal policy when $\delta f'(0) \leqslant 1$, it is necessary that $\delta f(x_M) \geqslant x_M$, which in turn implies that $\delta f'(x_M) \geqslant 1$.

In the case that $x = x_M = \delta f(x_M)$, consuming everything immediately, consuming $f(x_M) - x_M$ forever and consuming $f(x_M) - x_M$ for a finite number of periods and then consuming everything, all yield equal utility. To see this, note that to remain indefinitely at x_M yields consumption of $f(x_M) - x_M$ in each period. Hence, since $\delta f(x_M) = x_M$,

$$\sum_{t=0}^{\infty} \delta^t (f(x_M) - x_M) = \frac{(f(x_M) - x_M)}{1 - \delta} = \frac{f(x_M) - \delta f(x_M)}{1 - \delta} = f(x_M).$$

A similar argument is valid for any finite number of periods. However, in general these policies are not optimal unless $\delta f'(x_M) = 1$. This example illustrates the fact that optimal policies need not be unique in the nonclassical case.

In the general case, i.e. when $\delta f'(x_M) > 1$, there exist two points, $\bar{x}$ and $\bar{\bar{x}}$ (here $\bar{\bar{x}} < \bar{x}$) such that $\delta f'(\bar{x}) = \delta f'(\bar{\bar{x}}) = 1$. In this case there exist x_1 and x_2 ($x_1 < x_2 < \bar{x}$) such that if $x < x_1$ immediate extinction is optimal; if $x_1 < x < x_2$ pure accumulation is optimal; and for $x > x_2$ steady-state behavior, i.e. $c_0 = f(x) - \bar{x}$ initially and $\bar{c} = f(\bar{x}) - \bar{x}$ forever, is optimal. The general solution for $u(x) = x$ is depicted in fig. 4.3.

Unfortunately, the analysis under the more general assumption that the utility function is concave is even more complicated. The problem has been dealt with by Skiba (1978) for the continuous time case (in which linear approximations are used to analyze the "local" behavior of optimal policies) and in the discrete time case by Majumdar and Mitra (1980b) and, most notably, by Dechert and Nishimura (1980). Basically, as in the case of a linear utility function, the initial stock plays a crucial role in the behavior of the optimal dynamics, especially with respect to the eventual extinction or steady-state behavior of the stock. It will be assumed that $f'(0) > 1$ and that $u'(0) = +\infty$. Several cases, defined by the values of $f'(x)$ and $f(x)/x$, will be discussed.

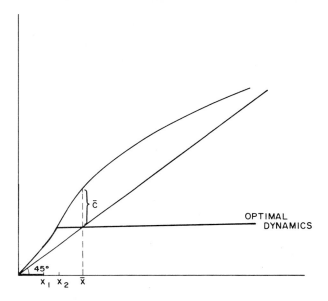

Figure 4.3

The basic conclusion of Dechert and Nishimura (1980) is that optimal paths converge monotonically to a steady state (perhaps the origin).

First consider the case in which $\delta f'(x) < 1$, for all $x > 0$ (note, this implies that $\delta f(x) < x$, for all x). For concave utility functions, as well as linear ones, there cannot be any optimal nonzero steady states. In fact, under an optimal policy the stock will converge to, but never reach, zero (if $u'(0) < \infty$, then it is possible that the stock will be depleted in finite time). At the other extreme, suppose that $\delta f'(0) \geqslant 1$. In this case there will exist a unique $\bar{x}$ such that $\delta f'(\bar{x}) = 1$, and for all $x > 0$ the optimal stock will converge to $\bar{x}$.

Hence, the most interesting cases are those for which $\delta f'(0) \leqslant 1$, but for some x, $\delta f'(x) > 1$. Under these circumstances there will, in general, be two solutions to the equation $\delta f'(x) = 1$. Let $\bar{x} < \bar{\bar{x}}$ be these solutions.

In this situation there exists a unique critical level x_c such that $x_c < \bar{\bar{x}}$, and such that if the initial value $x_0 < x_c$ and $\delta f(x_c) < x_c$, extinction in the limit is optimal, while if $x_0 > x_c$, the optimal stock converges to $\bar{\bar{x}}$. However, if $x_0 = x_c$, the optimal path is not unique. In fact there exist two optimal paths from x_c: one converging to zero and the other to $\bar{\bar{x}}$. Moreover, $\bar{x}$ cannot be an optimal steady state. The general optimal path is depicted as in fig. 4.4.

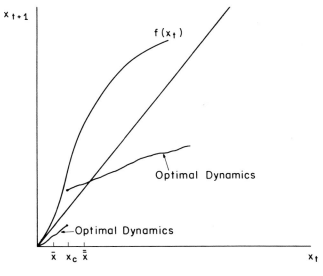

Figure 4.4

2. The relationship to nonconcavities in the utility function

The relationship between nonconcavities in the dynamics and the objective function as alluded to above can be clarified by studying a benefit function of the form

$$\sum_{t=0}^{T} \delta^t u(c_t). \tag{2}$$

Often, the end point, T, is endogenously determined. When c_t is the destructive use of some biomass, the optimal determination of T involves deciding whether the optimal exploitation of the biomass requires extinction of the biomass.

Define the "terminal utility" of a program as the level of utility implicitly achieved after the extinction of the resource, i.e. in periods $T+1, T+2, \ldots, \infty$. In the standard presentation "terminal utility" is taken to be zero. What may occur is that $u(0) = \lim_{\varepsilon \to 0} u(\varepsilon)$ is *not* equal to the level of terminal utility.

A divergence of terminal utility and $u(0)$ may arise in practical economic problems, like the following.

(1) In resource economics, if there is some social welfare associated with the survival of a genotype, $u(0)$ may exceed terminal utility.

(2) Certain government welfare programs offer minimal subsistence levels (Medicaid nursing homes) once one's assets are depleted. An agent solving a wealth allocation problem is in a situation where the guaranteed subsistence corresponds to terminal utility.

If, as often occurs, the level of terminal utility exceeds $u(0)$, there are incentives, which are not captured by the usual marginal conditions, for an optimizing agent to choose termination. An example will illustrate the point. There is a simple paradox in the exhaustible resource literature known as "the cake-eating problem". Suppose, goes the paradox, there is an optimizing agent with a concave utility function and neutral time preference. He has a cake of finite size, and wants to know the best way to eat it. Under the assumptions made he should consume very small amounts over long periods of time, e.g. ε in each period. But carried to the limit this means no

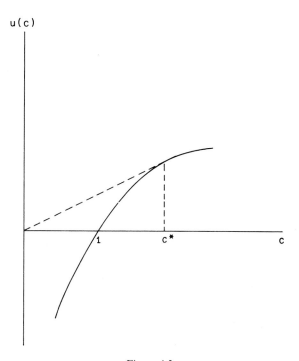

Figure 4.5

consumption – he never eats the cake! This result requires that terminal utility equal $u(0)$. As a simple counterexample consider the following, drawn from Koopmans (1974):

$$\max_{c_t, T} \sum_{t=0}^{T} \log c_t$$

subject to

$$c_t + x_t = x_{t-1}; \qquad x_t \geqslant 0, \quad x_0 = \bar{x}.$$

Here terminal utility is zero, but $u(0) = -\infty$. Consumption of one unit of cake provides zero utility, so it is clear that any optimal policy implies consuming more than one unit of cake in each period. The full solution (ignoring the corners introduced by discrete time) is to maximize average utility per unit of consumption, which occurs at c^* (see fig. 4.5). Termination is optimal after (roughly) $\bar{x}/c^*$ periods.

Precisely the same difficulty can arise in a different way. It is often recognized in resource economics that there is some minimal sustainable size of the biomass, say x. Often the growth rule for the biomass is assumed to be concave above x. A simple example of such a growth rule is the linear function

$$x_{t+1} = rx_t - b, \qquad r > 1, \quad b > 0$$

(see fig. 4.6). Suppose an agent's objective is

$$\max_{c_t, T} \sum_{t=0}^{T} \delta^t u(c_t)$$

subject to

$$x_{t+1} = rx_t - b - c_t; \qquad c_t \geqslant 0, \quad x_t \geqslant 0, \quad x_0 = \bar{x}.$$

Let $u(0) = 0$ so that there is no difficulty introduced in this way. Define $u^*(c^*)$ as a continuous and increasing function on $[0, \infty)$, where u^* is arbitrary[1] for $c^* < b$ and where $u^*(c^*) = u(c^* - b)$ for $c^* \geqslant b$. The equivalent problem is

$$\max \sum_{t=0}^{T} \delta^t u^*(c_t^*)$$

subject to

$$x_{t+1} = rx_t - c_t^*, \qquad c_t^* \geqslant b, \quad x_t > 0, \quad x_0 = \bar{x}.$$

---

[1] In fact in the optimal solution $c^* \geqslant b$.

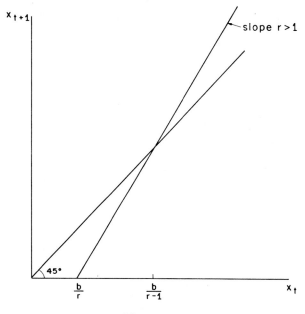

Figure 4.6

In this equivalent problem $u^*(0)$ is *not* equal to terminal utility, which is zero. Since consumption of b offers no more utility than termination, the constraint $c_t^* \geqslant b$ will not be binding.

Finally, the problem may arise in quadratic dynamic programming. The canonical problem in quadratic dynamic programming is

$$\min \sum_0^T x_t^T Q x_t + u_t^T R u_t$$

subject to

$$x_{t+1} = A x_t + B u_{t+1} + C + \varepsilon_{t+1},$$

where x is a vector of states (x^T is its transpose), u is a vector of controls, Q and R are positive definite matrices, A and B are matrices, and C is a column vector.

Even if in the initial formulation of the problem C is zero, it is often the case that the objective function involves terms that are products of control variables and state variables. The standard technique for reducing a problem of this form to the canonical form is by an appropriately chosen linear transformation

$$x' = x - k_0; \qquad u' = u - k_1,$$

which will induce a nonzero C in the dynamics for the revised coordinates.

This should demonstrate that the problems which arise when $u(0)$ is not equal to terminal utility also occur in a variety of other disguises – making the problem of substantial interest. When $u(0)$ is not equal to terminal utility the value function is no longer concave, so that the standard dynamic optimization techniques cannot be utilized. One interpretation of the example of this paper is that it generalizes Koopmans (1974) to the case where the resource can grow.

3. An example

Assume that $u(c) = c^{1/2}$ and let $0 < \delta < 1$ be the discount factor. Then

$$V(x) = \max_{\{c_0,\ldots,c_T, T\}} \sum_{i=0}^{T} \delta^i (c_i)^{1/2}$$

subject to

$$c_0 + x_0 = x,$$
$$c_i + x_i = \max\{rx_{i-1} - b, 0\}, \qquad i = 1, \ldots, T,$$
$$x_T = 0.$$

Here $r > 1$ and $b > 0$. The dynamics are depicted in fig. 4.6.

Let $V_t(x)$ be the maximum sum of discounted utility that can be achieved by consuming positive quantities for the first t periods and zero thereafter. Then $V(x)$ is the envelope of these functions, i.e.

$$V(x) = \max_t V_t(x).$$

The maximizing t is the optimal length of the program starting from x and the optimal consumption sequence is that which achieves $V_t(x)$.

It can, by an easy calculation, be shown that for $t \geq 1$:

$$V_t(x) = \left[x - \frac{b}{r} \left(1 + \cdots + \frac{1}{r^{t-1}} \right) \right]^{1/2} \left[1 + \cdots + (\delta^2 r)^t \right]^{1/2},$$

and that:[2]

$$V_\infty(x) = \left[x - \frac{b}{r}\left(1 + \cdots + \frac{1}{r^t} + \cdots\right)\right]^{1/2}\left[1 + \cdots + (\delta^2 r)^t + \cdots\right]^{1/2}.$$

Note that for convergence it must be the case that $r > 1$ and $\delta^2 r < 1$. However, we shall also assume that $\delta r > 1$.

The optimal program will be characterized as a partition of the x axis, i.e. values $x_1, \ldots, x_T$ such that if the initial stock $x \in [x_i, x_{i+1}]$, an optimal program is an i period program. If $x > x_T$, then an infinite program is optimal. To show this, consider the values x_t defined by the equation

$$V_t(x_t) = V_\infty(x_t),$$

i.e. the x_t are the points at which $V_t(x)$ and $V_\infty(x)$ cross.

To find x_t write

$$\left[x_t - \frac{b}{r}\left(1 + \cdots + \frac{1}{r^t} + \cdots\right)\right]^{1/2}\left[1 + \cdots + (\delta^2 r)^t + \cdots\right]^{1/2}$$

$$= \left[x_t - \frac{b}{r}\left(1 + \cdots + \frac{1}{r^{t-1}}\right)\right]^{1/2}\left[1 + \cdots + (\delta^2 r)^t\right]^{1/2}.$$

Squaring both sides and subtracting yields,

$$\left\{\left[1 + \cdots + (\delta^2 r)^t + \cdots\right] - \left[1 + \cdots + (\delta^2 r)^t\right]\right\}x_t$$

$$= \frac{b}{r}\left\{\left(1 + \cdots + \frac{1}{r^t} + \cdots\right)\left(1 + \cdots + (\delta^2 r)^t + \cdots\right)\right.$$

$$\left. - \left(1 + \cdots + \frac{1}{r^{t-1}}\right)\left(1 + \cdots + (\delta^2 r)^t\right)\right\}$$

---

[2] Let the value function for a t period program without the "fixed cost," i.e. $b = 0$, be $J(x, t)$. Then $J(x, t)$ is $V_t(x)$ without the term $(b/r)(1 + \cdots + 1/r^{t-1})$. Because of the linear dynamics this has a simple interpretation. The initial stock, x, has been divided into two portions. The first, $(b/r)(1 + \cdots + 1/r^{t-1})$, pays the fixed cost of b per period for t periods. The other, $(x - b/r)(1 + \cdots + 1/r^{t-1})$, will ultimately be consumed. Therefore this example can be extended to other utility functions provided the linear dynamics are retained. In general

$$V_t(x) = J\left(x - \frac{b}{r}\left(1 + \cdots + \frac{1}{r^{t-1}}\right), t\right).$$

and

$$(\delta^2 r)^{t+1}\left[1+\cdots+(\delta^2 r)+\cdots\right]x_t$$

$$=\frac{b}{r}\left\{\frac{1}{1-1/r}\cdot\frac{1}{1-\delta^2 r}-\frac{1-1/r^t}{1-1/r}\cdot\frac{1-(\delta^2 r)^{t+1}}{1-\delta^2 r}\right\}.$$

Hence,

$$\frac{(\delta^2 r)^{t+1}}{1-\delta^2 r}x_t=\frac{b}{r}\left\{\frac{1}{1-1/r}\frac{1}{1-\delta^2 r}-\frac{1-1/r^t}{1-1/r}\frac{1-(\delta^2 r)^{t+1}}{1-\delta^2 r}\right\}.$$

Finally,

$$x_t=\frac{b}{r-1}\left\{\frac{1}{r^t(\delta^2 r)^{t+1}}+1-\frac{1}{r^t}\right\}=\frac{b}{r-1}\left\{\frac{r}{(\delta^2 r^2)^{t+1}}+1-\frac{1}{r^t}\right\}.$$

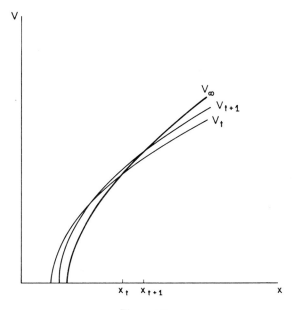

Figure 4.7

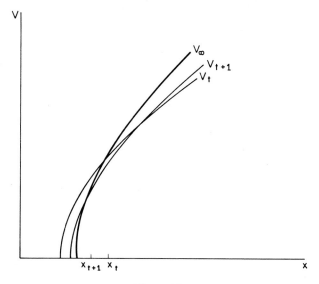

Figure 4.8.

Since $\delta r > 1$ by assumption, x_t is well defined. Note that as $t \to \infty$, $1/(\delta^2 r^2)^{t+1}$ decreases, while $1 - 1/r^t$ increases. Hence, x_t is not in general monotonic, but will first increase, then decrease. The first case, i.e. $x_{t+1} > x_t$, is depicted in fig. 4.7 while $x_t > x_{t+1}$ is depicted in fig. 4.8.

Let $\bar{T} = \max\{t: x_t \geqslant x_{t-1}\}$. For all $t > \bar{T}$, $\max_x\{V_{\bar{T}}(x), V_\infty(x)\} \geqslant V_t(x)$, for all x. This implies that no finite program of length greater than $\bar{T}$ is optimal. To determine $\bar{T}$ consider

$$x_t - x_{t-1} = \frac{b}{r-1}\left\{\frac{r}{(\delta^2 r^2)^{t+1}} - \frac{r}{(\delta^2 r^2)^t} - \frac{1}{r^{t-1}} - \frac{1}{r^t}\right\}$$

$$= \frac{b}{(r-1)r^{t-1}}\left\{\frac{1}{(\delta^2 r)^t}\left[\frac{1}{\delta^2 r^2} - 1\right] + 1 - \frac{1}{r}\right\}.$$

Hence, at the turning point, $\bar{t}$,

$$\left(\frac{1}{\delta^2 r}\right)^{\bar{t}} = \frac{1 - 1/r}{1 - 1/\delta^2 r^2} = \frac{\delta^2 r(r-1)}{\delta^2 r^2 - 1},$$

and $\bar{T}$ is the integer part of $\bar{t}$ where

$$\bar{t} = \log\left[\frac{\delta^2 r^2 - 1}{\delta^2 r(r-1)}\right] \cdot \left[\frac{1}{\log \delta^2 r}\right].$$

Here $\delta^2 r > 1$ implies that $\bar{T} \geqslant 0$. A similar argument may be made for the points x_t^* such that

$$V_t(x_t^*) = V_{t+1}(x_t^*).$$

It can be shown that

$$x_t^* = \frac{b}{r-1}\left\{1 + \frac{r-1}{(1-\delta^2 r)(\delta^2 r^2)^{t+1}} - \frac{1-\delta^2}{(1-\delta^2 r)r^t}\right\},$$

and that these values of x_t^* first increase, then decrease and are always increasing for $t \leqslant \bar{T}$. These points define the x_i in the optimal partition.

Finally, if $\delta r = 1$, there is no finite t, i.e. for any finite T there is some initial value x for which the length of the optimal program from x is t periods. Note that the infinite program is optimal only if $x \geqslant [(r+1)/(r-1)]b$, where clearly $[(r+1)/(r-1)]b > b/(r-1)$. This implies that even from sustainable initial stocks a finite path may be optimal.

References

Clark, C.W. (1971) "Economically Optimal Policies for the Utilization of Biologically Renewable Resources", *Mathematical Biosciences*, 17, 245–268.

Dechert, W.D. and K. Nishimura (1980) "A Complete Characterization of Optimal Growth Paths for an Aggregated Model with a Non-Concave Production Function", September.

Koopmans, T. (1974) "Proof for a Case where Discounting Advances the Doomsday", *Review of Economic Studies*, 41, 117–120.

Majumdar, M. and T. Mitra (1980a) "On Optimal Exploitation of a Renewable Resource in a Non-convex Environment and the Minimum Safe Standard of Conservation", Working Paper 223, Department of Economics, Cornell University.

Majumdar, M. and T. Mitra (1980b) "Intertemporal Allocations with a Non-convex Technology: The Aggregative Framework", Working Ppaer 221, Department of Economics, Cornell University.

Skiba, A. (1978) "Optimal Growth with a Convex-Concave Production Function", *Econometrica*, 46, 527–540.

CHAPTER 5

Optimal use of renewable resources with nonconvexities in production

TRACY R. LEWIS and RICHARD SCHMALENSEE

1. Introduction

In most of economic theory, convexity of tastes and technologies is assumed so that agents' optimization problems have smooth, interior solutions. Much of the work on renewable resources has followed in this tradition. But the technology of harvesting any particular renewable resource, such as an ocean fishery, may in fact display various kinds of nonconvexities. For example, the reproduction of the population itself may exhibit increasing returns to scale for small stock sizes. Or, increases in the resources devoted to harvesting the stock may produce more than proportionate increases in yield, perhaps because of (flow) fixed costs of harvesting. Finally, start-up costs may be incurred whenever harvesting begins after a period of unimpeded population growth, or there may be shutdown costs if the fishery is temporarily or permanently abandoned.

These sorts of nonconvexities are of interest to resource economists for both theoretical and practical reasons. It is well known that nonconvex preferences or technologies cause problems in most branches of economic theory. The properties of optimal solutions to dynamic resource and investment problems with nonconvex technologies are not yet fully understood. Such problems offer a number of unconventional challenges to theorists. On the practical side, we do know that the presence of nonconvexities can radically alter the form of optimal strategies in some simple models. It thus may be very important to deal with real nonconvexities in order to formulate sound resource use policies.

Essays in the economics of renewable resources, edited by L.J. Mirman and D.F. Spulber
© *North-Holland Publishing Company, 1982*

This chapter reviews some recent work on optimal production from a natural resource subject to a nonconvex technology. Our focus is on a continuous time model of optimal resource management, though results of discrete time analysis are also reported. Adopting the notation used in Lewis and Schmalensee (1975, 1977, 1979), and elsewhere in the literature, assume that a planner chooses $H(t)$, the harvest rate over time, in order to maximize

$$V = \int_0^\infty [B(H, S) - F] e^{-rt} \delta(t) \, dt + \sum_{i=0}^\infty e^{-r\tau(i)} R, \qquad (1)$$

subject to the non-negativity of H and S and to the growth equation

$$\dot{S} = g(S) - H, \qquad (2)$$

given the initial value of S. Time arguments are omitted here and below where no confusion should result.

In (1), B is the short-run profit or benefit function that depends on the harvest rate and the physical size of the resource stock, S. Presumably, B is increasing in S, since the cost of harvesting declines with greater resource abundance, but B is frequently assumed to be independent of S in the literature. It is natural to assume that $B(0, S) = 0$ for all S. F is a non-negative (possibly zero) fixed cost that is incurred (as a flow) whenever the industry is operating, so that net benefit or profit is $[B - F]$. The variable $\delta(t)$ equals one when the industry is operating and equals zero when it is shut down. R is a non-negative (possibly zero) cost of starting up the industry after a period of shutdown, and $\tau(i)$ is the time of the ith such start-up.[1] (Formally, the $\tau(i)$ are the set of times at which $\delta(t)$ switches from zero to one.) The variable r is a positive, constant discount rate, and the function $g(S)$ in eq. (2) gives the natural rate of growth of the resource stock, with no harvesting by man. A natural assumption here is $g(0) = 0$.

When $F = R = 0$ and both B and g are concave functions, the preceding two paragraphs describe a standard, well-behaved resource management problem of the sort considered by Plourde (1970, 1971) and Quirk and Smith (1970), for instance. Our concern here is with the kinds of policies that are optimal when the problem is nonclassical because one or more of

---

[1] We follow the literature and do not explicitly consider shutdown costs. Such costs will have a qualitative effect on the analysis if they are sufficiently large as to prevent the fishery from becoming idle when it otherwise would.

these assumptions fails to hold.[2] There turn out to be three basic types of optimal management policies then: (a) to exhaust the resource in finite time, then abandon it forever; (b) to harvest the resource on a sustained basis, with $\delta(t)=1$ forever; and (c) to harvest the resource cyclically, with $\delta(t)$ changing value regularly forever. The first two optimal policy types also occur in the classical problem with full convexity, but the third does not.

The next section surveys the existing literature on optimal harvesting *without* full convexity and reports conditions under which each of these three basic strategies is optimal. Section 3 analyzes the limiting case in which F is positive but R is zero. In this case the problem can be rendered convex by allowing for a limiting form of cyclical harvesting, and the properties of the corresponding optimal policies can be compared with those arising in the more difficult problems that are the focus of section 2.

2. Nonconvexities and optimal policy types

Let us examine the consequences of relaxing the classical convexity assumptions one at a time. We first focus on nonconvexities in reproduction, then in the net benefit function. The final subsection shows how positive start-up or re-entry costs serve to magnify nonconvexities from these sources.[3]

2.1. Reproduction

Let us assume for now that B is concave with respect to H and that $F = R = 0$. Two sorts of nonconvexities in the growth function, $g(S)$, are considered in the literature. Lewis and Schmalensee (1975, 1977, 1979) examine the case where there is some positive minimum viable population size, $\underline{S}$. For $S < \underline{S}$, the population declines to zero even with no harvesting by man. Lewis and Schmalensee assume that g is twice continuously differentiable for positive S, with $g'' < 0$ there. A discontinuity at the origin is required to satisfy $g(0)=0$. A growth function of this sort is drawn in fig.

---

[2] The control-theoretic problem posed above is a highly simplified aggregate representation of the fishery management problem. Because they are not central to our analysis, we are abstracting from such complexities as stock uncertainty, the definition of property rights, and interactions among different resource populations.

[3] It is instructive to compare these forms of nonconvexity with those that Davidson and Harris (1981) argue arise naturally in investment models.

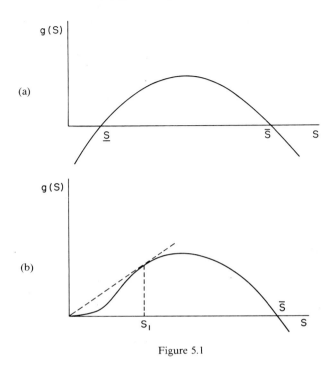

Figure 5.1

5.1(a). In the absence of harvesting by man, the stock reaches its maximum sustainable size, $\bar{S}$, in the limit. If $\underline{S} = 0$ there is clearly full convexity.

Clark (1971) and Majumdar and Mitra (1980a) examine a second type of nonconvexity, illustrated in fig. 5.1(b), in which there are increasing returns to reproduction at small stock sizes. As fig. 5.1(b) illustrates, $g(S)$ is positive for all positive S and continuous for non-negative S. In that figure the average rate of growth of the population, $g(S)/S$, is increasing for $0 \leqslant S \leqslant S_1$; this is referred to as "depensation growth". (See, for instance, Clark, 1976, p. 16.) The marginal increase in growth owing to an increase in S, $g'(S)$, reaches a maximum at some stock size below S_1.

There are two varieties of optimal programs when the growth function is the source of nonconvexity: abandonment and continuous harvesting. Three distinct cases appear in the literature, depending on the discount rate.[4]

---

[4] For many of the cases discussed in this paper, the existence of an optimal solution has not been rigorously established. Majumdar and Mitra (1980a, 1980b) have proven existence in their discrete-time analysis, however.

First, if the discount rate is large relative to the marginal productivity of the stock in reproduction (specifically, if r exceeds the maximum value of $g'(S)$), and if harvesting remains profitable as $S \to 0$,[5] then it is optimal to drive the stock size to zero and abandon the resource for every initial stock size.[6] Lewis and Schmalensee (1977) also demonstrate that extinction is economically optimal, regardless of the rate of discount, if the initial stock size is sufficiently close to $\underline{S}$ so that it is barely viable.

Secondly, if the discount rate is small relative to the reproductive capacity of the resource, than a sustained yield program is optimal. That is to say, it is optimal to drive the stock to a unique size (given the initial conditions) and maintain that level forever. The steady state is reached in finite time if there are no depletion effects (B is independent of S); otherwise the steady-state stock size is reached only asymptotically.[7]

Thirdly, if the discount rate is moderate, falling between the two ranges just discussed, the optimal program generally depends on the initial stock size. Extinction is optimal for small stocks, while a sustained yield program is optimal if S_0 is large. Majumdar and Mitra (1980b) note that there may be more than one sustained harvesting program that satisfies all the necessary conditions for optimality. Skiba (1978) and Davidson and Harris (1981) encounter a similar phenomenon in continuous time investment models. They devise an ingenuous way to choose among different candidate paths that permits simple calculation of discounted present values.

2.2. Benefit function

Two forms of benefit or profit function nonconvexity have been examined in the literature. Jacquette (1974), Reed (1974), and Lewis and Schmalensee (1975, 1977, 1979) assume a positive flow of fixed costs associated with harvesting, with gross benefits, $B(H, S)$, strictly concave in the harvesting rate. Such fixed costs occur if there is a minimum scale of fleet required for efficient fishing or if certain dockside support facilities must be operating whenever a fishery is being harvested. Since $H = 0$ implies zero net benefits, there is a discontinuity at the origin in this case. The second form of benefit

[5] Lewis (1979) gives conditions for profitable harvesting as S goes to zero with depletion effects.

[6] Wherever appropriate, we report the continuous-time analogues of relevant discrete-time results. The analyses of Clark (1971) and Majumdar and Mitra (1980a, 1980b) are in discrete time.

[7] See Salant et al. (1980).

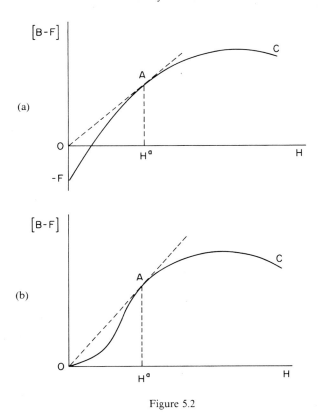

Figure 5.2

function nonconvexity, analyzed by Lewis (1981), occurs if there are initially increasing marginal returns from harvesting. (See also Hannesson, 1975.) The fixed cost and increasing returns forms of nonconvexity are depicted in figs. 5.2(a) and 5.2(b), respectively. For the general case in which B is a function of both S and H, these figures should be understood to be drawn holding S constant at some arbitrary value.

   If nonconvexity enters through the benefit function, the optimal harvesting policy depends on whether the analysis is done in continuous or discrete time. The difference arises because in continuous models, with $R = 0$ and no additional complications, it is possible to change the harvesting rate infinitely often, while in discrete time it can only be changed once a period. If H can be changed infinitely rapidly, one can "convexify" the benefit functions in figs. 5.2(a) and 5.2(b) by having the harvest rate ocillate infinitely rapidly between zero and H^a. This makes all points along the dotted line OA attainable as time averages. (Formally, this resembles use of mixed strategies to convexify strategy sets in game theory.) Points closer to A (to O) are achieved by setting H equal to zero (to H^a) a greater proportion of the time. Moreover, by sufficiently rapid oscillation between these values, one can approximate to any desired degree the average benefit/harvest relation along OA. Policies that involve rapid switching of this sort are called "chattering controls".[8] We will use the term "vibrating" to refer to the limiting case in which switching occurs infinitely rapidly.

Strictly speaking, an optimal program will generally fail to exist when the profit function is nonconcave and $R = 0$, since one can always improve on any well-defined chattering control by switching a bit more rapidly under some circumstances. (This is formally a type of "open set" problem.) However, it is possible to find solutions to the "convexified" problem, in which the net benefit function is replaced by the nonstrictly concave function with graph OAC in figs. 5.2(a) and 5.2(b). Then one can show that the value of the optimal vibrating program for the convexified problem can be approached arbitrarily closely by following a chattering policy (with sufficiently rapid oscillation) that is feasible for the original non-convex problem. This is established formally by Davidson and Harris (1981) for a model slightly different from ours. Section 3 explores the properties of the limiting chattering policy (i.e. the vibrating solution to the convexified problem) in the situation depicted by fig. 5.2(a).

In the discrete-time analyses of Jacquette (1974), Hannesson (1975), Reed (1975), and Lewis (1981), this convexification device is not helpful, since there is a limit to how often the harvest rate can be changed. In discrete time, significant benefit function nonconcavity implies the optimality of what was called in section 1 a cyclical harvesting strategy, which Clark (1976, p. 250) calls a "pulsed fishing" strategy. Under such a program, the population is harvested only after it reaches a sufficiently large size, whereupon it is rapidly drawn down to some lower limit, harvesting ceases, and the cycle begins once again. This resembles the "Ss" policies that arise in inventory theory because of fixed ordering costs.

2.3. Re-entry costs

A positive re-entry cost, R, penalizes the use of chattering to offset benefit function nonconvexities. This cost is assumed here to be incurred whenever the industry switches from a nonoperating to an operating mode. R might

---

[8]See Clark (1976, p. 171) and Davidson and Harris (1981) for discussions and references.

represent the cost of transporting a fishing fleet to a new area, or the costs of re-opening a fishery, for instance.

Lewis and Schmalensee (1975, 1977, 1979) consider a model with positive re-entry cost and a fixed-cost nonconcavity in the benefit function of the sort depicted in fig. 5.2(a). They investigate conditions under which strategies of each of the types mentioned in section 1 are optimal. If R is very large, it will either be optimal to harvest the resource on a sustained basis or to extinguish it in finite time. Other strategy types, which must involve re-entry, can always be ruled out by making R large enough. Large values of F or growth function nonconcavities tend to make harvesting uneconomical at small stock sizes and so tend to make it more likely that a strategy of extinction and abandonment will dominate sustained harvesting. (High discount rates also favor abandonment; see Clark, 1973, and Lewis and Schmalensee, 1977.)

If R is relatively low, on the other hand, policies involving some re-entry may be optimal. Positive values of R serve to rule out the infinitely rapid chattering discussed above and analyzed in section 3. If F is large enough, it may be optimal to follow what Lewis and Schmalensee (1979) term a "regeneration" strategy: to cease harvesting immediately in order to avoid fixed costs, and then to follow a sustained harvesting strategy as soon as the stock is large enough. Or, it may be optimal to follow an "exploitation/regeneration" policy: to harvest the resource for a while, then to cease harvesting and follow a regeneration strategy. If some re-entry is optimal but neither of these variants of sustained harvesting is optimal, Lewis and Schmalensee (1979) show that all optimal policies must be cyclical.

A cyclical policy involves alternating periods of operating and nonoperating states for the industry forever. During operating periods, the population is harvested and the stock is drawn down to some lower limit. At this point (or for smaller stock sizes if the industry is just starting) the industry shuts down to avoid fixed costs, and the population is allowed to grow until it reaches a fixed upper limit. At this point (or for larger stock sizes if the industry is just starting) harvesting begins and another cycle starts. Lewis and Schmalensee (1979) show that increases in F tend to reduce the time optimally spent operating. Such reductions may be associated with shifts from sustained harvesting to a cyclical policy or with more intense harvesting during operating periods of a cyclical strategy. If cyclical policies are optimal, increases in R tend to increase the time taken on each cycle and to increase the distance between the upper and lower bounds on stock size. This is consistent with the discussion of chattering above, since one can think of infinitely rapid chattering when $R = 0$ as a cyclical policy with cycle length zero. As we show below, regeneration strategies may also be optimal when $R=0$, though exploitation/regeneration policies can be ruled out then.

This overview of the literature should make it clear that the presence of nonconvexities in resource management problems (as elsewhere) can induce important *qualitative* changes in the nature of optimal policies. One cannot expect intuition or computation based on a fully convex model to be reliable except in a fully convex world.

3. Chattering to convexify when $R=0$

Our concern here is with maximization of the present value functional V defined by eq. (1) above when $R=0$, $F>0$, and B and g are concave, with $\underline{S}=0$ (see fig. 5.1(a)) for simplicity. This section will illustrate the use of chattering to convexify a problem with a nonconcave benefit function. It further exhibits a limiting form of cyclical policy and indicates how optimal regeneration policies can arise. Detailed proofs of some of the assertions that follow may be found in Lewis and Schmalensee (1975), which is available from either author.

We proceed formally by defining a new control variable, $w(t)$, the fraction of the time the industry is operating. By following a vibrating policy, entering and leaving infinitely rapidly (and incurring thereby no extra cost, since $R=0$), w can be made to take on any value in the closed interval $[0, 1]$. Referring to fig. 5.2(a), the ability to choose w in the open interval $(0, 1)$ makes it possible to attain all points along the dotted line OA. This transforms the effective net benefit function from a nonconcave function with a discontinuity at the origin to a concave function with a linear segment for $H \in [0, H^a]$. By the strict concavity of $B(H, S)$, the slope of this segment is the largest value of marginal benefit, $B_H(H, S)$, for any particular stock size, S.

With complete freedom to enter and leave, the resource manager's problem can be written as follows: choose control variables $w(t)$ and $H(t)$, along with horizon T, in order to maximize

$$V = \int_0^T w[B(H, S) - F]e^{-rt}dt, \tag{1'}$$

subject to the revised equation of motion S,

$$\dot{S} = g(S) - wH, \tag{2'}$$

the non-negativity of H, S, w, and $(1-w)$, and the initial condition $S(0) = S_0$.

The necessary conditions for this problem require the existence of a continuous function $\lambda(t)$, along with functions $\alpha_1(t)$, $\alpha_2(t)$, $\beta_1(t)$, and $\beta_2(t)$, continuous at all points of continuity of $H(t)$ and $w(t)$, such that the constraints are satisfied along with the following:

$$wB_H(H, S) - w\lambda = \alpha_2 - \alpha_1, \tag{3a}$$

$$B(H, S) - F - \lambda H = \beta_2 - \beta_1, \tag{3b}$$

$$\dot{\lambda} = \lambda[r - g_S(S)] - wB_S(H, S), \tag{3c}$$

$$\alpha_1 \geqslant 0; \qquad \alpha_1 H = 0, \tag{3d}$$

$$\alpha_2 \geqslant 0; \qquad \alpha_2 S = \alpha_2[g(S) - H] = 0, \tag{3e}$$

$$\beta_1 \geqslant 0; \qquad \beta_1 w = 0, \tag{3f}$$

$$\beta_2 \geqslant 0; \qquad \beta_2[1 - w] = 0, \tag{3g}$$

$$\lim_{t \to T} e^{-rt}\{w[B(H, S) - F] + \lambda[g(S) - wH]\} = 0, \tag{3h}$$

and, if the optimal T is finite,

$$\lim_{t \to T} e^{-rt}\lambda(t) \geqslant 0, \tag{3i}$$

$$\lim_{t \to T} e^{-rt}\lambda(t)S(t) = 0. \tag{3j}$$

In the analysis of Lewis and Schmalensee (1977), R is assumed to be infinite. Under that assumption, re-entry is ruled out, so that $w = 1$ at all times before T. Then conditions (3b), (3f), and (3g), which relate to the optimal choice of w, can be deleted. With these changes, conditions (3) above become necessary conditions (3) in Lewis and Schmalensee (1977).

The critical harvest rate H^a depicted in fig. 5.2(a) is defined implicitly by

$$D[H^a(S), S] = B[H^a(S), S] - F - H^a(S)B_H[H^a(S), S] = 0. \tag{4}$$

The first equality defines the function $D(H, S)$, which is increasing in H. From condition (3a), the value of the costate variable, λ, corresponding to H^a is given by

$$\lambda^a(S) = B_H[H^a(S), S]. \tag{5}$$

For any S, increases in F raise H^a and lower λ^a. If B is increasing in S, as we will assume, $\lambda^a(S)$ is an increasing function. If it is possible to earn positive net benefits by harvesting at stock size S, $\lambda^a(S)$ is positive.

The discussion of convexification in section 2 above indicated that it would never be optimal to operate the industry with a harvest rate below H^a. To prove this, assume that for some S we have $0 < H < H^a(S)$ and

$w > 0$. (Unless w and H are both positive, the industry is not operating.) Then $\alpha_1 = \beta_1 = 0$, $\alpha_2 = 0$ if S is positive. Conditions (3a) and (3b) then imply that whenever the industry is operating,

$$D(H, S) = \beta_2 \geqslant 0.$$

But this is a contradiction, since $H < H^a$ implies $D(H, S) < D(H^a, S) = 0$. Thus, it is indeed never optimal to set H below $H^a(S)$.

If the industry is operating, with w, H, and S positive, condition (3a) implies that $B_H = \lambda$. Substituting into (3b), the latter condition may be rewritten as

$$D(H, S) = \beta_2 - \beta_1. \tag{6}$$

Now suppose that for some S the industry is operating, conditions (3) are satisfied, and $0 < \lambda < \lambda^a(S)$. Since B is concave in H, condition (3a) then implies $H < H^a(S)$ and, from (4), $D(H, S) > 0$. But this implies $w = 1$ from (6), (3f), and (3g). Thus, for $0 < \lambda < \lambda^a(S)$, as long as $S > 0$, conditions (3) require harvesting at all times, with $w = 1$ and system evolution exactly as described by Lewis and Schmalensee (1977) under the assumption that re-entry is impossible.

If $\lambda > \lambda^a(S)$, on the other hand, (3a) cannot be satisfied with positive w, since $B_H(H, S)$ can then only exceed $\lambda^a(S)$ if $H < H^a(S)$, and we have shown that this cannot be optimal. Thus, $w = 0$ whenever $\lambda > \lambda^a(S)$, and no harvesting occurs. In the borderline case $\lambda = \lambda^a(S)$, conditions (3a)–(3g) are satisfied with $H = H^a(S)$ and *any* value of w in the closed interval $[0, 1]$.

In problems of this sort, the costate variable, λ, can be interpreted as the shadow value of marginal increases in the corresponding state variable, here the resource stock, S. In a convex world, one would always operate with $B_H = \lambda$, thus equating the marginal benefit from harvesting to the marginal cost of reducing the stock. Here the effective net benefit function is given by OAC in fig. 5.2(a), and marginal benefits are bounded above by $\lambda^a(S)$. If the marginal value of the stock exceeds this quantity, it is optimal not to harvest at all. If $\lambda = \lambda^a(S)$, all points along the flat segment OA satisfy the marginal condition.

On this interpretation of λ, $D(H, S)$ can be interpreted as the *real* net benefit flow from harvesting, taking into account the value of the stock removed.[9] It is thus clear why $D(H, S)$ must always be non-negative if harvesting is optimal. Similarly, condition (3h), the first-order condition for

---

[9] It is correct to use the marginal value of the *stock*, λ, to compute the shadow cost of the entire harvesting *flow* at any instant, since for finite H any instant's harvesting causes only an infinitesimal change in S.

optimal choice of T, can be interpreted as requiring that *real* total net
benefit (defined to allow for $w < 1$ and including the value of stock growth)
goes to zero if the resource is abandoned forever after a finite time. (For T
infinite, this condition is satisfied if all variables approach finite limits.)

The implications of these results may be illustrated by consideration of
figs. 5.3(a) and 5.3(b). In both figures the curve labeled SS' is the $\dot{S} = 0$
locus when re-entry is impossible, obtained by setting $w = 1$ in conditions
(3). Similarly, $\lambda\lambda'$ is the corresponding $\dot{\lambda} = 0$ locus. If re-entry were impossible, the optimal infinite horizon (sustained harvesting) strategy would
involve following the unique trajectory of the modified conditions (3) that
approaches point E in the limit. If re-entry is impossible, the only alternative is to harvest the resource for a finite time and then abandon it forever.
(These two policy types correspond to local maxima of the objective
functional with respect to T.) In fig. 5.3(a), optimal abandonment would

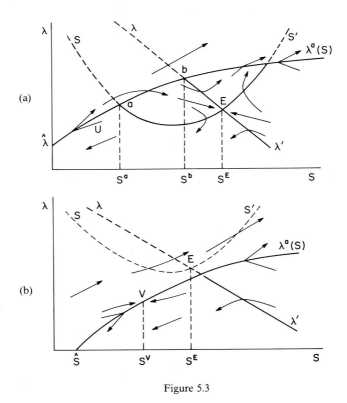

Figure 5.3

involve following the unique trajectory terminating at the point $S = 0$, $\lambda = \hat{\lambda}$, while in fig. 5.3(b), which is drawn for a larger value of F, optimal abandonment drives the system to the point $S = \hat{S}$, $\lambda = 0$.[10]

Such abandonment policies may also be optimal when $R = 0$. If so, they involve approaching the same points as when re-entry is impossible.[11] But with the possibility of using vibrating to mitigate the effects of fixed cost, it becomes less likely that the best finite-T (i.e. abandonment) policy is better than the best infinite-T strategy. (If $F = 0$, abandonment cannot be optimal even if re-entry is impossible unless $\underline{S} > 0$; see Lewis and Schmalensee, 1977, proposition 5.) If it is not optimal to have T finite, condition (3h) indicates that the limiting values of H, S, w, and λ must be finite. Figs. 5.3(a) and 5.3(b) illustrate the possible infinite horizon policies satisfying conditions (3) when $R = 0$. The discussion below assumes abandonment is not optimal in order to simplify exposition.

In fig. 5.3(a) it is optimal to approach point E for all initial stock sizes above S^E, setting $w = 1$ and ignoring the possibility of free exit and re-entry. For stock sizes only slightly below S^E ($S_0 > S^b$ is sufficient), such an approach to point E is also optimal. But if the initial stock size is small enough ($S_0 < S^a$ is sufficient), it will not be possible to approach E in this fashion and satisfy conditions (3). If S is below S^a, all trajectories of (3) with $w = 1$ involve declining S. For small S_0, a regeneration policy may be optimal. Such a policy involves setting $\lambda > \lambda^a$ initially and letting the stock grow with no harvesting by man. One can show by analysis of limiting values of trajectory slopes that all points along the $\lambda^a(S)$ locus between points a and b can be reached in finite time in this fashion. It is thus possible to reach the unique $w = 1$ path approaching point E from the left. (If such a policy is followed, $\lambda = \lambda^a(S)$ only for an instant, and the choice of w at that instant does not matter.)

Paths like the u-turn trajectory labeled U in fig. 5.3(a) may also satisfy conditions (3). This means that it may be optimal to harvest for a while,

---

[10] If $\underline{S}$ is positive, it will generally be optimal to reach the $S = 0$ axis at a point below $\lambda^a(0)$ in fig. 5.3(a). See Lewis and Schmalensee (1977), especially the discussion of fig. 5.1, for the details of the analysis of conditions (3) with $w = 1$ on which this paragraph is based. It is shown there that a sufficient condition for the existence of a saddlepoint like E is $r < g(\underline{S})$, which is assumed to hold in the discussion here.

[11] Moreover, it is shown in Lewis and Schmalensee (1975) that the comparative static results on abandonment policies stated in propositions 7 and 8 of Lewis and Schmalensee (1977) carry over to the case $R = 0$. (This is done by showing that for all times near the optimal abandonment time, T, w is optimally equal to one.) If $\underline{S}$ is positive, abandonment can be shown to be optimal for initial stock sizes sufficiently close to $\underline{S}$ by slight modifications of the proof of proposition 9 in Lewis and Schmalensee (1977).

then to cease harvesting when the $\lambda^a(S)$ locus is reached from below, and finally to resume harvesting and approach E as before when the $\lambda^a(S)$ locus is reached from above. This corresponds to what we have called an exploitation/regeneration policy. Note that such a strategy involves encountering a range of stock sizes twice, first with a low value of λ, then with a higher value. But by the stationarity of the problem, the optimal choice of λ (and thus of H) at any instant can depend only on the stock size, S, and not on time. One thus must be exactly indifferent between starting on the upper part of an optimal path like U and starting on the lower part. But starting on the upper part amounts to adopting a regeneration policy. Thus, if an exploitation/regeneration policy is optimal, there is a regeneration policy that yields exactly the same discounted net benefits. We therefore lose nothing by ruling out exploitation/regeneration when $R=0$. (We suspect that this is also true when R is positive and finite, but, as the discussion in Lewis and Schmalensee, 1979, indicates, we have not been able to prove it.)

In fig. 5.3(b) the sustained harvesting equilibrium stock size S^E is optimally maintained with $H = g(S^E) < H^a(S^E)$ if re-entry is impossible. When $R=0$, this cannot be optimal, even if it yields positive net benefits. (Operation at E may be profitable, since the set of points at which operation with $w=1$ and $B_H = \lambda$ produces $B < F$ is strictly above the $\lambda^a(S)$ locus.) As fig. 5.3(b) is drawn, any optimal rest point of the system must lie on the $\lambda^a(S)$ locus. Any such point must be maintained by choosing w strictly between zero and one, thus exploiting the possibility of following a vibrating policy.

In order to see what this implies, it is useful to define

$$w^a(S) = g(S)/H^a(S). \tag{7}$$

This is the value of w required to keep the stock constant at S on the $\lambda^a(S)$ locus with $H = H^a(S)$. Similarly, λ is held constant at such a point if w is equal to

$$w^b(S) = \lambda^a(S)[r - g_S(S)]/B_S[H^a(S), S]. \tag{8}$$

If it is possible to stay at a point like V in fig. 5.3(b) and satisfy conditions (3), it clearly must be that $w^a(S^V) = w^b(S^V)$. Moreover, analysis of second-order conditions establishes that w^a must intersect w^b from above at that point if it is to be an optimum. It is shown in Lewis and Schmalensee (1975) that if all sustained harvesting equilibria like point E in fig. 5.3(b) lie above the $\lambda^a(S)$ curve, then at least one vibrating equilibrium point like point V in fig. 5.3(b) satisfying these conditions must exist.

Since the optimal rest point V in fig. 5.3(b) is not an equilibrium point of the differential equations implied by (3) when $w=1$ or $w=0$, it is reached in finite time. (That it actually can be reached from both the left and the right is established by analysis of trajectory slopes.) It is optimally maintained thereafter by holding $w = w^a(S^V) = w^b(S^V)$. (Note that here, as in general, w changes discontinuously when the $\lambda^a(S)$ locus is reached.) This is a limiting form of the cyclical policies described above. Since entry and exit occur infinitely rapidly at a vibrating equilibrium, the upper and lower bounds on the stock size coincide. As was noted above, this is consistent with the results of Lewis and Schmalensee (1979) that the distance between these bounds and the time between successive re-entries in optimal cyclical policies both drop when R decreases.

A vibrating equilibrium point like V in fig. 5.3(b) may also exist under the conditions depicted in fig. 5.3(a). If one does exist, it must lie to the left of point a on the $\lambda^a(S)$ curve. If no such point exists, then either regeneration or sustained harvesting must be optimal for all initial stock sizes.

If R is infinite, changes in F do not affect the optimal infinite horizon policy, though they generally change the optimal finite horizon (abandonment) policy and increase the likelihood that abandonment is globally optimal. When $R = 0$, however, increases in F have two sorts of effects on optimal infinite horizon policies. First, they shift the $\lambda^a(S)$ curve down. This increases the stock size at which re-entry is optimal for a regeneration policy, consistent with the more general result that (discounted) operating time is nonincreasing in F (Lewis and Schmalensee, 1979, proposition 3). This shift also tends to transform situations like fig. 5.3(a) into situations like fig. 5.3(b) by rendering sustained harvesting equilibrium points nonoptimal. Secondly, increases in F change the location of vibrating equilibrium points like V in fig. 5.3(b). While the change in the corresponding stock size cannot be signed, one can establish that a small increase in F lowers the equilibrium value of w at such points. When re-entry is impossible, increases in F make it more likely that a finite horizon, abandonment policy is optimal. When $R = 0$, however, this is no longer true, since abandonment is no longer the only way to avoid fixed costs.

Equilibrium points like V are also shifted by changes in the discount rate, r. Increases in r raise $w^b(S)$ for all stock sizes, and w^a must intersect w^b from above at an optimum, so that increases in r lower the corresponding equilibrium stock sizes. Lewis and Schmalensee (1977, proposition 2) establish this same result for sustained harvesting equilibria like E in fig. 5.3(a).[12]

Even in the limiting case considered in this section, the full range of optimal policy types described above appear. Because of the possibility of

---

[12]Lewis and Schmalensee (1975) show that the sustained harvesting comparative dynamics given in propositions 2–4 basically carry over to the case $R = 0$.

following a vibrating policy when $R = 0$, we are able to rule out exploitation/regeneration as redundant and to show that optimal cyclical policies must be of a special, limiting sort. Because vibrating does not produce strict concavity of the effective net benefit function, it does not eliminate all complexity. When R is positive, exploitation/regeneration cannot be ruled out, and nondegenerate cyclical policies may be optimal. The control-theoretic tools employed here are much less helpful then. The analysis of this section should provide some insight into the way nonstandard optimal policy types arise in the presence of nonconvexity, as well as some feel for their properties and the relations among them.

References

Clark, C.W. (1971) "Economically Optimal Policies for the Utilization of Biologically Renewable Resources", *Mathematical Biosciences*, 17, 245–268.

Clark, C.W. (1973) "Profit Maximization and the Extinction of Animal Species", *Journal of Political Economy*, 81, 950–961.

Clark, C.W. (1976) *Mathematical Bioeconomics* (Wiley, New York).

Davidson, R. and R. Harris (1981) "Non-Convexities in Continuous Time Investment Theory", *Review of Economic Studies*, 48, forthcoming.

Hannesson, R. (1975) "Fishery Dynamics: A North Atlantic Cod Fishery", *Canadian Journal of Economics*, 8, 151–173.

Jacquette, D.L. (1974) "A Discrete-Time Population-Control Model with Setup Cost", *Operations Research*, 22, 298–303.

Lewis, T.R. (1979) "The Exhaustion and Depletion of Natural Resources", *Econometrica*, 47, 1569–1572.

Lewis, T.R. (1981) *Optimal Resource Management under Conditions of Uncertainty* (University of Washington Press, Seattle), forthcoming.

Lewis, T.R. and R. Schmalensee (1975) "Nonconvexities and the Theory of Renewable Resource Management", Discussion Paper 75-16, Department of Economics, University of California, San Diego.

Lewis, T.R. and R. Schmalensee (1977) "Nonconvexity and Optimal Exhaustion of Renewable Resources", *International Economic Review*, 18, 535–552.

Lewis, T.R. and R. Schmalensee (1979) "Nonconvexity and Optimal Harvesting Strategies for Renewable Resources", *Canadian Journal of Economics*, 12, 677–691.

Majumdar, M. and T. Mitra (1980a) "On Optimal Exploitation of a Renewable Resource in a Non-Convex Environment and the Minimum Safe Standard of Conservation", Working Paper 223, Department of Economics, Cornell University.

Majumdar, M. and T. Mitra (1980b) "Intertemporal Allocation with a Non-Convex Technology: The Aggregative Framework", Working Paper 221, Department of Economics, Cornell University.

Plourde, C.G. (1970) "A Simple Model of Replenishable Natural Resource Exploitation", *American Economic Review*, 60, 518–522.

Plourde, C.G. (1971) "Exploitation of Common-Property Replenishable Resources", *Western Economic Journal*, 9, 256–266.

Quirk, J. and V. Smith (1970) "Dynamic Economic Models of Fishing", in: A. Scott, ed., *Economics of Fisheries Management: A Symposium* (University of British Columbia, Institute of Animal Resource Ecology, Vancouver).

Reed, W.J. (1974) "A Stochastic Model for the Economic Management of a Renewable Animal Resource", *Mathematical Biosciences*, 22, 313–337.

Salant, S., M. Eswaran and T.R. Lewis (1980) "The Length of Optimal Extraction Programs when Depletion Affects Extraction Costs", Mimeographed, Federal Trade Commission.

Skiba, A.K. (1978) "Optimal Growth with a Convex-Concave Production Function", *Econometrica*, 46, 527–540.

PART IV

OPTIMAL HARVESTING OF RENEWABLE
RESOURCES UNDER UNCERTAINTY

Introduction to Part IV

Managers of fisheries are confronted with variability in stock levels and yields. Uncertainty may be present with regard to the location and quantity of fish available as well as the age, weight and sex composition of the stock. Random environmental disturbances are also present in the form of climate, currents, water temperature, pollution, available food supply and the presence of predators. The fishery manager must plan harvest and escapement levels taking into account environmental uncertainty. Harvest levels may also be affected by the need to learn about unknown biological and environmental parameters which affect the growth of the fish stock.

Spulber's chapter, "Adaptive Harvesting of a Renewable Resource and Stable Equilibrium", examines optimal harvesting of a lumped-parameter renewable resource when random environmental uncertainty affects the resource growth function. Given linear marginal harvesting costs and fixed set-up costs, pulse-fishing policies are shown to be optimal. The observation that an optimal escapement level is a recurrent state for the harvested population is used to demonstrate convergence to a unique, steady-state probability distribution on yields. This distribution is seen to be the proper stochastic analogue to the optimal sustained yield in the deterministic case. The form of the steady-state distribution is examined for different parameter values of the environmental disturbance function. This type of analysis within an uncertainty framework should have implications for applied work on modelling fisheries subject to environmental randomness.

Majumdar's chapter, "A Note on Learning and Optimal Decisions With a Partially Observable State Space", demonstrates the existence of a stationary optimal policy in a planning problem with incomplete information regarding the state of the system. This problem is encountered by a fisheries manager with imperfect knowledge regarding some aspect of the current state of the fishery. The chapter considers an example in which the stock of fish is not known precisely so that the decision on how much to harvest must depend upon an estimate. The chapter yields insights into the structure of optimal policies with partial information and suggests the need for further investigation of alternative forms of partial information encountered in fisheries management.

CHAPTER 6

Adaptive harvesting of a renewable resource and stable equilibrium

DANIEL F. SPULBER*

1. Introduction

Equilibrium harvest and optimal sustainable yield concepts need to be re-examined when biological or environmental uncertainty is present. Failure to revise harvesting plans to take into account new information about environmental disturbances, population density and variability of the yield may lead to increased variability and possibly to unintended collapse of the population.[1] A firm managing a particular resource will increase its profits by adaptive harvesting policies which adjust for changes in the environment and the state of the resource. In population biology, the stochastic analogue to the equilibrium population concept found in deterministic problems is the time-independent probability distribution on population size.[2] For economists, the stochastic analogue to the concept of optimal sustained yield must be the time-invariant probability distribution on yields from a resource harvested so as to maximize expected present discounted value.

*Revised August 1979. The support of the National Science Foundation under Grant SOC 79-07201 is gratefully acknowledged. Preliminary research was performed under National Science Foundation Grant SOC 76-20953 (Principal Investigator, John Ledyard, Northwestern University). I also wish to thank Harl Ryder, Brown University, for helpful discussions. I would like to thank Marion Wathey for expert typing.

[1] Beddington and May (1977) note that: "For a population harvested for sustained yield in a randomly fluctuating environment, the relative variability in the population magnitude, and hence in the yield, increases systematically as the harvesting effort increases."

[2] May (1974, p. 110) observes that, in randomly fluctuating environments, "[The] equilibrium probability distribution is to the stochastic environment as the stable equilibrium point is to the deterministic one."

Essays in the economics of renewable resources, edited by L.J. Mirman and D.F. Spulber
© *North-Holland Publishing Company, 1982*

This chapter examines the long-run equilibrium of an optimality harvested resource stock subject to environmental uncertainty and biological variability. Optimal harvesting rules are derived for a firm managing a fishery and conditions are stated under which a policy of pulse-fishing is optimal. Given a policy of pulse-fishing, the stochastic process describing the state of the resource stock is shown to pass through a recurrent state over time. This observation is then used to demonstrate convergence to a unique invariant probability distribution on the state of the renewable resource, in this case, the biomass. The invariant distribution on the resource biomass and the (known) distribution of environmental disturbances, when taken together with the optimal harvesting policy, induce an invariant distribution on the yield of the resource. This is of interest for two reasons. First, the distribution is the stochastic analogue to the optimal sustained yield result obtained in deterministic analyses. Secondly, the empirically observable results of the firm's decisions, the harvests, may be considered as random draws from the invariant distribution on yields. This result is important for applied work on renewable resource management. Comparative static-type results on expected yields may be obtained in terms of economic parameters and degree of environmental uncertainty.

The lumped-parameter fishing problem is examined using discrete-time stochastic dynamic programming techniques. The pulse-fishing policy is examined with and without fixed set-up costs of harvesting. As in Jaquette (1972b, 1974) and Reed (1974), a feedback (S, s) policy is shown to be optimal.[3] The results of Jaquette and Reed are generalized to the case of Markovian disturbances, and a direct proof of the existence and optimality of the (S, s) policy is provided using the theory of contraction operators on Banach spaces. The optimal escapement level is shown to be a recurrent state for the stochastic process of stock levels. This implies convergence to a unique equilibrium probability distribution on the biomass level of the fish population.

The paper is organized as follows. Section 2 examines adaptive harvesting policies for the case of fixed set-up costs, with linear marginal harvesting costs. Section 3 demonstrates convergence to the equilibrium probability distribution on biomass levels and yield. In section 4, an example is analyzed. The logistic growth model is examined when the intrinsic growth rate and population carrying capacity are random, so as to observe the effects of economic and biological parameters upon the probability distribution on yields. Conclusions are presented in section 5.

---

[3] See Jaquette (1972a, b, 1974) for additional references.

2. Optimal harvesting with linear and fixed costs

Stock adjustment models with nonconvex costs have been applied to the study of optimal management of renewable resources as well as to the control of disease and pests. The similarities of these models to those used in dynamic inventory theory[4] has been stressed by Jaquette (1972a, b, 1974), and Reed (1974). Using a contraction operator approach developed in Easley and Spulber (1979), a direct proof of the existence and optimality of an inventory-type harvesting policy for the infinite horizon case is given in the appendix. This method of analysis allows us to bypass consideration of the finite horizon policy analyzed by Jaquette (1972b) and Reed (1974) and extends their results to the case of Markov environmental disturbances.

The manager of the resource is assumed to be a competitive firm taking the market price of the resource p as given. Suppose that marginal harvesting costs c are linear and let $q = p - c > 0$ be the net marginal return to harvesting.[5] Let h_t, a_t and y_t denote harvest, escapement and biomass at date t, where $h_t + a_t = y_t$. The firm also faces a fixed set-up cost of harvesting K. The optimal harvesting policy will be examined for $K > 0$ and $K = 0$.

Let $x_t \in R_+$ represent the parent stock and let $w_t \in E$ be the environmental disturbance observed at time t. The growth function for the resource is given by $y_t = g(x_t, w_t)$. We assume that there is a minimum sustainable population level $\underline{x} \geqslant 0$ a maximum attainable population level $\bar{x}$ which is finite.

Assumption 1. The growth function g: $[\underline{x}, \bar{x}] \times E \to [\underline{x}, \bar{x}]$ is continuous and nondecreasing in x and w and concave in x.

This assumption admits a wide range of biological growth functions. In particular, it allows the growth function to have linear segments.

Environmental disturbances are considered for the case of a general Markov process and for the case where disturbances are independently and identically distributed in each period. The general Markov case is of interest since varying environmental conditions such as currents, weather, pollution, and predation may be dependent upon previously observed conditions.

---

[4] For stock-adjustment models in economics and operations research see Arrow, Karlin and Scarf (1958), Arrow, Karlin and Suppes (1960), and Scarf, Gilford and Shelly (1963).

[5] Given a number of additional assumptions, the results in this paper may be generalized to the case of stock-dependent harvesting costs of the form $\int_{y-h}^{y} c(z)\,dz$, where $c(z)$ is the marginal cost of harvesting. See Reed (1974).

When (w_t) is a Markov process, the disturbance w_{t+1} has the distribution $\phi(\cdot \mid w_t)$. When disturbances are independently and identically distributed, w_{t+1} has distribution $\phi(\cdot)$.

Assumption 2. Disturbances take values in E, a complete, separable metric space. The distribution ϕ takes E into the space of probability measures on E, $P(E)$ continuously when $P(E)$ is endowed with the weak topology.

This assumption admits a very general range of disturbances.

The firm's problem is to maximize the expected present discounted value of profits over an infinite planning horizon, discounted by a factor α, $0 < \alpha < 1$. The firm must solve

$$\max_{(h_t, a_t)} E\left[\sum_{t=1}^{\infty} \alpha^{t-1}\left(q \cdot h_t - \delta_{h_t} \cdot K \right) \right] \tag{1}$$

subject to x_1 and w_1 given, and

$$h_t + a_t = y_t,$$
$$y_t = g(x_t, w_t),$$
$$x_{t+1} = a_t, \qquad t = 1, 2, \ldots,$$

where δ is an indicator function. The problem may easily be restated in the recursive form of dynamic programming. Let $V(x, w)$ be the value of the resource when the parent stock is x and the last observed environmental disturbance is w. The value function $V(x, w)$ is defined by

$$V(x, w) = \max_{h, a} \left[q \cdot h - \delta_h \cdot K + \alpha \int_E V(a, w') \, d\phi(w' \mid w) \right] \tag{2}$$

subject to $h + a = g(x, w)$.

The optimal value function and harvesting policies may now be characterized.

Proposition 1. Given $K > 0$ and assumptions 1 and 2, an optimal value function V exists satisfying eq. (2) that is continuous and bounded in x and w and is nondecreasing and K-concave in x. There exist optimal measurable policies $h = h(x, w)$ and $a = a(x, w)$. The harvesting policy is given by

$$h = \begin{cases} 0, & \text{if } y \leqslant s(w), \\ y - S(w), & \text{if } y > s(w), \end{cases}$$

where $y = g(x, w)$, and $\underline{x} \leqslant S(w) \leqslant s(w) \leqslant \bar{x}$.

The proof of this result is given in the appendix. Thus, when the recruitment is large enough for the returns from harvesting to cover fixed costs, the population should be harvested to the optimal escapement $S(w)$. Note that the critical population size for harvesting, $s(w)$, is dependent on the last observed disturbance. In deciding whether or not to harvest, future disturbances are taken into account. Also, the size of the harvest $(y - S(w))$ will depend on expectations of future disturbances since the optimal escapement is dependent on w. We obtain the following corollaries.[6]

Corollary 1. Given $K = 0$, an optimal value function exists satisfying eq. (2) that is continuous and bounded in x and w and nondecreasing and concave in x. There exist optimal continuous policies $h = h(x, w)$ and $a = a(x, w)$. The harvesting policy is given by

$$h = \begin{cases} 0, & \text{if } y \leqslant S(w), \\ y - S(w), & \text{if } y > S(w), \end{cases}$$

where $y = g(x, w)$ and $\underline{x} \leqslant S(w) \leqslant \bar{x}$.

When the assumption of Markov disturbances is relaxed we obtain:

Corollary 2. When disturbances are independently and identically distributed;

(a) for $K > 0$, the optimal harvest policy is given by

$$h = \begin{cases} 0, & \text{if } y \leqslant s, \\ y - S, & \text{if } y > s; \end{cases}$$

(b) for $K = 0$, the optimal harvest policy is given by

$$h = \begin{cases} 0, & \text{if } y \leqslant S, \\ y - S, & \text{if } y > S, \end{cases}$$

where $y = g(x, w)$ and $\underline{x} \leqslant S \leqslant s \leqslant \bar{x}$.

This result follows immediately from proposition 1.

If we assume that the biological growth function $g(x, w)$ is differentiable and strictly concave in x, the harvesting policy obtained in corollary 1 may

---

[6]A result similar to corollary 2 is obtained as the limit of a finite horizon plan by Jaquette (1972b) and Reed (1974). Reed assumes that population growth is *linear* in environmental disturbances.

be derived using Kuhn-Tucker analysis. Rewriting eq. (2) as

$$L = q \cdot h + \alpha \int V(a, w') \, d\phi(w' \mid w) + \lambda_1(g(x, w) - h - a)$$
$$+ \lambda_2 h + \lambda_3 a, \tag{3}$$

the first-order conditions are then

$$q - \lambda_1 + \lambda_2 = 0, \tag{4}$$

$$\alpha \int V_x(a, w') \, d\phi(w' \mid w) - \lambda_1 + \lambda_3 = 0, \tag{5}$$

$$g(x, w) - h - a = 0, \tag{6}$$

$$\lambda_2 h = 0, \qquad \lambda_2 \geqslant 0, \tag{7}$$

$$\lambda_3 a = 0, \qquad \lambda_3 \geqslant 0. \tag{8}$$

Note that the derivative of the value function may be obtained explicitly:

$$V_x(x, w) = q \cdot g_x(x, w). \tag{9}$$

So, eq. (5) becomes

$$\alpha \int q \cdot g_x(a, w') \, d\phi(w' \mid w) - \lambda_1 + \lambda_3 = 0. \tag{10}$$

Assuming that $g(x, w) > 0$, then $\lambda_2 > 0$ and $\lambda_3 > 0$ are inconsistent. To rule out the case where both $\lambda_2 = 0$ and $\lambda_3 > 0$ occur, assume that

$$1/\alpha \leqslant \int g_x(a, w') \, d\phi(w' \mid w), \quad \text{for all } a \in [\underline{x}, \bar{x}]; \tag{11}$$

i.e. assume that the expected marginal product of the stock exceeds the inverse of the discount factor. Now consider the case where $\lambda_2 > 0$ and $\lambda_3 = 0$. Then $h = 0$ and $a = g(x, w)$ and

$$1/\alpha \leqslant \int g_x(g(x, w), w') \, d\phi(w' \mid w). \tag{12}$$

When $\lambda_2 = \lambda_3 = 0$, then $a = S(w)$ which solves

$$1/\alpha = \int g_x(S(w), w') \, d\phi(w' \mid w). \tag{13}$$

By the concavity of g, this holds for a when $g(x, w) \geqslant S(w)$.

With a number of additional assumptions, we may examine the effect of the current environmental disturbance w on the optimal escapement. Suppose that w is a positive scalar. Suppose also that $g_{xw} \geqslant 0$ and $\phi(\cdot \mid w)$ is stochastically increasing in w, i.e. for $w_2 \geqslant w_1$, $\phi(\cdot \mid w_2)$ stochastically dominates $\phi(\cdot \mid w_1)$. Then, for S fixed, the right-hand side of (13) will be nondecreasing in w. Therefore, since g is concave, the optimal escapement will be nondecreasing in environmental disturbances.

3. (S, s) policies and stable equilibrium

When pulse-fishing is pursued, the fish population periodically exceeds the optimal size for harvesting, and is then harvested down to the optimal escapement. Suppose we consider the stock levels of the fish population subject to random environmental disturbances as observations of a stochastic process. Pulse-fishing ensures that the optimal escapement level is a *recurrent state* for this stochastic process. This observation will now be used to demonstrate that there is a stable equilibrium probability distribution on the size of the fish stock in any period which is *independent* of any previous fish stock or environment disturbance.

Let us formally describe the stochastic process of fish biomass levels. For the case of Markov environmental disturbances, the biomass levels and disturbances taken together form a Markov process, although the sequence of biomass levels itself will not, in general, be Markovian. Let $Z = X \times E$ be the relevant state space with Borel σ-algebra Ω. Let $a: X \times E \to X$ be the optimal escapement policy given by

$$a(x, w) = \begin{cases} g(x, w), & g(x, w) < s(w), \\ S(w), & g(x, w) \geqslant s(w). \end{cases} \tag{14}$$

The probability that $(a(x_t, w_t), w_{t+1}) \in B$, where $B \in \Omega$, given $(x_t, w_t) = z$, is given by the transition probability measure $P: Z \times \Omega \to [0, 1]$. The measure P is defined as follows:

$$
\begin{aligned}
P(z, B) &\equiv \phi\big(\{w_{t+1} \in E: (a(x_t, w_t), w_{t+1}) \in B\} \mid w_t\big) \\
&= \delta_{a(z)}(x) \circ \phi\Big(\underset{E}{\text{proj }} B \mid w_t\Big),
\end{aligned} \tag{15}
$$

where δ is an indicator function and $x \in X$. For the case of independent and identically distributed environmental disturbances, the sequence of biomass levels alone does form a Markov process so the transition probability P is defined on $X \times \chi$, where χ is the Borel σ-algebra of X. The measure P is defined as follows:

$$P(x, B) \equiv \phi(\{w \in E: a(x, w) \in B\}), \tag{16}$$

for $x \in X$ and $B \in \chi$. Given the transition probability P, the concept of a recurrent state may be formalized.

Definition 1. A point $\bar{z} \in Z$ is a recurrent state if there is an integer $n > 0$ and a number $\beta > 0$, such that $P^n(z, A) \geqslant \beta > 0$, for all $z \in Z$, and for all measurable sets A containing $\bar{z}$.

The purpose of this section is to show the existence of a unique stable probability distribution $F: \chi \to [0,1]$ which indicates the probability that the biomass of the fish population is in some interval at any time regardless of any past stock levels or environmental disturbances. For the Markov disturbances case we will show the existence of a unique stable probability distribution satisfying

$$\eta(B) = \int_B \int_Z P(z, dz') \, d\eta(z), \tag{17}$$

for $z \in Z$, $z' \in B$ and $B \in \Omega$. The stable distribution on biomass levels is then defined by $F(A) \equiv \eta(a^{-1}(A))$, for all $A \in \chi$, where a^{-1} is the inverse of the optimal escapement policy. For the i.i.d. disturbances case, the stable distribution satisfies

$$F(A) = \int_A \int_X P(x, dx') \, dF(x), \tag{18}$$

for $x \in X$, $x' \in A$ and $A \in \chi$.

A joint condition must be placed on the growth function g and the distribution of environmental disturbances ϕ to insure that the resource is viable when it is left *undisturbed*. For the Markov case, the condition insures that at least *one* disturbance occurs with positive probability such that the resource may approach its maximum attainable population level in a finite number of steps. For the i.i.d. case, the condition insures that for some *set* of environmental disturbances, the resource may approach its maximum attainable population level. These restrictions are much weaker than requiring the population to approach its maximum attainable level with certainty.

Assumption 3. (a) Choose $\varepsilon > 0$. When disturbances are Markov, there exists a disturbance $\bar{w} \in E$ satisfying $\phi(\bar{w} \mid w) \geqslant \gamma > 0$, for all $w \in E$, such that for the sequence (y_n) defined by $y_n = g(y_{n-1}, \bar{w})$, for all $y_0 \in X$, there exists an integer N such that $y_N \geqslant \bar{x} - \varepsilon$.

(b) Choose $\varepsilon > 0$. When disturbances are i.i.d., there exists a set $A \in E$ satisfying $\phi(A) \geqslant \gamma > 0$ such that for the sequence (y_n) defined by $y_n = g(y_{n-1}, w_{n-1})$, for all y_0 and for any $w_n \in A$, there exists an integer N such that $y_N \geqslant \bar{x} - \varepsilon$.

This assumption is not restrictive and permits a wide range of growth functions. An additional assumption is needed for the case of Markov disturbances.

Assumption 4. The Markov process of environmental disturbances (w) is stochastically bounded, i.e. there exists an integer N such that for any $\varepsilon > 0$ there is a compact set $C \subseteq E$ such that $M^N \lambda(C) \geqslant 1 - \varepsilon$, for all probability measures λ on E, where $M\lambda(A) = \int \phi(A \mid dw)\lambda(dw)$ and $A \in \mathcal{E}$.

This assumption guarantees that the Markov environmental disturbances are somewhat well behaved but is less restrictive than bounding disturbances into a compact set.[7]

The proof of the main result depends on a theorem of Easley and Spulber (1979)[8] which states that a stochastically bounded Markov process with a recurrent state has a unique, stable invariant probability. We now state the result for the case of Markov environmental disturbances.

Proposition 2a. Given assumptions 3(a) and 4, the transition probability defined by (15) converges to a unique probability measure $\eta \colon \Omega \to [0, 1]$ with the optimal escapement $S(\bar{w})$ and the disturbance $\bar{w}$ as a recurrent state if $s(\bar{w}) < \bar{x}$, for $K > 0$, and $S(\bar{w}) < \bar{x}$, for $K = 0$.

Proof. The proof will be stated only for $K > 0$. The case of $K = 0$ follows immediately. Since (w) is a stochastically bounded Markov process by assumption 4 and $a(x, w)$ is bounded for all $(x, w) \in Z$, the Markov process defined by eq. (15) is stochastically bounded. Since $s(\bar{w}) < \bar{x}$ by assumption, there is an N such that $y_N > s(\bar{w})$, for any $y_0 \in X$, by assumption 3(a). Therefore, $a(y_N, \bar{w}) = S(\bar{w})$. So, $(S(\bar{w}), \bar{w})$ is reached with probability greater than or equal to $\gamma \cdot (N + 1) > 0$, from any point in the state space and is thus a recurrent state for the stochastic process (x, w). This implies the existence of a unique stable invariant probability $\eta \colon \Omega \to [0, 1]$.

The result is also obtained for i.i.d. disturbances.

Proposition 2b. Given assumption 3(b) and the transition probability defined by (16), the sequence of probability measures on stock levels converges to a unique probability measure $F \colon \chi \to [0, 1]$ with the optimal escapement S as a recurrent state, if $s < \bar{x}$, for $K > 0$, and $S < \bar{x}$, for $K = 0$.

The proof is similar to the proof of proposition 2a.

---

[7]It is important to note that assumptions 3(a) and 4 are sufficient to guarantee that the Markov process of disturbances is ergodic. However, the Markov case must be treated as distinct from the i.i.d. This is because any decision-maker treating the invariant distribution of Markov disturbances as a distribution of independent disturbances would not be making full use of available information. Furthermore, it must be stressed that the process of biomass levels taken alone is still not a Markov process.

[8]The theorem shows that Doeblin's condition is satisfied. See Neveu (1965, p. 185).

Given the invariant distribution on parent stocks and environmental disturbances, η, and the optimal harvest policy h: $X \times E \to [0, \bar{x}]$, the steady-state distribution ξ on the yield of the resource is given by

$$\xi(A) = \eta(h^{-1}(A)),\tag{19}$$

for all $A \in B([0, \bar{x}])$, the Borel σ-algebra of $[0, \bar{x}]$. While this expression is the distribution of yields in a period in which harvesting occurred, it is equivalently the distribution of yields expected in *any* period. Thus, since h is the optimal pulse-fishing policy, ξ is the stochastic analogue to the optimal sustainable yield. Finally, the distribution η can be used to generate the equilibrium probability distribution on the value of the resource to the firm in any period:

$$\theta(A) = \eta(V^{-1}(A)),\tag{20}$$

where V is the optimal value function defined in (2).

4. An example: The logistic growth model

4.1. In this section we examine how the economic and biological parameters of the optimal harvesting problem affect the form of the steady-state probability distribution on the stock of fish. The fish population is assumed to grow according to the well-known logistic growth equation introduced by Verhulst (1838) (see also Schaefer, 1957, and Clark, 1976). Let x_t represent the stock of fish at time t and let k be the environmental carrying capacity. Given the intrinsic growth rate, ρ, $0 \leq \rho \leq 1$, the population is assumed to grow by discrete increments:

$$x_{t+1} - x_t = \rho x_t(1 - x_t/k).\tag{21}$$

We will examine in turn the cases where the intrinsic growth rate ρ and the environmental carrying capacity k are subject to random environmental disturbances.[9]

4.2. The intrinsic growth rate ρ is assumed to be affected by random disturbances $w \in [0, \infty]$, where $\rho(w) = e^{-w}$. The growth function has the

---

[9]For a discussion of logistic growth in continuous time with environmental randomness, see May (1974) and Levins (1969). Levins allows variability in both the environmental carrying capacity and in the intrinsic growth rate.

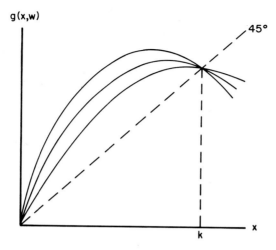

Figure 6.1

form

$$g(x,w)=x+e^{-w}x(1-x/k) \tag{22}$$

(see fig. 6.1). Environmental disturbances are assumed to be exponentially distributed with mean $1/\lambda$, so that the intrinsic growth rate varies between 0 and 1 with mean $\lambda/(1+\lambda)$.

Consider the case where the set-up costs of harvesting equal zero. The assumptions needed for corollary 2 are then satisfied. The optimal escapement S solves the Euler equation (13) for the decision-maker's maximization problem:

$$1 = \frac{1}{1+r} \int_0^\infty \left[1 + e^{-w}\left(1 - \frac{2S}{k}\right)\right] \lambda e^{-\lambda w} dw, \tag{23}$$

where $\alpha = 1/(1+r)$ is the discount factor and r is the rate of interest. Solving for S we obtain:

$$S = \tfrac{1}{2}k\left(1 - r\left(\frac{1+\lambda}{\lambda}\right)\right). \tag{24}$$

For $S>0$, the expected intrinsic growth rate of the population $\lambda/(1+\lambda)$ must exceed the rate of interest. Note that $S<\tfrac{1}{2}k$.

To find the explicit form of the invariant distribution, we first state the Markov transition probability for the fish population not subject to harvesting:

$$P(x, b) = \phi(\{w \in [0, \infty): x + e^{-w}x(1 - x/k) \leq b\})$$

$$= \phi\left(\left\{w \in [0, \infty): w \geq \ln\left(\frac{b - x}{x(1 - x/k)}\right)^{-1}\right\}\right)$$

$$= \int_{\ln\left(\frac{b - x}{x(1 - x/k)}\right)^{-1}}^{\infty} \lambda e^{-\lambda w}\, dw$$

$$= \left[\frac{b - x}{x(1 - x/k)}\right]^{\lambda}. \tag{25}$$

For $x = S$, the transition probability is given by

$$P(S, b) = \left[\frac{b - S}{S(1 - S/k)}\right]^{\lambda}. \tag{26}$$

Since the logistic growth function has the property that the population never decreases for any parent stock below k, for any constant growth rate ρ, $0 \leq \rho \leq 1$, the optimality harvested population will never fall below S. Thus, given the pulse-fishing policy, the population size is independently and identically distributed in each period, and the transition probability (26) is identical to the invariant probability distribution $F(x)$:

$$F(x) = \frac{1}{[S(1 - S/k)]^{\lambda}}(x - S)^{\lambda}, \tag{27}$$

defined on the interval $[S, S + S(1 - S/k)]$. The steady-state probability density $f(x) = dF(x)$ is then

$$f(x) = \frac{1}{[S(1 - S/k)]^{\lambda}}\lambda(x - S)^{\lambda - 1}. \tag{28}$$

Note that the distribution is well-defined since $\lambda > 0$. The form of the distribution depends upon the parameter of the distribution of environmental disturbances. For $0 < \lambda < 1$, the distribution of disturbances is downward sloping and convex. For $\lambda = 1$, the distribution is uniform on $[S, S + S(1 - S/k)]$. For $1 < \lambda < 2$, the distribution is upward sloping and concave and for $2 < \lambda$, the distribution is upward sloping and convex (see fig. 6.2 (a–d)).

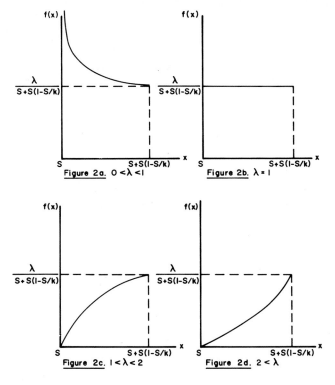

Figure 6.2

Given the equilibrium distribution we may calculate the expected stock in the steady state:

$$Ex = \int_{S}^{S+S(1-S/k)} xf(x)\,dx$$

$$= S + S\left(1 - \frac{S}{k}\right)\left(\frac{\lambda}{1+\lambda}\right). \tag{29}$$

The expected yield h_e is simply

$$h_e = Ex - S$$

$$= S\left(1 - \frac{S}{k}\right)\left(\frac{\lambda}{1+\lambda}\right). \tag{30}$$

Substituting for

$$S = \tfrac{1}{2}k\left(1 - r\left(\frac{1+\lambda}{\lambda}\right)\right)$$

into (30), we obtain

$$h_e = \frac{k}{4}\left(\frac{\lambda}{1+\lambda}\right)\left(1 - r^2\left(\frac{1+\lambda}{\lambda}\right)^2\right). \tag{31}$$

The effects of the parameters r, k, and λ on the optimal escapement S and the expected harvest h_e are the same. Both S and h_e are increasing and linear in the carrying capacity k, and decreasing and convex in the mean environmental disturbance $1/\lambda$. The escapement S is linear and decreasing in the rate of interest and the expected harvest h_e is concave and decreasing in the rate of interest. Cross effects of r, $\bar{x}$, and λ on S and h_e are also similar. For h_e we observe

$$\frac{\partial}{\partial \lambda}\left(\frac{\partial h_e}{\partial r}\right) = \frac{r}{4}\frac{1}{\lambda^2} > 0, \tag{32}$$

$$\frac{\partial}{\partial k}\left(\frac{\partial h_e}{\partial r}\right) = \frac{-r}{4}\left(\frac{1+\lambda}{\lambda}\right) < 0, \tag{33}$$

$$\frac{\partial}{\partial k}\left(\frac{\partial h_e}{\partial \lambda}\right) = \frac{1}{4}\left(\frac{1}{(1+\lambda)^2} + \frac{r^2}{\lambda^2}\right) > 0. \tag{34}$$

Thus, the effects of higher interest on expected yield (and on the optimal escapement) are lessened by a higher mean disturbance $1/\lambda$ and by a higher carrying capacity k. A higher carrying capacity lessens the effect of a higher mean disturbance.

4.3. We now assume that the intrinsic growth rate of the population ρ is constant, and that the environmental carrying capacity is an increasing function of environmental disturbances, where $k = \gamma/(1+e^{-w})$. The growth function has the form

$$g(x, w) = x + x\rho\left(1 - \frac{x(1-e^{-w})}{\gamma}\right). \tag{35}$$

Environmental disturbances are exponentially distributed with mean $1/\lambda$ as before, so the carrying capacity varies between $\gamma/2$ and γ. Note that when the environmental carrying capacity is variable, the population size may fall for any parent stock above $\gamma/2$ (see fig. 6.3).

Given the logistic growth function with a variable carrying capacity, and linear harvesting costs, the optimal escapement S solves the following Euler

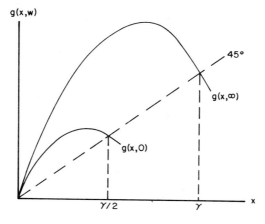

Figure 6.3

equation:

$$1 = \frac{1}{1+r} \int_0^\infty \left[1 + \rho - \frac{2x}{\gamma}(1+e^{-w}) \right] \lambda e^{-\lambda w} dw. \tag{36}$$

Solving for S, we obtain:

$$S = \frac{\gamma}{2}(\rho - r)\left(\frac{1+\lambda}{1+2\lambda} \right). \tag{37}$$

For S to be positive we require the intrinsic growth rate ρ to exceed the rate of interest. Note that since $(\rho - r) < 1$ and $(1+\lambda)/(1+2\lambda) < 1$, then $S < \frac{1}{2}\gamma$. Therefore, when the population is harvested back to S, it will always increase in the next period and will again be subject to harvesting. So, the population size will again be independently and identically distributed in each period. This will immediately yield the invariant cumulative probability distribution:

$$F(x) = \phi\left(\left\{ w: S + S\rho\left(1 - \frac{S}{\gamma}(1+e^{-w}) \right) \leq x \right\} \right)$$

$$= \int_0^{\ln\left[\frac{\gamma}{S}\left(1 - \frac{x-S}{S\rho} \right) - 1 \right]^{-1}} \lambda e^{-\lambda w} dw$$

$$= 1 - \left[\frac{\gamma}{S}\left(1 - \frac{x-S}{S\rho} \right) - 1 \right]^\lambda, \tag{38}$$

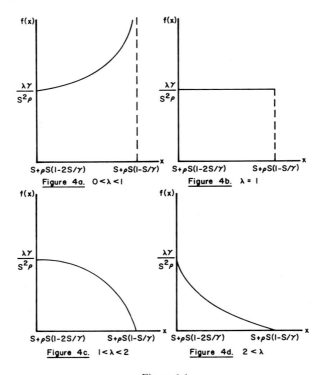

Figure 6.4

with domain $[S + S\rho(1 - 2S/\gamma), S + S\rho(1 - S/\gamma)]$. The invariant probability distribution is then

$$f(x) = \lambda \left[\frac{\gamma}{S} \left(1 - \frac{x - S}{S\rho} \right) - 1 \right]^{\lambda - 1} \frac{\gamma}{S^2 \rho}. \tag{39}$$

See fig. 6.4(a–d) for the form of $f(x)$ for different parameter values of λ.

The optimal escapement S is linear and increasing in γ and ρ, linear and decreasing in r, and convex and decreasing in λ. The expected harvest is found as before:

$$h_e = \rho S \left(1 - \frac{S}{\gamma} \left(\frac{1 + 2\lambda}{1 + \lambda} \right) \right). \tag{40}$$

Substituting for S we obtain

$$h_e = \frac{\gamma}{2} \left(\frac{1 + \lambda}{1 + 2\lambda} \right) \rho(\rho - r) \left(1 - \frac{\rho - r}{2} \right). \tag{41}$$

Note that h_e is linear and increasing in γ, decreasing and convex in λ, decreasing and concave in r and increasing in ρ and convex in ρ for $\rho \leqslant 2/3$.

5. Conclusion

A unique stable probability distribution on biomass levels was shown to exist for natural populations harvested by pulse-fishing. This distribution was found to yield empirical implications for explicit parameterization of the population growth function and the probability distribution of environmental disturbances. The approach taken here would seem to extend in a straightforward manner to the adaptive harvesting rules for populations where members are distinguished by sex for harvesting and growth (see Mann, 1970). Also, the approach may be applied to the study of multi-cohort and multi-species fisheries where pulse-fishing is often found to be desirable. In the multi-cohort fishery, environmental disturbances may cause wide variations in cohort size. Hannesson (1975, p. 162) notes the "very substantial fluctuations in recruitment which occur in cod fisheries." Consideration of the stable distribution on the vector of cohort biomass levels and on yields may be analytically more tractable than solving the deterministic problem. In the case of a multi-species fishery, the stable distribution approach is particularly interesting when there is, as May (1974, p. 138) notes, "tension between the stabilizing population interactions and destabilizing environmental fluctuations".

Appendix

The characterization of the optimal value function and optimal harvesting policy draws upon the properties of K-concave functions. See Scarf (1960) and Reed (1974).

Definition (Scarf). Let $K \geqslant 0$. The function f is (*strictly*) K-*concave* if

$$K(>) \geqslant f(y+x) - f(x) - y \cdot \left[\frac{f(x) - f(x-b)}{b} \right], \qquad (A.1)$$

where $y > 0$, $x > 0$ and $b > 0$.

The following theorem of Reed (1974) will be useful.

Theorem (Reed).   Suppose $f(x)$ is continuous and strictly K-concave on $[\underline{x}, \bar{x}]$ and let $N = \sup_{[\underline{x}, \bar{x}]} f(x)$ and $S = \inf\{y: f(y) = N, \ y \in [\underline{x}, \bar{x}]\}$. Then there exists at most one s, $S \leqslant s \leqslant \bar{x}$ such that $f(s) = N - K$ and, further, if such an s exists $f(x) < N - K$ for $x \in (s, \bar{x}]$.

The proof of proposition 1 uses the contraction mapping technique of dynamic programming (see Maitra, 1968, and Hinderer, 1970). The proof is similar to the technique introduced in Easley and Spulber (1979) for the inventory control problem. Let $B(X \times E)$ be the space of bounded and measurable functions on $X \times E$. The space $B(X \times E)$ is a Banach space under the sup norm. Let $D_K(X \times E)$ be the space of non-negative, continuous and bounded functions on $X \times E$ which are also non-decreasing and K-concave on X. We begin by stating and proving three lemmata.

Define the operator $G: B(X \times E) \to B(X \times E)$ by

$$(Gv)(x, w) = \max_{a \in [\underline{x}, y]} \left[q(y - a) - \delta_{(y-a)} \cdot K + \alpha \int_E v(a, w') \, \mathrm{d}\phi(w' \mid w) \right],$$

(A.2)

where $v \in B(X \times E)$ and $y = g(x, w)$. Clearly, G is a contraction operator on the Banach space $B(X \times E)$ (see Maitra, 1968). Any closed subset of the Banach space $B(X \times E)$ which is mapped by G into itself, will have a fixed point.

Lemma 1.   The space $D_K(X \times E)$ is complete.

Proof.   We need only show that $D_K(X \times E)$ is a closed subset of the complete space $B(X \times E)$. It is sufficient to show that $(f_n) \subset D_K(X \times E)$ and $f_n \to f$ in the sup norm implies that $f \in D_K(X \times E)$. Clearly, f is a nonnegative, nondecreasing, continuous and bounded function, so we need to show that f is K-concave. Since $f_n \in D_K(X \times E)$

$$K \geqslant f_n(x + y) - f_n(x) - y \cdot \left[\frac{f_n(x) - f_n(x - b)}{b} \right], \quad \forall x, y, b,$$

and $f_n \to f$ implies $f_n(x) \to f(x)$, $f_n(x + y) \to f(x + y)$, and $f_n(x - b) \to f(x - b)$, hence

$$K \geqslant f(x + y) - f(x) - y \cdot \left[\frac{f(x) - f(x - b)}{b} \right] \geqslant 0.$$

Thus, $f \in D_K(X \times E)$.

Lemma 2. For $K>0$, the operator G on $B(X \times E)$ given in eq. (A.2) takes the space $D_K(X \times E)$ into itself.

Proof. Clearly, (Gv) is non-negative and bounded in (x, w). Since v is continuous and K-concave, the term $\alpha \int v(a, w') d\phi(w'/w)$ is continuous and strictly K-concave in a since $0 < \alpha < 1$. So, the conditions of Reed's theorem are satisfied. Let $N(w)$ be defined by

$$N(w) = \sup_{a \in [\underline{x}, \bar{x}]} \left[-q \cdot a + \alpha \int_E v(a, w') d\phi(w' \mid w) \right] \tag{A.3}$$

and let $S(w)$ be defined by

$$S(w) = \inf \left\{ u: \left[-q \cdot u + \alpha \int_E v(u, w') d\phi(w' \mid w) \right] = N(w), u \in [\underline{x}, \bar{x}] \right\}. \tag{A.4}$$

Note that by the maximum principle (Berge, 1963), $N(w)$ is continuous. Then, there exists at most one $s(w)$, where $\underline{x} \leqslant S(w) \leqslant s(w) \leqslant \bar{x}$ such that

$$-q \cdot s(w) + \alpha \int v(s(w), w') d\phi(w' \mid w) = N(w) - K, \tag{A.5}$$

and further, if such an $s(w)$ exists,

$$-q \cdot u + \alpha \int v(u, w') d\phi(w' \mid w) < N(w) - K, \tag{A.6}$$

for $y \in (s(w), \bar{x}]$. If such an $s(w)$ does not exist let $s(w) = \bar{x}$. The maps $s(w)$, $S(w)$ will be measurable in w. Thus, (Gv) may be rewritten as

$$(Gv)(x, w) = \begin{cases} \alpha \int_E v(g(x, w), w') d\phi(w' \mid w), \\ \quad \text{if } g(x, w) \leqslant s(w), \\ q \cdot (g(x, w) - S(w)) - K + \alpha \int_E v(S(w), w') d\phi(w' \mid w), \\ \quad \text{if } g(x, w) > s(w). \end{cases} \tag{A.7}$$

The function (Gv) will now be shown to be continuous in x and w. For $g(x, w) < s(w)$, (Gv) is continuous in x and w by the continuity of $\phi(\cdot \mid w)$ in the weak topology and by the continuity of v and g. Also, for $g(x, w) \geqslant s(w)$, using eq. (A.3),

$$(Gv)(x, w) = q \cdot g(x, w) - K + N(w),$$

which is continuous by the continuity of $N(w)$. Finally, note that since

$$-q \cdot s(w) + \alpha \int_E v(s(w), w') \, d\phi(w' \mid w) = N(w) - K$$

$$= -q \cdot S(w) - K + \alpha \int v(S(w), w') \, d\phi(w' \mid w), \qquad (A.8)$$

from (A.4) and (A.5), then rearranging terms yields

$$\alpha \int v(s(w), w') \, d\phi(w' \mid w) = q \cdot (s(w) - S(w)) - K$$

$$+ \alpha \int v(S(w), w') \, d\phi(w' \mid w). \qquad (A.9)$$

This implies that (Gv) is continuous for x, w such that $g(x, w) = s(w)$. So, (Gv) is continuous in x, w. By similar arguments, (Gv) is nondecreasing in x.

It will now be shown that (Gv) is K-concave in x for all w. Let w be fixed. For x such that $g(x, w) < s(w)$, (Gv) is strictly K-concave since v is nondecreasing and K-concave in x, g is nondecreasing and concave in x and $0 < \alpha < 1$. For x such that $g(x, w) \geq s(w)$, (Gv) is strictly K-concave since it is the sum of a constant term and $q \cdot g(x, w)$ which is concave in x. Now consider the interval $[x, y]$, where x and y are such that $g(x, w) < s(w)$ and $g(y, w) \geq s(w)$. Let $x = y - a$. We wish to show that for w chosen arbitrarily,

$$(Gv)(y - a) - (Gv)(y) + a \left[\frac{(Gv)(y + b) - (Gv)(y)}{b} \right] \leq K, \qquad (A.10)$$

where $a, b > 0$. Writing (Gv) explicitly and adding and subtracting $q \cdot g(y - a, w)$ yields

$$\alpha \int v(g(y - a), w') \, d\phi(w' \mid w)$$

$$- \left[q \cdot (g(y, w) - S(w)) - K + \alpha \int v(S(w), w') \, d\phi(w' \mid w) \right]$$

$$+ \frac{a}{b} \left[\left[q \cdot (g(y + b) - S(w)) - K + \alpha \int v(S(w), w') \, d\phi(w' \mid w) \right] \right.$$

$$\left. - \left[q \cdot (g(y, w) - S(w)) - K + \alpha \int v(S(w), w') \, d\phi(w' \mid w) \right] \right]$$

$$= K + \left[\left[-q \cdot g(y - a, w) + \alpha \int v(g(y - a, w), w') \, d\phi(w' \mid w) \right] \right.$$

$$\left. - \left[-q \cdot S(w) + \alpha \int v(S(w), w') \, d\phi(w' \mid w) \right] \right]$$

$$+ q \left[g(y - a, w) - g(y, w) + \frac{a}{b} [g(y + b, w) - g(y, w)] \right]$$

$$\leq K. \qquad (A.11)$$

This holds since the first term in brackets is nonpositive by the definition of $S(w)$ and the second term in brackets is nonpositive by the concavity of g. So, (Gv) is K-concave in x for all w.

Lemma 3. For $K > 0$, and the operator G given in eq. (A.2), there exists a unique $V^* \in D_K(X \times E)$ such that $GV^* = V^*$.

Proof. Since G is a monotone operator and $0 < \alpha < 1$, G is a contraction mapping on $B(X \times E)$. Since $G: D_K(X \times E) \to D_K(X \times E)$ and $D_K(X \times E) \subset B(X \times E)$, G is also a contraction mapping on $D_K(X \times E)$. Hence, by the Contraction Mapping Principle, there is a unique point $V^* \in D_K(X \times E)$ such that $GV^* = V^*$ (see Liusternik and Sobolev, 1974).

Proof of Proposition 1. With each Borel measurable map $a: X \times E \to X$, associate the operator $H(a): D_K(X \times E) \to D_K(X \times E)$ defined by

$$(H(a)v)(x,w) = q \cdot (g(x,w) - a(x,w)) - \delta_{(g(x,w) - a(x,w))} \cdot K$$
$$+ \alpha \int v(a(x,w), w') \, d\phi(w' \mid w), \qquad (A.12)$$

for $v \in D_K(X \times E)$. Since $H(a)$ is a monotone linear operator and $0 < \alpha < 1$, it is a contraction on $C(X \times E)$, the space of continuous and bounded functions on $X \times E$. By an argument similar to lemma 3, $H(a)$ has a unique fixed point $I(a)$ in $D_K(X \times E)$.

By a Selection Theorem of Dubins and Savage (1965) (see Maitra, 1968), there is a Borel measurable map $a: X \times E \to X$ such that $GV = H(a)V$. Hence, $H(a)V = V$ and $V = I(a)$, since $I(a)$ is the unique fixed point of $H(a)$. Therefore, $GV = V$ can be rewritten as

$$I(a)(x,w) = \max_{a \in [\underline{x}, g(x,w)]} \left[q \cdot (g(x,w) - a) - \delta_{(g(x,w) - a)} \cdot K \right.$$
$$\left. + \alpha \int V(a,w') \, d\phi(w' \mid w) \right].$$

Thus, $I(a)$ satisfies the optimality equation and the stationary plan $(a, a, a, \ldots)$ is optimal (see Blackwell, 1965).

Since $V = I(a)$ and $V \in D_K(X \times E)$, the optimal return is non-negative, continuous and bounded on $X \times E$ and is also nondecreasing and K-concave on X. Since $0 < \alpha < 1$, the term the planner seeks to minimize, if the decision is made to harvest,

$$-q \cdot a + \alpha \int V(a,w') \, d\phi(w' \mid w),$$

is continuous and strictly K-concave in a. Hence, by Reed's Theorem, the optimal escapement policy has the form

$$a = \begin{cases} g(x,w), & \text{if } g(x,w) \leqslant s(w), \\ S(w), & \text{if } g(x,w) > s(w). \end{cases}$$

References

Arrow, K. J., S. Karlin and H. Scarf (1958) *Studies in the Mathematical Theory of Inventory and Production* (Stanford University Press, Stanford, California).

Arrow, K. J., S. Karlin and P. Suppes (1960) *Mathematical Methods in the Social Sciences* (Stanford University Press, Stanford, California).

Beddington, J. R. and R. M. May (1977) "Harvesting Natural Populations in a Randomly Fluctuating Environment," *Science*, 197, 29 July, 463–465.

Berge, C. (1963) *Topological Spaces* (Macmillan, New York).

Blackwell, D. (1965) "Discounted Dynamic Programming", *Annals of Mathematical Statistics*, 36, 226–235.

Clark, C. W. (1976) *The Optimal Management of Renewable Resources* (John Wiley and Sons, New York).

Dubins, L. E. and L. J. Savage (1965) *How to Gamble if You Must* (McGraw-Hill, New York).

Easley, D. and D. F. Spulber (1979) "Optimal Policies and Steady-State Solutions for Inventory Problems with Markovian Uncertainty", Northwestern University, Center for Mathematical Studies, Discussion Paper no. 353.

Hannesson, R. (1975) "Fishery Dynamics, A North Atlantic Cod Fishery", *Canadian Journal of Economics*, 8, 151–173.

Hinderer, K. (1970) *Foundations of Non-Stationary Dynamic Programming with Discrete Time Parameter*, Lecture Notes in Operations Research and Mathematical Systems, vol. 33 (Springer-Verlag).

Jaquette, L. (1972a) "Mathematical Models for the Control of Growing Biological Populations: A Survey", *Operations Research*, 20, 1142–1151.

Jaquette, L. (1972b) "A Discrete-Time Population-Control Model", *Mathematical Biosciences*, 15, 231–252.

Jaquette, L. (1974) "A Discrete-Time Population Control Model with Setup Cost", *Operations Research*, 22, 298–303.

Levins, R. (1969) "The Effect of Random Variations of Different Types on Population Growth", *Proceedings of the National Academy of Sciences*, 62, 1061–1065.

Liusternik, L. A. and V. J. Sobolev (1974) *Elements of Functional Analysis* (John Wiley and Sons, New York).

Maitra, A. (1968) "Discounted Dynamic Programming on Compact Metric Spaces", *SANKHYA*, Ser. A, 30, Part 2, 211–216.

Mann, S. H. (1971) "A Mathematical Theory for the Control of Pest Populations", *Biometrics*, 27, 357–368.

May, R. M. (1974) *Stability and Complexity in Model Ecosystems*, 2nd edn. (Princeton University Press, Princeton).

Neveu, J. (1965) *Mathematical Foundations of the Calculus of Probability* (Holden-Day, San Francisco).

Reed, W. J. (1974) "A Stochastic Model of the Economic Management of a Renewable Animal Resource", *Mathematical Biosciences*, 22, 313–337.

Scarf, H. (1960) "The Optimality of (S, s) Policies in the Dynamic Inventory Problem", in: *Mathematical Methods in the Social Sciences* (Stanford University, Stanford, California).

Scarf, H., D. M. Gilford and M. W. Shelly (1963) *Multistage Inventory Models and Techniques* (Stanford University Press, Stanford, California).

Schaefer, M. B. (1957) "Some Considerations of Population Dynamics and Economics in Relation to the Management of Marine Fisheries", *Journal of the Fisheries Research Board of Canada*, 14, 669–681.

Verhulst, P. F. (1838) "Notice sur la Loi que la Population Suit Dans son Accroissement", *Correspondence Mathématique et Physique*, 10, 113–121.

CHAPTER 7

A note on learning and optimal decisions with a partially observable state space

MUKUL MAJUMDAR

1. Introduction

"The basic need for a special theory to explain the behavior under conditions of uncertainty arises from two considerations: (1) subjective feelings of
imperfect knowledge when certain types of choices, typically commitments
over time, are made; (2) the existence of certain observed phenomena, of
which insurance is the most conspicuous example, which cannot be explained on the assumption that individuals act with subjective certainty"
(Arrow, 1974, p. 44). An impressive literature on intertemporal resource
allocation under uncertainty has attempted to deal formally with the first
type of problems that Arrow was concerned with: the *actions* of an agent
may not determine the *consequences*, which are allowed to depend on *the
state of the environment*, whose occurrence the agent cannot control. An
action may be a microeconomic decision by an individual or a family on
how much to save and invest, and what type of portfolios to choose when
making that investment;[1] or, it may be a macroeconomic decision imple-

*March 1980. Financial support from the National Science Foundation is gratefully
acknowledged. A preliminary version of the paper was presented at the Conference on The
Economics of Renewable Resource Management organized at Brown University in October
1979. I wish to thank E. Dynkin, D. Easley, T. Mitra, L. Mirman, D. Ray and D. Spulber for
their useful comments. I have drawn heavily on the numerous conversations I had with Gautam
Bhattacharya who has followed up some of the ideas presented in this chapter. I have a much
better understanding of the problems thanks to his help. Finally, thanks are due to Dean Alain
Seznec for approving of an arrangement that facilitated the completion of this manuscript.
[1]See, for example, Phelps (1962) or Levhari and Srinivasan (1969).

Essays in the economics of renewable resources, edited by *L.J. Mirman and D.F. Spulber*
© North-Holland Publishing Company, 1982

mented by the Central Planning Board on the aggregate volume of invest-ment and choice of techniques.[2] The consequences are nondeterministic, since the returns to an investment of a particular individual may depend on a complex set of factors linked to the overall state of the economy that the individual cannot control. Similarly, the aggregate output resulting from macroeconomic decisions may be influenced by climatic forces or condi-tions in the international markets that are beyond the control of the Central Planning Board. A rather large class of optimization problems in which the planner is subjected to this type of uncertainty has been attacked by using the techniques of stochastic dynamic programming developed by Blackwell, Maitra and others. The recursive structure of the decision-making process has been exploited to derive interesting properties of optimal actions.[3]

Yet another type of uncertainty is imperfect knowledge about the state of the system itself when actions are taken, even though the consequences of the actions may well be determinate. In the literature on optimal extraction and management of exhaustible or renewable resources, the importance of such an element of uncertainty has been recognized by Gilbert (1979), Loury (1978), and others. But examples from other areas also come to mind very naturally. It is not unusual that decisions over time are often made neither with a complete knowledge about the state of the environment nor under total ignorance, but only on the basis of some signals or messages that come to the planner. In a model with sequential decisions, such signals also enable the planner to learn (at least in principle) more about the environment with the passage of time. To establish interesting optimality properties of specific types of learning behavior, or even to prove the existence of an optimal sequence of decisions relying on some precise learning rules, has always been one of the more difficult analytical problems in the economics of uncertainty. It is not surprising that even in the recent literature, existence questions are often side-stepped, or treated on an ad hoc basis, exploiting whenever possible the special structures of the model.[4] The modest purpose of this note is to draw attention to the theory of

---

[2] See, for example, Majumdar (1977) and Brock and Majumdar (1978) for a discussion of the stochastic version of Ramsey's optimal savings problem and the various "turnpike" theorems.
[3] See, for example, Maitra (1968) for a list of references to the important earlier papers by Blackwell and Strauch. The paper by Majumdar and Radner (1979) contains a stochastic intertemporal allocation model and an application of the dynamic programming arguments.
[4] Loury's analysis (1978) is interesting from many angles; however, he did not face up to the existence problem. Also, there was no distinction between the true actual stock and the known stock, a distinction which is of some importance. From that point of view, I find Gilbert's approach (1979) more satisfying.

stochastic dynamic programming with a partially observable state space (developed by Dynkin, Yushkevich and others), and to point out that by using that logical framework, one can develop a systematic and unified approach towards identifying a class of stochastic optimization problems in which a Bayesian type learning mechanism generates an optimal policy. In section 2, the basic mathematical model is reviewed very briefly. In section 3 I discuss two particular applications of the statistical theory to the analysis of problems arising in the theory of natural resources. It is conceded right at the beginning that the specific examples are highly oversimplified partial equilibrium exercises. First, we consider the question of optimal harvesting of a fishery when the owner does not know the true stock, but acts on the basis of messages received about the total reserve. The biological evolution of the fish stock is assumed to be random (the stochastic law of evolution is considered to be of a simple type). Secondly, we consider the problem of optimal extraction of a resource when the true stock is not known, and the discovery in any period is random. The common elements of the underlying logical structures in the two models are easy to identify once one has the general framework in proper perspective. It is perhaps useful to mention some other applications in quite different contexts. Bhattacharya (1980) has tried to derive the main result in Rothschild's two armed bandit theory (1974) of market pricing with imperfect information about demand conditions. The question of optimal resource extraction when there is a possibility of development of a "backstop" technology (that neutralizes the importance of the resource and guarantees a steady flow of consumption stream) discussed by Dasgupta and Heal (1974) can also be treated by similar methods. Mirman has pointed out that the techniques can be applied to the theory of Bayesian consumers and information production that has been developed by Grossman, Kihlstrom and Mirman (1977).[5]

Of course, it is small consolation to know that in a model of decision-making under uncertainty, the planner does have an optimal sequence of actions. One ought to be alarmed about the consistency of the logical structure if such existence questions cannot be settled. One would like to go further, and to derive qualitative properties of optimal policies: so far, this seems to be feasible only in special examples. But this really is another research project.

---

[5] Bhattacharya's thesis (1980) provides a detailed discussion of (a) the resource extraction example, (b) the question of the backstop technology, (c) the two armed bandit theory as a special case of the dynamic programming and theory of the type that we are concerned with in this note, and (d) the Grossman–Kihlstrom–Mirman theory of Bayesian consumers.

Notation and organization

In what follows R and R_+ denote the sets of real numbers and non-negative real numbers, respectively. The discussion that follows presupposes a knowledge of the theory of stochastic dynamic programming with a completely observable state space and the theory of weak convergence of probability measures on metric spaces. Because of space limitations, I have omitted the technical details in most of the proofs.

2. The basic statistical model

We recall only the relevant definitions and results from the statistical literature. The reader interested in a more detailed discussion is referred to Sawarigi and Yoshikawa (1970), Yushkevich (1976) and Rhenius (1974).

In what follows the Cartesian product of Borel sets A and B is denoted by AB, and its generic element by ab. All the metric spaces are endowed with the usual Borel σ-field (see, for example, Billingsley, 1968, for the definitions).

A discounted dynamic programming model with incomplete information about the state space can be described in terms of the following elements.

(AI)   A complete separable metric space M of all possible *observations* (or messages) available to the decision-maker.

(AII)   A complete separable metric space S of *true (unobservable) states.*

(AIII)   A compact metric space A of all possible *actions.*

(AIV)   A continuous correspondence ϕ from M into A such that for all m in M, $\phi(m)$ is a compact subset of A; we interpret $\phi(m)$ as the set of all *feasible actions* when the observation is m.

(AV)   A *transition function* $\mathcal{P}(ds\,dm/sma)$ which determines the joint stochastic law of $(s_{t+1}m_{t+1})$ in any period $t+1$ given $(s_t m_t a_t)$ – the state, message and action in period t, respectively. Thus, $\mathcal{P}(ds\,dm/sma)$ is the *stochastic law of motion* of the system which is assumed to satisfy the following properties

(AVa)   For any Borel subset T of SM, $\mathcal{P}(T/\cdot)$ is measurable in sma.

(AVb) $\mathcal{P}(\cdot/sma)$ is a probability distribution on the Borel σ-field of *SM*.

(AVI)   A one-period *return* or *utility* function u defined on $\{ma: a \in \phi(m)\}$ with values in R such that u is continuous and bounded; the *discount factor* δ satisfies $0 < \delta < 1$.

At $t = 0$, an initial observation m_0 and an a priori distribution ν_0 on S are given. The planner chooses an action a_0 in $\phi(m_0)$. The system moves to a new state s_1 and the planner receives an observation m_1 according to the distribution $\mathcal{P}(ds_1 dm_1 / s_0 m_0 a_0)$; also, a return of $u(m_0 a_0)$ is generated. The same decision-making problem is faced by the planner in the next period, except that at the time of choosing an action, his information is restricted to the observations m_0 and m_1 along with his initial "beliefs" formally expressed as ν_0 and his action a_0. A *policy* (or *a program*) $\pi = (\pi_t)$ is a sequence of decision functions where each π_t is a measurable function of the *observed past* $h_t = (m_0 \nu_0 a_0 m_1 a_1 \ldots m_{t-1} a_{t-1} m_t)$ such that $\pi_t(h_t)$ is in $\phi(m_t)$ for all $t \geqslant 0$. The set of all policies is denoted by Z. The goal of the planner is to maximize the discounted sum of expected returns starting from any $m_0 \nu_0$, i.e. to choose a policy π^* such that

$$E_{\pi^*} \left[\sum_{t=0}^{\infty} \delta^t u(m_t a_t^*) \right] \geqslant E_{\pi} \left[\sum_{t=0}^{\infty} \delta^t u(m_t a_t) \right] \tag{1}$$

for all π in Z. Such a policy π^* (satisfying (1)) is called an *optimal policy*.

This model of decision-making under uncertainty with partial information about the state space can be transformed into another model in which there is complete knowledge about a suitably defined state space. Roughly speaking, the approach is as follows: at time $t = 0$, we have the message m_0 and the a priori distribution ν_0; at any time t, we try to define the "state" so as to incorporate all the information at our disposal. It is natural, for example, to look at the pair $(m_t \nu_t)$, where m_t is the message arriving in period t, and ν_t is the a posteriori probability distribution for the (unobserved) true state s_t, taking into account the entire observed history. With a finite or countable number of states, we can formally express the successive revisions in terms of the well-known Bayesian formula. With a general state space, one can appeal to a fundamental result on the existence of regular conditional distributions depending measurably on a parameter. We state the precise result for the sake of completeness.

Theorem 2.1.   Assume that to each u in the measurable space U there corresponds a probability measure $\mathcal{P}(dx \, dy / u)$ on the product of the Borel

spaces XY which is measurable with respect to u. Then to each pair ux in UX one can associate a probability measure $\lambda(dy/ux)$ on Y such that
(a) $\lambda(dy/ux)$ is measurable with respect to ux; and
(b) for each u, $\mathcal{P} = (dxdy/u) = \mu(dx/u) \cdot \lambda(dy/ux)$,
where $\mu(dx/u)$ is the measure on X induced by $\mathcal{P}(dxdy/u)$, i.e. $\mu(dx/u)$ is the conditional marginal distribution on X.

Proof. See Parthasarathy (1967, ch. V, theorem 8.1).

To describe the "transformed problem" formally, let N be the set of all probability distributions on S. Endowed with the weak topology, N is a complete separable metric space. Consider a dynamic programming problem defined as follows:
(i) the state space is given by MN (endowed with the product topology, it is a complete separable metric space);
(ii) the set of all possible actions is given by A (a compact metric space);
(iii) a correspondence $\hat{\phi}$ from MN into A defined as $\hat{\phi}(m\nu) = \phi(m)$ (a continuous correspondence such that $\hat{\phi}(m\nu)$ is a compact subset of A);
(iv) a one-period return function $\hat{u}$ from MNA into R defined as $\hat{u}(m\nu a) = u(ma)$;
(v) a transition function $\hat{\mathcal{P}}(dm_{t+1}d\nu_{t+1}/m_t\nu_t a_t)$ obtained by first setting

$$\overline{\mathcal{P}}(ds_{t+1}dm_{t+1}/m_t\nu_t a_t) = \int_S \mathcal{P}(ds_{t+1}dm_{t+1}/s_t m_t a_t)\nu(ds_t)$$

and applying theorem 2.1 to get the factorization

$$\overline{\mathcal{P}}(ds_{t+1}dm_{t+1}/m_t\nu_t a_t) = \hat{\mathcal{P}}(dm_{t+1}/m_t\nu_t a_t) \cdot \nu(ds_{t+1}/m_t\nu_t a_t m_{t+1}),$$
$$(2)$$

where the first factor on the right-hand side of (2) is the marginal distribution of m_{t+1} induced by $\overline{\mathcal{P}}$ and the second factor is an element of N, which is measurable with respect to the collection $(m_t\nu_t a_t m_{t+1})$; finally, by defining $\hat{\mathcal{P}}(dm_{t+1}d\nu_{t+1}/m_t\nu_t a_t)$ from (2) with $\hat{\mathcal{P}}(dm_{t+1}/m_t\nu_t a_t)$ as the distribution of m_{t+1} and with

$$\nu_{t+1}(ds_{t+1}) \equiv \nu(ds_{t+1}/m_t\nu_t a_t m_{t+1}).$$
$$(3)$$

Let $\hat{Z}$ be the set of all policies in the transformed dynamic programming model. Given any policy π in Z (for the model with a partially observable state space), we can get a policy $\hat{\pi}$ in $\hat{Z}$ by setting

$$\pi_t(m_0\nu_0 a_0 m_1 \cdots) = \hat{\pi}_t(m_0\nu_0 a_0 \cdots a_t m_t\nu_t).$$
$$(4)$$

and conversely, given any policy $\hat{\pi}$ in $\hat{Z}$ we can get a policy π in Z by using (4). One can also show that the formula (4) leaves the average expected return per period the same (between π and $\hat{\pi}$). It follows that if π^* is an optimal policy (or, ε-optimal policy) in Z, the corresponding policy $\hat{\pi}^*$ is optimal (ε-optimal) in $\hat{Z}$. Thus, we are able to apply the Blackwell–Strauch results on the existence of optimal or ε-optimal policies. Finally, we record the following basic result on the existence of a stationary optimal policy function:

Theorem 2.2. Suppose that
   (a) M is countable;
   (b) S is a locally compact, σ-compact metric space; and
   (c) the transition function $\mathcal{P}(\mathrm{d}s\,\mathrm{d}m\,/sma)$ is continuous with respect to sma in the weak topology.
   Then there is an optimal policy function $g: MN \rightarrow A$ such that $g(m\nu) \in \phi(m\nu)$ and $\pi^* = (g^\infty)$ is a stationary optimal policy.

3. Two possible applications

Among the many possible applications of the basic statistical theory reviewed in the previous section, I shall sketch only two examples of decision-making under uncertainty from the economic theory of natural resource utilization.

3.1. The model of a fishery[6]

Let (r_t) be a sequence of independent, identically distributed random variables with a common distribution θ, the support of which is a closed interval $[\theta_1, \theta_2]$ of positive reals.

Let s_t be the true stock of fish in period t; if a_t is the "harvest" in period t, the stock in the next period, s_{t+1}, is determined according to the stochastic relation

$$s_{t+1} = f(s_t - a_t; r_{t+1}).\tag{5}$$

The function f in (5) is assumed to have the following properties:

(BI) $f: R_+ \times [\theta_1, \theta_2] \rightarrow R_+$ is continuous, with $f(0, r) = 0$ for all r in $[\theta_1, \theta_2]$.

---

[6]For references to the literature on the management of fisheries, see Clark (1976).

(BII)   For each r in $[\theta_1, \theta_2]$, $f(x, r)$ is strictly increasing in x.

(BIII) $r' > r$ implies $f(x, r') > f(x, r)$ for all $x > 0$. There is some positive constant $\beta > 0$ such that $f(x, \theta_1) > x$ for all x in $[0, \beta]$; there is some $\hat{x} > 0$ such that $f(\hat{x}, \theta_2) = \hat{x}$ and $f(x, \theta_2) < x$ for all $x > \hat{x}$.

We denote the interval $[0, \hat{x}]$ by S. Suppose that we are not able to observe the true stock of fish in period t, denoted by s_t, but can only get an estimate m_t which indicates that the true stock is at least m_t. The decision on how much to harvest depends only on the estimate. Let us assume that

(BIV) M, the set of all possible estimates, is a countable subset of S.

For any m in M, define $\phi(m) = [0, m]$. Our feasibility constraint requires that in any period t, the harvest a_t must be in $\phi(m_t)$. The one-period return from harvesting is generated according to a function u, and let us assume that

(BV) $u: R_+ \to R$ is bounded and continuous.

Actually, it is enough for u to be continuous on S in this framework. Thus, we *can* allow for a linear function.

From (5) we can define $p(ds_{t+1}/s_t m_t a_t)$, the conditional distribution of the true stock s_{t+1} in period $t+1$, given the true stock, the harvest and the estimate in period t. According to the formulation (5), this distribution does *not* depend directly on m_t, a fact that should be kept in mind in verifying the continuity properties asserted in the following proposition:

Proposition 3.1.   Under (BI) through (BIII), the family $p(ds/sma)$ has the following properties:
    (1) for any sma, $p(ds/sma)$ is a probability distribution on the Borel σ-field of Y;
    (2) for any A in the Borel σ-field of Y, $p(A/sma)$ is measurable in sma;
    (3) if a sequence $s^n m^n a^n$ converges to sma, the corresponding sequence $p(ds/s^n m^n a^n)$ converges weakly to $p(ds/sma)$.

A detailed verification of properties (1) through (3) involves careful arguments of the type spelled out in Majumdar and Radner (1979).
    For simplicity of exposition, we describe the relationship between the true stock s_{t+1} in period $t+1$ and the message m_{t+1} in period $t+1$ in terms of

another family of conditional distributions $F(dm_{t+1}/s_{t+1})$. We impose the following regularity properties on this family:

(BVIa)   For any s in S, $F(dm/s)$ is a probability distribution on M, and for any subset A of M, $F(A/s)$ is measurable in s.

(BVIb)   If s^n converges to s, the corresponding sequence $F(dm/s^n)$ converges weakly to $F(dm/s)$.

(BVIc)   For any i in M, let $F(i/s)$ be the probability density of i; then

$$\sum_{\substack{i \leqslant s \\ i \in M}} F(i/s) = 1. \tag{6}$$

In view of (6), which ensures that the estimate in any period is no greater than the true stock with probability one, and the feasibility constraint that the amount harvested cannot exceed the estimate, we are sure that any planned harvest can actually be carried out. Nevertheless, the framework does seem somewhat artificial, since one can conceive of experiments generating overestimates of the true stock. Also, if all the messages can be recorded and remembered, the message received on any particular date may or may not be informative to the decision-maker. At the cost of some more involved notation, some more realistic structures can be introduced. For example, it is better to let the message in period $t+1$ depend on s_t, m_t and a_t, explicitly and to ensure that the message m_{t+1} is at least as good an estimate as $f(s_t - a_t, \theta_1)$. But I have chosen to keep the simplest, although quite unsatisfactory, formulation.

The "joint" conditional distribution of $(s_{t+1} m_{t+1})$, given $s_t m_t a_t$, is defined through the families $p(ds_{t+1}/s_t m_t a_t)$ and $F(dm_{t+1}/s_{t+1})$ in the usual way (see, for example, Loeve, 1963, p. 358). Formally, for any Borel subset $K_1 K_2$ of SM, one has

$$\mathcal{P}(K_1 K_2/s_t m_t a_t) = \int_{K_1} F(K_2/s_{t+1}) p(ds_{t+1}/s_t m_t a_t). \tag{7}$$

In order to obtain the existence results reviewed in section 2, one has to verify the different continuity and compactness conditions appearing in the various assumptions. These are mostly routine; the properties summarized in proposition 3.1 are useful, and the following "weak" continuity property is also basic:

Proposition 3.2. If $(s_t^n m_t^n a_t^n)$ converges to $(s_t m_t a_t)$, the sequence of conditional distributions $\mathscr{P}(ds_{t+1} dm_{t+1}/s_t^n m_t^n a_t^n)$ converges weakly to $\mathscr{P}(ds_{t+1} dm_{t+1}/s_t m_t a_t)$.

Proof. Let f be a bounded continuous real-valued function on SM. To show the desired weak convergence, we must show that if $(s_t^n m_t^n a_t^n)$ converges to $(s_t m_t a_t)$, the sequence

$$\int_{SM} f(s_{t+1} m_{t+1}) \mathscr{P}(ds_{t+1} dm_{t+1}/s_t^n m_t^n a_t^n)$$

must converge to

$$\int_{SM} f(s_{t+1} m_{t+1}) \mathscr{P}(ds_{t+1} dm_{t+1}/s_t m_t a_t).$$

We write

$$\int_{SM} f(s_{t+1} m_{t+1}) \mathscr{P}(ds_{t+1} dm_{t+1}/s_t^n m_t^n a_t^n)$$

$$= \int_S \left[\int_M f(s_{t+1}, \cdot) F(dm_{t+1}/s_{t+1}) \right] p(ds_{t+1}/s_t^n m_t^n a_t^n)$$

Clearly, if $\int_M f(s_{t+1}, \cdot) F(dm_{t+1}/s_{t+1})$ is a continuous function of s_{t+1}, the result follows from the standard property of the weak convergence (since f is bounded and we have proposition 3.1). But, continuity of $\int f(s_{t+1}, \cdot) F(dm_{t+1}/s_{t+1})$ is a direct consequence of Royden (1968, proposition 18, ch. 1) in view of our assumptions.   Q.E.D.

Remark. In the more general case when the model is specified directly in terms of $F(dm_{t+1}/s_t m_t a_t)$, one needs the following continuity property. Suppose $f(uv)$ is a bounded continuous real-valued function on UV, where U is a compact and V is a locally compact, σ-compact metric space. Then $\int_V f(uv)(dv)$ is continuous on $U\mathscr{N}(V)$, $\mathscr{N}(V)$ being the set of all probability measures on V endowed with the weak topology.

3.2. Optimal extraction of a resource with unknown stock[7]

Consider the case in which there is a nonproducible resource (a natural source of energy) and the planner does not know the *exact* amount in which

---

[7]A more detailed discussion of this and related examples is in Bhattacharya (1980).

it is available. The initial beliefs are summarized by an a priori probability distribution ν_0 with a support $[\gamma_1, \gamma_2]$ of positive reals; γ_1 is to be interpreted as the most pessimistic view of the total stock and γ_2 as the most optimistic estimate of the total stock. Of course, if s_t happens to be the true stock in period t, and the amount extracted in that period is a_t, $0 \leqslant a_t \leqslant s_t$, the true stock in the next period becomes

$$s_{t+1} = s_t - a_t \geqslant 0. \tag{8}$$

Denote the interval $[0, \gamma_2]$ by S.

While the planner cannot observe the exact stock in *any* period, a (random) message is received about the quantity of the remaining stock. The amount of extraction depends on this estimate m_t, and we assume that

$$0 \leqslant a_t \leqslant m_t,$$
$$m_t \leqslant s_t. \tag{9}$$

The return or utility from the extracted amount is generated according to a function $u: R_+ \to R$ which is assumed to be continuous and bounded.

In any period t, the message or the estimate m_t about the remaining stock reflects the outcome of exploration activities undertaken in the past. We keep the exposition simple by treating the problem in a very partial equilibrium set-up, and by ignoring the question of how the levels of those activities are determined. Instead, we denote by Δ_t the amount of the resource discovered during period t as

$$m_{t+1} = m_t + \Delta_t - a_t.$$

If $\Delta_t = 0$, there is no discovery, and no new addition to our knowledge about the total stock available; thus, m_{t+1} is simply $m_t - a_t$, the estimate in period t *minus* the extraction a_t. If $\Delta_t = s_t - m_t$, we do have a significant discovery, and are able to estimate the remaining stock accurately. Thus, Δ_t must be in the interval $[0, s_t - m_t]$; in other words, m_{t+1} must be in the interval $[m_t - a_t, s_t - a_t]$. We assume that m_{t+1} is a random variable whose conditional distribution, given $s_t m_t a_t$, denoted by $F(\mathrm{d} m_{t+1} / s_t m_t a_t)$, has a support equal to the interval $[m_t - a_t, s_t - a_t]$. Moreover, we make the following assumptions:

(CI) M, the set of all possible messages, is a countable subset of $[0, \gamma_2]$.

(AII)   For any (sma), $F(\cdot / sma)$ is a probability distribution over M, and for any subset A of M, $F(A/sma)$ is measurable in (sma).

(CIII)   If a sequence $(s^n m^n a^n)$ converges to (sma), the corresponding sequence $F(\mathrm{d} m / s^n m^n a^n)$ converges weakly to $F(\mathrm{d} m / sma)$.

The stochastic transition function $\mathcal{P}(ds_{t+1}\,dm_{t+1}/s_t m_t a_t)$ can easily be defined: note that if $a_t \leqslant s_t$, s_{t+1} is determined according to (8), and formally, we set $s_{t+1} = 0$ if $a_t > s_t$. Thus, s_{t+1} is determined deterministically, given $s_t a_t$. The behavior of m_{t+1}, given $(s_t m_t a_t)$, is random, and it is described in terms of the family of conditional distributions F. One can verify the relevant continuity properties, and appeal to theorem 2.2 to assert the existence of an optimal policy function.

In a few simple examples (with an explicit form of the utility function) one is able to compare the optimal policy with a Bayesian revision scheme with some other situations:

(i) when there is complete certainty that (a) the resource stock is γ_1 or (b) that it is γ_2; and

(ii) when the planner starts with a given ν_0 and does not revise ν_0. Typically, uncertainty or lack of information leads to a *more conservative* initial extraction (i.e. lower a_0^*).

4. Concluding comments

While "partial" or "incomplete" observation does introduce an element of realism in modeling optimization behavior under uncertainty, the question of existence of an optimal policy is nothing more than the first step. One would like to have as much insight into the qualitative behavior of optimal policies as possible, and would like to characterize the role of information in a precise manner. It remains to be seen how far one can go in comparing alternative formalizations of a decision-making process before one makes drastic simplifications and works with special examples.

References

Arrow, K.J. (1974) *Essays in the Theory of Risk Bearing* (North-Holland, Amsterdam).
Bhattacharya, G. (1980) "Two Essays in the Economics of Uncertainty: The Importance of Learning in Planning with Exhaustible Resources and Optimality of Equilibrium with Incomplete Markets", Ph.D. Thesis at the University of Rochester.
Billingsley, P. (1968) *Convergence of Probability Measures* (John Wiley and Sons, New York).
Brock, W. and M. Majumdar (1978) "Global Asymptotic Stability Results for Multisector Models of Optimal Growth under Uncertainty when Future Utilities are Discounted", *Journal of Economic Theory*, 18, 2, 225–243.
Clark, C.W. (1976) *Mathematical Bioeconomics* (John Wiley and Sons, New York).
Dasgupta, P. and G. Heal (1974) "The Optimal Depletion of Exhaustible Resources", *The Review of Economic Studies*, Symposium, 3–28.

Gilbert, R. (1979) "Optimal Depletion of an Uncertain Stock", *The Review of Economic Studies*, 46, 47–58.

Grossman, S., R. Kihlstrom and L. Mirman (1977) "A Bayesian Approach to the Production of Information and Learning by Doing", *The Review of Economic Studies*, 44, 533–547.

Levhari, D. and T. Srinivasan (1969) "Optimal Savings under Uncertainty", *The Review of Economic Studies*, 36, 153–164.

Loeve, M. (1963) *Probability Theory*, 3rd edn. (D. Van Nostrand Company Inc., Princeton).

Loury, G. (1978) "The Optimal Exploitation of an Unknown Reserve", *The Review of Economic Studies*, 45, 621–636.

Maitra, A. (1968) "Discounted Dynamic Programming on Compact Metric Spaces", *Sankhya*, 30, 211–216.

Majumdar, M. (1977) "On Some Turnpike Results in the Theory of Optimal Allocation under Uncertainty", Cornell University Working Paper no. 160 (presented at the New York Meetings in December 1977).

Majumdar, M. and R. Radner (1979) "Stationary Optimal Policies with Discounting in a Stochastic Activity Analysis Model", Cornell University Working Paper no. 186.

Parthasarathy, K. (1967) *Probability Measures on Metric Spaces* (Academic Press, New York).

Phelps, E. (1962) "The Accumulation of Risky Capital: A Sequential Utility Analysis", *Econometrica*, 30, 729–743.

Rhenius, D. (1974) "Incomplete Information in Markovian Decision Models", *The Annals of Statistics*, 2, 1327–1334.

Rothschild, M. (1974) "A Two Armed Bandit Theory of Market Pricing", *Journal of Economic Theory*, 10, 185–202.

Royden, H. (1968) *Real Analysis* (The Macmillan Company, London).

Sawarigi, Y. and T. Yoshikawa (1970) "Discrete Time Markovian Decision Process with Incomplete State Observation", *Annals of Mathematical Statistics*, 41, 78–86.

Yushkevich, A. (1976) "Reduction of a Controlled Markov Model with Complete Information in the case of Borel State and Control Spaces", *Theory of Probability and Its Applications*, 21, 153–157.

PART V

INDUSTRY STRUCTURE AND RESOURCE USE

Introduction to Part V

The structure, conduct and performance approach of Industrial Organization may be profitably applied to the study of the commercial fishing industry. The harvest and stock levels depend upon firm harvesting costs and entry costs, as well as the number and size of firms in the industry. Given alternative arrangements of property rights, firm harvesting levels will depend upon their conduct in the market place, i.e. whether or not the firms are price-takers. Total harvest levels also depend upon the strategic interaction between the firm's harvesting policies. The number and size of firms in the fishery and their strategic interaction will affect the allocation of the fishery resource over time. Part V presents several aspects of the effects of market structure on resource use: it examines competitive free access, monopoly in the harvesting sector, bilateral monopoly in harvesting and processing, the multi-purpose fleet and finally harvesting in the recreational fishery.

Hartwick's chapter, "Free Access and the Dynamics of the Fishery", employs a lagged entry framework to evaluate the dynamic stability of the competitive, free-access fishery. In a discrete-time framework, Hartwick demonstrates that the fishery is overexploited at the common property equilibrium and shows that this entails a deadweight welfare loss. The dynamics of the fishery are examined in detail within a continuous-time framework. Stability is shown to depend upon demand elasticity and elasticity of firm harvest size with respect to the stock level.

The harvesting time path for a sole owner with market power is examined by Levhari, Michener and Mirman in "Dynamic Programming Models of Fishing: Monopoly". The monopoly harvesting problem is considered both when the cost function is and is not stock-dependent. In Chapter 10, "Bilateral Monopoly and Optimal Management Policy", Munro assumes that a monopolistic harvesting firm faces a monopsony firm in the processing sector. The two firms choose their output levels at an equilibrium of a Nash bargaining game. Munro discusses the possible departure of the bilateral monopoly harvesting path from the social optimum, and the difficulties facing a regulatory authority.

157

158 *The economics of renewable resources*

In "The Economics of Multipurpose Fleet Behavior", Anderson examines the allocation of fishing effort between two independent species for competitive firms in a free access fishery. The analysis, which is static, examines firm decision-making for the case in which the total fishing time is limited and alternatively the case in which the length of the fishing season for each species is constrained. The free-access multi-species fishery is shown to result not only in an incorrect number of vessels but also in a distorted allocation of effort between each species by each vessel.

McConnell and Sutinen consider the recreational fishery in Chapter 12, "Using the Household Production Function in Bioeconomic Models". Anglers are assumed to maximize their net benefits from recreational fishing by choosing the number of fishing trips and the number of fish to be caught per trip. The use of household production functions for days of fishing and for catch per trip allows a comparative statics analysis of the effects of input prices on angler behavior and on the steady-state fish stock. The introduction of household production functions and the derived cost functions suggest a close relation between the structure of commercial and recreational fishing models.

CHAPTER 8

Free access and the dynamics of the fishery

JOHN M. HARTWICK*

1. Introduction

The recent control by national governments of exploitation of fish stocks, by means of the regulation of vessels within 200 miles of a nation's shores, indicates that the old regime of free access was presaging some kind of disaster. Presumably there was a feeling that open access[1] to world fish stocks would result either in steady-state harvests that were undesirably small or in the extinction of many species. Free entry to a depletable stock has a well-known instability associated with it. If entry is motivated by the prospect of reaping positive rent on profit and entry degrades the stock, then harvests fall, prices rise and further entry is induced, provided costs of production do not rise faster than prices. This is a classical economic instability.[2] Is the world fishery operating in this environment?

*This work was done at Stanford University. I am indebted to the Humanities and Social Sciences Research Council of Canada for financial support. Professor Robert Solow made invaluable critical comments which got the work back on track. My thanks to him. He should not be implicated in views or errors in this work.

[1] Three terms have been used with reference to the same phenomenon with regard to the fishery: common property (Gordon, 1954), free access (Weitzman, 1974) and open access (Clark, 1976). We will also use the term "free entry" to mean the same as the other terms. The idea is that no individual, collectivity or planner controls the amount of exploitation activity directed to the stock of fish. Access or entry to the stock is free or open or the stock is exploited in common by all "owners".

[2] Plourde (1971) has a model of open access to the fishery which exhibits dynamic instability. It is a two-commodity model of labor allocation between a fisheries industry and another industry. The focus of attention is completely different from that in our one-sector model which focuses attention in large part on the dynamics of free access. Of some interest perhaps is that Plourde chose to specify our $\psi(\cdot)$ function below as Cobb–Douglas.

Essays in the economics of renewable resources, edited by L.J. Mirman and D.F. Spulber
© North-Holland Publishing Company, 1982

Smith (1968, pp. 415–418) has analyzed the situation and has concluded the contrary – that open access or free entry to the fish stock can be associated with a dynamically stable outcome in which the steady-state harvest (and stock) and inputs are positive. We might refer to this as Smith's Law: "Harvesting depletes the stock, costs rise, and, *ceteris paribus*, discourages harvesting with the possibility if not a guarantee of an equilibrium [which is interior and dynamically stable]" (p. 418). This leads to the question: If the fishery is stable, why are national and international agencies regulating harvest sizes and entry to the fishery? If it is unstable, what actions are appropriate in order to improve welfare? We set out a more general version of the model of Smith (1968), Clark (1976) and others and readily isolate cases of stability and instability. We argue that though stability in the sense of Smith seems to be the plausible case, the stable equilibrium has been drifting toward lower world stocks as a result of technical progress and population (demand) growth. Regulation is apparently required to prevent biological collapse of the fish stocks. We point out that a special case of our model is the Lotka–Volterra dynamic system, but this fact is really a *curiosum* and the details are relegated to an appendix.

Common-property resources are interesting in an indirect way from the point of view of capital theory. An owner of a capital good attempts to maximize his returns over a period of time and so he regulates the intensity of use of the good, say a piece of land. Free entry, however, is inherently myopic. The users of the capital good, say the fish stock, have no concern for the productivity of the capital good "tomorrow" since it is presumed that any restraint on exploitation today in the interest of having more tomorrow will result in gains that will be totally dissipated among tomorrow's exploiters. Individual restraint today cannot be capitalized in individual gain tomorrow. Now there has been developed (e.g. Shell–Stiglitz) some tentative results on the stability of capital accumulation models, but these results turn on *owners* of goods *managing* them in the interest of a good's value and productiveness tomorrow. However, since no one is managing a capital good under open access such as the fishery, we cannot appeal to known arguments for assurance about the stability of the stock exploitation program over time. If the biological dynamics in combination with the entry and exploitation dynamics are not stable, we cannot turn to considerations of capital goods management for another line of investigation. It is then the free access property of certain fisheries models which removes them from the realm of capital theory to a distinct area of inquiry.[3]

---

[3] Gordon (1954) developed the notion of the dissipation of economic rent under free access to a fish stock. His analysis was formally static. Weitzman (1974) compared relative welfare

Before turning to an analysis of entry and exit by harvesters, and growth and decline of stock, we examine the nature of "market failure" resulting from free access to the fishery. We observe the intertemporal externality: agent *i*, by forgoing fishing today, can only reap, the discounted average payoff to his restraint rather than the discounted marginal payoff. This externality results in the *steady-state* stock under free access being lower than the socially optimal value and of course results in lower social welfare under free access than under a competitive or optimal planning regime. We establish these two propositions in the section 2 below. We then turn to the question of the stability and existence of free access equilibria in a simple dynamic model.

2. Free access and private ownership steady states in a discrete-time framework

We compare the free-access or common-property outcome with two agents to the planning solution for the problem. (The $N>2$ agent problem is discussed below.) Each agent under the common-property regime maximizes discounted profits from fishing in

$$\pi^i = \sum_{t=0}^{\infty} \left(\frac{1}{1+r} \right)^t \{ p - c(Z_t, q_t^i) \} q_t^i \qquad (i=1,2)$$

where

π^i = the present value of profit for agent *i*,
r = the interest or discount rate,
p = the price of a unit of fish caught,
Z_t = the stock of fish exploited at time *t*,
q_t^i = the quantity of fish caught by agent *i* at time *t*,
$c(\cdot,\cdot)$ = the cost per unit of fish caught, which depends on the stock (a proxy for the "density" of fish in the fishing ground) and on the current quantity caught. We explicitly omit the familiar interdependency of current costs of *i* on current catches of *i* *and j* emphasized by, for example, Dasgupta and Heal (1979, pp. 55–73). We are attempting to focus attention on the intertemporal interdependencies.[4] It is assumed that $\partial c / \partial Z_t \equiv c_{Z_t} < 0$, $\partial c / \partial q_t^i \equiv c_{q_t^i} \geq 0$.

---

levels of participants in a one-commodity world under free access and private ownership. His entry relation was in increasing function of individual return. Gordon considered inputs (labor) to be infinitely elastic at a fixed "wage".

[4] Dasgupta and Heal have the most detailed development of the micro-foundations of free access to a stock or of a common property solution in a steady state. Their analysis is entirely

The exploitation–biological growth dynamics are represented by

$$Z_{t+1} - Z_t = \phi(Z_t) - q_t^1 - q_t^2 \qquad (t = 0, \ldots, \infty),$$

where $\phi(Z_t)$ is the natural growth of the stock indicating net births over deaths of fish. We will appeal to the familiar logistic form below: $\phi(Z_t) \equiv aZ_t(1 - (Z_t/M))$ where $a > 0$ and $M > 0$ is the "carrying capacity" of the fishing ground. Note that $\phi(0) = \phi(M) = 0$ and $d\phi/dZ_t \equiv \phi_{Z_t} \gtreqless 0$ as $Z_t \lesseqgtr (M/2)$.

The interdependency leading to an intertemporal externality in the above model is that agent i's costs in period $t + 1$ are affected adversely by agent j's catch in period t. The effects are reciprocal and we assume here that the size of the agents and their costs are the same.

The first-order conditions for profit maximization yield the simultaneous recursive equations

$$\left[\frac{1 + \phi_{Z_{t+1}}}{1 + r}\right]\left[p - c(Z_{t+1}, q_{t+1}^i) - q_{t+1}^i c_{q_{t+1}^i}\right]$$

$$= \left[p - c(Z_t, q_t^i) - q_t^i c_{q_t^i}\right] + \left(\frac{1}{1+r}\right) q_{t+1}^i c_{Z_{t+1}} \qquad (i = 1,2). \qquad (1)$$

We now move to consider steady-state solutions. Let $\hat{q}$ be the steady output *for one agent* and $\hat{Z}$ be the steady-state stock. Now $\hat{q} = \phi(\hat{Z})/2$. The basic equation characterizing our common property steady state is then, from (1),

$$\left[\frac{1 + \phi_{\hat{Z}}}{1 + r}\right]\left[p - c\left(\hat{Z}, \frac{\phi}{2}\right) - \hat{q}c_{\hat{q}}\right] = \left[p - c\left(\hat{Z}, \frac{\phi}{2}\right) - \hat{q}c_{\hat{q}}\right] + \left(\frac{1}{1+r}\right)\hat{q}c_{\hat{Z}}.$$

$$(2)$$

One can, by the same procedure above, obtain the basic equation for the socially optimum steady state (one treats the problem as if there is just one

static. The current explicit interdependence of agent i's output on the levels of output of other agents results in the market failure. The framework is very similar to that of road congestion and the solution is, as with road congestion, to apply a tax on the output of agent i. Our approach to the micro-foundations is explicitly dynamic. Khalatbari (1977) has a dynamic common-property model dealing with two exploiters of an exhaustible pool of oil. The model and the context are quite different from ours for the fishery, but Khalatbari also observes that the presence of a common-property setting leads to overexploitation of the stock – in this latter case, overly rapid exploitation relative to that under a socially optimal plan. See Dasgupta and Heal (1979, pp. 372–375). We note also that Clark (1976, p. 43) points out that for some models the common-property equilibrium can be viewed as the socially optimal outcome in which the discount rate tends to infinity. Our model is an attempt to provide micro-foundations for why common property regimes display a "bias" to the present (high discount rates) relative to the future.

firm maximizing profits, i.e. the private ownership solution.) It is[5]

$$\left[\frac{1+\phi_Z}{1+r}\right]\left[p-c(Z,\phi)-qc_q\right]=\left[p-c(Z,\phi)-qc_q\right]+\left(\frac{1}{1+r}\right)qc_Z. \quad (3)$$

The existence of interior solutions requires additional assumptions on the properties of $\phi(Z)$ and $c(Z,q)$. We proceed to specialize without searching for generality at this point. We let $\phi(Z)$ be the logistic set out above and $c(Z,q)\equiv q/Z$ or ϕ/Z in a steady under optimal planning. This form for costs is used extensively in Clark (1976). Our steady-state equations (2) and (3) become:

$$\left[\frac{1+\phi_{\hat{Z}}}{1+r}\right]\left[p-\frac{\phi}{\hat{Z}}\right]=\left[p-\frac{\phi}{\hat{Z}}\right]-\left(\frac{1}{1+r}\right)\left(\frac{\phi}{2\hat{Z}}\right)^2 \quad (4)$$

and

$$\left[\frac{1+\phi_Z}{1+r}\right]\left[p-\frac{2\phi}{Z}\right]=\left[p-\frac{2\phi}{Z}\right]-\left(\frac{1}{1+r}\right)\left(\frac{\phi}{Z}\right)^2, \quad (5)$$

respectively, where $\phi_Z=a[1-(2Z/M)]$ and $\phi/Z=a[1-(Z/M)]$.

Note that $(\phi/Z)=0$ for $Z=M$ and $(\phi/Z)=\phi_Z=a$ for $Z=0$. We manipulate (4) and (5) to obtain the same R.H.S., namely

$$\left[p-\left(\frac{2\phi}{Z}\right)\right]-\left(\frac{1}{1+r}\right)\left(\frac{\phi}{Z}\right)^2,$$

plotted as schedule *hb* in fig. 8.1. It increases in Z. The new L.H.S. of (4) is

$$\left(\frac{1+\phi_Z}{1+r}\right)\left[p-\frac{\phi}{Z}\right]-\left(\frac{\phi}{Z}\right)-\left[\frac{3}{4}\left(\frac{1}{1+r}\right)\left(\frac{\phi}{Z}\right)^2\right]$$

plotted as schedule *ef* in fig. 8.1. The L.H.S. of (5) is

$$\left(\frac{1+\phi_Z}{1+r}\right)\left[p-\frac{2\phi}{Z}\right],$$

plotted as schedule *gf* in fig. 8.1. Routine calculation reveals each schedule to be concave in Z.[6] *hb* reaches a value of p as $Z=M$. *gf* and *ef* reach a

---

[5] This of course can be made into the familiar steady-state intertemporal arbitrage rule if r is placed on the R.H.S.

[6] The slope of schedule *hb* is

$$\frac{2a}{(1+r)M}\left[1+r+a-\frac{aZ}{M}\right];$$

of schedule *ef* is

$$\frac{2a}{(1+r)M}\left[\frac{9a}{4}+1-p+\frac{r}{2}-\left(\frac{11}{4}\right)\frac{aZ}{M}\right];$$

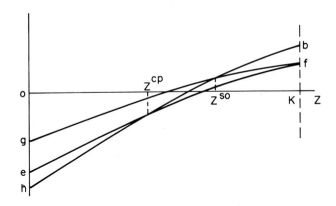

Figure 8.1

value of $((1-a)/(1+r))p$ for $Z = M$ at f; clearly, $((1-a)/(1+r))p > 0$ for $0 < a < 1$ and $p > 0$, which we assume. If $p - 1 + a < 0$, then gf and ef will be increasing in Z provided g and e are negative at $Z = 0$. Now g corresponds to a negative value provided $p - 2a < 0$, which we assume. Point e corresponds to a value less than g if $r > \frac{1}{4}a$. Finally, point e lies above point h if $r/a > (2a - p)/(3a - p)$. (These conditions are satisfied, for example, if $r = 0.7$, $a = 0.8$, and $p = 0.1$). We have, in light of fig. 8.1,

Proposition 1 (Over exploitation of the stock under common property). $Z^{cp} < Z^{so}$, where Z^{cp} and Z^{so} are the stocks in steady state under common property and social optimality, respectively.

In a free-access/common-property equilibrium (steady state), agents, assumed identical, will enter until $[p - c(Z, \phi/N)] = 0$, where N is the number of agents. One can work out the equilibrium for any $N > 2$ by replacing $\phi(Z)/2$ above by $\phi(Z)/N$. The welfare result is of course that consumer and producer surplus is higher under a socially optimal plan than under free access/common property. We can demonstrate this result for $N = 2$ and

---

and of schedule gf is

$$\frac{2a}{(1+r)M}\left[3a + 1 - p - \frac{4aZ}{M}\right];$$

all *linear in Z*. Thus, given our other assumptions on parameter values, no two schedules can intersect more than once. Also, as $Z \rightarrow M$, the positive slope of ef must exceed the positive slope of gf. Given point g above point e by assumption, schedules gf and ef cannot intersect.

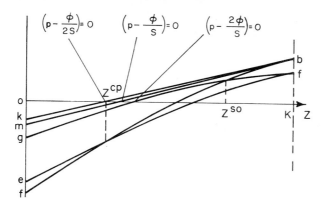

Figure 8.2

$[p-(\phi/2Z)]=0$ in fig. 8.2. Existence of $0<Z<M$ for $[p-(\phi/2Z)]=0$, given our form for $\phi(Z)$ above, requires $0<(a-2p)/a<1$; then $Z=((a-2p)/a)M$. We insert the linear schedule kb in fig. 8.2 corresponding to $[p-(\phi/2Z)]$. In fig. 8.2 we assume that the steady state under common property has entry "complete" at two agents so that Z^{cp} satisfies $[p-(\phi/2Z)]=0$. Linear schedule mb corresponds to $[p-\phi/Z]$. Scrutiny of fig. 8.2 yields

Proposition 2 (Welfare cost of common-property equilibrium). If Z^{cp} corresponds to a situation of zero profit for an agent (i.e. $p-(\phi/2Z)=0$), then Z^{so} corresponds to a situation of positive producer and consumer surplus (i.e. $(p-\phi/Z>0$).

One could obviously rework the analysis with the familiar static common property externalities inserted. One could have current catch of agent i affected by the current catch of agents other than i and/or the current catch of agent i affected by the number of agents currently exploiting the resource. Then there would be two sources of market failure under common property – a static externality and our intertemporal externality.

We note, as a postscript, the forgoing fishing is a form of saving and of investment in the stock for future use. However, our model differs essentially from a general many-person consumption–savings analysis involving the pooling of savings. In our model the *stock* enters directly into each element in the sum in the objective function and the pooling of savings affects the magnitude of the stock. There are no such direct "stock effects" in a many-person Ramsey-type model of accumulation and overconsumption does not occur in these models.

3. Dynamics of the fishery under free access in a continuous-time framework

We assume that the rate of growth of the stock is a decreasing function of the density of the stock or the "carrying capacity" of the environment.[7] We are now in a continuous-time framework,

$$\frac{\dot{Z}}{Z} = a\left(1 - \frac{Z}{M}\right), \tag{6}$$

where Z is the stock[8] at time t, $\dot{Z} \triangleq dZ/dt$. This equation can be solved to yield $Z(t) = M/(1 + ce^{-at})$, where $c = (M - Z_0)/Z_0$.

We postulate that current harvest is an increasing function of the inputs in fishing exploitation (say a composite of labor and capital in a fixed relation to each other) and an increasing function of the current size of the stock: $H = \psi(E, Z)$, where H (rather than q above) is now the current harvest at time t, E is the input in fish exploitation,[9] and Z is the current stock. Our stock dynamics are then, with exploitation, $\dot{Z} = aZ(1 - Z/M) - \psi(E, Z)$. Letting ψ_E depend on stock size, Z can be interpreted as a congestion effect (Smith, 1968, p. 418). (ψ_E denotes the derivative of $\psi(\cdot)$ with respect to E, etc.) On a world-wide scale, congestion seems to be irrelevant and so we specialize $\psi(E, Z)$ to the form $Eg(Z)$ with $g_Z > 0$.

---

[7] An interesting variation on this growth form is the Frisch–Holme equation

$$\frac{\dot{Z}}{Z} = a\left[1 - \frac{Z(t-T)}{M}\right]$$

in which T is the lag interval. Thus, the current growth rate in the stock depends on the density at some interval back in time. See May (1973, pp. 95–96) for a report on the properties of this equation.

[8] We have in mind an approximately homogeneous stock of fish when we speak of harvest H and stock Z. We abstract from details of the age profile and the species types. Exploitation presumably involves harvesting those types with highest profitability first. Thus, decline in stocks presumably involves certain species being depleted first. By the fishery, we have in mind an aggregate of different geographically distinct fishing grounds or banks. Thus, the depletion of one area with relatively high profitability leads to exploitation of the next most profitable area and so on. It seems then that there is little significant loss at this stage from working with our aggregates.

[9] The input E has been referred to as fishing "effort". We have in mind resources entering and exploiting fish stocks. We sometimes refer to E as "boats," presumably of a standardized type.

Thus, our growth–exploitation dynamics are

$$\dot{Z} = aZ\left(1 - \frac{Z}{M}\right) - Eg(Z).$$ (7)

Our free access mechanics are inspired directly by Gordon's (1954) analysis. Resources enter the fishery as long as rent is positive. There is a supply of inputs at price $w(E)$ dollars per unit with $w_E > 0$. Hence,

$$\dot{E} = k\left\{\frac{p(H)\cdot H}{E} - w(E)\right\},$$ (8)

where $p(H)$ is the inverted demand schedule for harvested fish. Whether $p(H)\cdot H$ rises or falls in response to a small increase in H depends on whether the demand schedule is locally inelastic or elastic (elastic being $|\varepsilon| > 1$ where $\varepsilon \triangleq (\mathrm{d}H/\mathrm{d}p)\cdot(p/H)$ and inelastic being $|\varepsilon| < 1$). k is a positive constant; we set it equal to unity subsequently.

Consider an interior solution or steady state for the dynamic system in (7) and (8) at (E^*, Z^*). That is, $\dot{Z}(E^*, Z^*) = \dot{E}(E^*, Z^*) = 0$. We analyze the local dynamics by expanding to a linear approximation in the neighborhood of (E^*, Z^*) and observe the key matrix of coefficients to be

$$\begin{bmatrix} a\left(1 - \dfrac{2Z^*}{M}\right) - E^* g_Z, & -g \\[2ex] g_Z p\left[1 + \dfrac{1}{\varepsilon}\right], & \dfrac{pg}{E^*}\left[\dfrac{1}{\varepsilon}\right] - w_E \end{bmatrix}.$$ (9)

Given the well-known conditions for stability,[10] we have

Proposition 3. The fishery (in (7) and (8)) is dynamically stable about (E^*, Z^*) if $Z^* > M/2$.

Observe a key property of the region $Z > M/2$. Consider eq. (7) in isolation for the moment with $\dot{Z} = 0$. If for the value of E, exogenous for the moment, Z^* satisfying $\dot{Z} = 0$ lies in $(M/2, M)$, then a *small increase (decrease) in E implies that total harvest Eg(Z) increases (decreases)*. However, if for a given value of E, Z^* lies in $(0, M/2)$, then a *small increase (decrease) in E implies that total harvest Eg(Z) decreases (increases)*. Now the first situation is an "efficient" or "stable" one: more inputs (increase in E) imply more output (increase in H) and the second situation, with $0 < Z^* < M/2$ is

---

[10] Necessary and sufficient conditions for stability are (a) the trace negative and (b) the determinant positive for the matrix in (9).

"inefficient" or "unstable", loosely speaking. We carry this argument one step further. Introduce our results immediately above into (8). In the "stable" case, an exogenous rise in E implies that H increases and Z decreases. This implies that $p(H)$ decreases, $g(Z)$ decreases and $w(E)$ increases. *Hence the assumed exogenous rise in E in eq. (7) leads to an unambiguous $\dot{E}<0$ in eq. (8) for the "stable" ($M/2<Z^*<M$) case.* However, by the same reasoning one finds that one *cannot* predict a priori the effect on $\dot{E}$ in eq. (8) arising from an assumed exogenous change in E in eq. (7) for the "unstable" case ($0<Z^*<M/2$). We thus have an informal picture of the nature of the result in proposition 3. We can also see why relative magnitudes will be crucial for determining the nature of the dynamics of the system in the region ($0<Z^*<M/2$).

The condition on stock size in proposition 3 is not related to cost of exploitation directly. We can gain further insight by rewriting $a(1-2Z^*/M)-E^*g_Z$ in (9) as $-aZ^*/M+E^*g/Z^*(1-\eta)$, where $\eta \stackrel{\triangle}{=} (\mathrm{d}g/\mathrm{d}Z)\cdot(Z^*/g)$. That is, η is the local elasticity of "boat-catch" with respect to stock size and indicates indirectly the current cost of exploitation. This leads to a different sufficiency condition for local stability. We can now infer instability also.

Proposition 4. The fishery (in (7) and (8)) is dynamically stable about (E^*, Z^*) if $\eta \geqslant 1$ *and* $|\varepsilon| \geqslant 1$.

The condition $\eta>1$ implies that a decline in stock leads to a more than proportionate decline in boat-catch. On its own this condition suggests that exit will be encouraged by a decline in Z at current prices. This is a "stablizing force". Also, the elasticity of demand $|\varepsilon|>1$ is also a "stabilizing force" since a decline in harvest will result in a decline in industry revenue, thus dampening the potential inflow of new entrants attracted by a higher price per unit of harvest.

From (9) and its determinant we observe that a sufficient condition for instability is $|\varepsilon| \leqslant 1$ *and* $a(1-2Z^*/M)>E^*g_Z$. Since from (7) $E^*=(rZ^*/g(Z^*))[1-Z^*/M]$, we have

Proposition 5. The fishery (in (7) and (8)) is locally dynamically unstable about (E^*, Z^*) if $|\varepsilon| \leqslant 1$, $\eta<K(Z^*)$ (where $K(Z^*)=[1-2Z^*/M]/[1-Z^*/M]$) for $Z^*/M<\frac{1}{2}$.

Note that the stock Z must lie between 0 and M in order for there to be a positive harvest. We require $Z^*/M<\frac{1}{2}$ in proposition 5 since η is assumed to be positive. It is not difficult to illustrate a case of instability with an example. Consider the constant elasticity fishery: the inverted demand schedule is $p = \alpha H^{-\beta}$, the catch per "boat" is $g(Z) \stackrel{\triangle}{=} bZ^\eta$ and the supply schedule for "boats" is $w(E) \stackrel{\triangle}{=} \gamma E$ for α, β, b, η, and γ non-negative. Setting eq. (7) equal to zero and substituting, we obtain

$$E = \frac{aZ^{1-\eta}}{b}\left(1 - \frac{Z}{M}\right), \tag{10}$$

and setting eq. (8) equal to zero and substituting, we obtain

$$E = \left[\frac{\alpha b^{1-\beta} Z^{\eta(1-\beta)}}{\gamma}\right]^{1/(1+\beta)}. \tag{11}$$

One observes that for the constant elasticity model, eq. (10) appears as illustrated in fig. 8.3 (a–c) for the cases indicated. In fig. 8.3 (d–f) we observe that $\dot{E} = 0$ in eq. (11) under different assumptions for the values of the elasticities η and β. If the schedules do not intersect in the positive quadrant, then of course we have no economically meaningful stationary solution. This nonexistence of a solution can plausibly be associated with the extinction of the stock. This point has been emphasized by Smith (1975) in his discussion of the extinction of mammoths and bisons.

We note that for the case $\eta < 1$ and $\beta = 1$, a combination of fig. 8.3 (b) and (d) can provide us with an example of instability. For example, if $\eta = \frac{1}{2}$ then by varying the parameters in the $\dot{E} = 0$ equation one can satisfy the

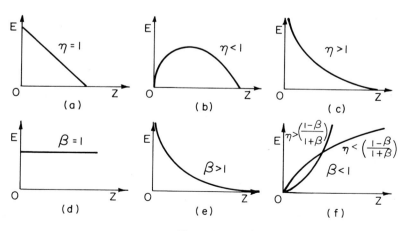

Figure 8.3

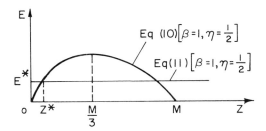

Figure 8.4

condition for instability, namely $[1-2Z/M]/[1-Z/M]>\eta$ and $Z<M/2$. There will be two positive solutions for this case and the unstable one will occur for the case $Z<M/2$.

In fig. 8.4 the equilibrium at (E^*, Z^*) is unstable for the case corresponding to the choice of parameters above. The special case $\eta=1$ results in eq. (10) being a straight line with slope $-a/M$ in the (E, Z) plane.

Given the constant elasticity specification above, the stable case, $|\varepsilon|>1$ and $\eta>1$, has eqs. (10) and (11) convex to the origin in the (E, Z) plane. Schedule (10) cuts the Z axis at M and otherwise both schedules are asymptotic to the axes. One can show that a solution with E^* and Z^* positive exists.[11] Whether the equilibrium exists for Z^* near M or Z^* near 0 is obviously the question concerning those involved with the world fishery.

If one treats price p as a parameter, one can construct a supply response schedule indicating for any p how much harvest will be forthcoming in a steady state. (We ignore issues of stability in this detour.) We treat boat supply as infinitely elastic at price w. Clark (1976, p. 153) constructs one such "supply schedule" for the case $g(Z)=Z$. We will let $g(Z)=bZ^{\eta}$. Our entry–exit equation becomes, assuming price fixed,

$$pbZ^{\eta} - w = 0.$$

This gives us an expression for Z in terms of p and from the biological

---

[11]One can verify that there exists a solution with E and Z positive and finite. To do this, substitute E in (11), using (10) and one obtains

$$\frac{a}{b}Z^{1-\eta}\left(1-\frac{Z}{M}\right)=\left[\frac{\alpha}{\gamma}a^{1-\beta}Z^{\eta(1-\beta)}\right]^{1/(1+\beta)}.$$

For $\beta=2$ and $\eta=6/5$ one has a quadratic $Z^2+BZ+C=0$ with $B>0$ and $C<0$. Hence, a positive solution exists. Nonexistence of a solution with positive and finite (E^*, Z^*) is a plausible situation for the collapse of the world fishery under free access.

dynamics harvest equation, assuming a steady state, we have

$$H = aZ\left(1 - \frac{Z}{M}\right)$$

or

$$H = a\left(\frac{w}{bp}\right)^{1/\eta}\left[1 - \frac{1}{M}\left(\frac{w}{bp}\right)^{1/\eta}\right]. \tag{12}$$

In fig. 8.5 we graph this "supply schedule", eq. (12), for three hypothetical values of $\eta (= \frac{1}{2}, 1, 2)$ and $c \stackrel{\triangle}{=} w/b$. One can imagine a demand schedule superimposed in each panel of fig. 8.5 and note the possible steady state equilibria.

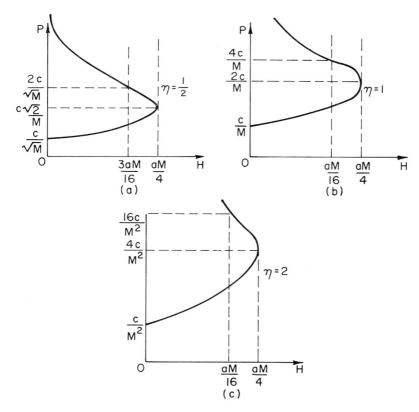

Figure 8.5

Note that large values of p correspond to small values of steady-state stock Z in fig. 8.5. From proposition 3 we have then: as long as the solution lies in the region where the demand schedule cuts the rising (to the north-east) part of the "supply schedule" in fig. 8.5, the equilibrium is locally dynamically stable. Recall that equilibria with $Z > Z_{MSY}(= M/2)$ were stable (proposition 3). Note also that $H_{MSY} = aM/4$ is that value of harvest corresponding to $Z_{MSY} = M/2$). As proposition 3 is expressed in fig. 8.5 it has a Marshallian echo about: *if the supply curve is sloping "upward" (to the NE) where it is intersected by the demand curve, then the equilibrium is stable.* Of course our model has no structural affinities with the Marshallian model of price adjustment as far as I can tell.

Observe that propositions 3, 4, and 5 are valid if $w_E = 0$ or the supply of "boats" is infinitely elastic at the prevailing opportunity cost for boats. This assumption of infinitely elastic supply seems more in keeping with Gordon's original analysis and has considerable appeal from the point of view of "causal empiricism". At an aggregate level, the supply of resources to the fishing industry would seem not to affect the prices of those resources. Also, Gordon had in mind virtually zero set-up costs for entry into the fishery. Entry and exit were presumed to be relatively costless and thus relatively rapid in response to changed conditions.

We can summarize our findings in table 8.1. From the sign pattern (and "region" of equilibrium in row 1) for the matrix in (9) and its determinant, we have determined the local stability (S) and instability (U) for cases I, II, V, VI, VII, VIII, and IX. Two cases, III and IV, require detailed knowledge of the "region" of equilibrium in order to determine the stability properties of the equilibrium.[12]

It appears that harvested fish are subject to an elastic demand schedule. There are many substitute foodstuffs available. One can also make a good case for contending that the elasticity of catch per boat with respect to stock size is greater than unity. Declining stocks imply relatively rapidly declining catches per boat. Thus, case IX seems to characterize the world fishery today and over long periods in the past. The equilibrium in such a case is stable as Smith argued from a slightly different vantage point. However, over time various parameters have been changing causing the stable equilibrium value of stock Z^* to drift slowly down. This drift may have become more rapid in recent decades as a result of population and demand growth and technical progress in the techniques of locating, netting and preserving fish at sea. The decline in stock sizes has pushed a number of species to thresholds of biological collapse. No individual or agency is choosing to

---

[12] The case of $\eta = 1$ and $\beta = -\infty$ was analyzed in detail in Clark (1976, pp. 203–204).

Table 8.1[a]

η ⟍ $\lvert\varepsilon\rvert$	<1	$=1$	>1
$< K(Z^*) < 1$	I, U	II, U	III, ?
$= 1$	IV, ?	V, S	VI, S
> 1	VII, S	VIII, S	IX, S
	(for $\eta > 1$ and $\eta\lvert 1/\varepsilon\rvert$)		

[a] $K(Z^*) = [1 - 2Z^*/M]/[1 - Z^*/M]$.

exhaust certain stocks in an optimal plan (see Clark, 1976, pp. 60–61). However, the equilibrium may be drifting into zones or stock sizes which are close to levels below which the stocks will die out naturally. This is presumably one motivation for national and international agencies to take action restricting harvest sizes and entry to the industry. One also has to consider that nations may be acting like individual owners of a capital good and are now changing the regime from free access to their stocks to regulated management in the familiar way private ownership involves.

Appendix: The Lotka–Volterra fishery

A specialization of our dynamic model of the fishery under free access is the well-known Lotka–Volterra predator–prey model. The specialization is as follows.

(a) Let the biological dynamics be of the simple form

$$\dot{Z} = aZ$$

rather than of the logistic form above. This new form indicates that in the absence of harvesting the stock grows exponentially at the rate a. This is clearly unreasonable for all stocks, but in the neighborhood of an equilibrium stock level, may not be inappropriate.

(b) Let the harvesting function be of the form

$$H = EbZ.$$

This form has harvest per "boat", namely bZ, linear in the stock size. E is the number of "boats" or units of inputs.

(c) Let the revenue function be infinitely price elastic in terms of the harvest. The specialized form is now

$$pH \quad \text{or} \quad p \cdot EbZ,$$

where p is a positive and constant price. b is a parameter of the harvest per "boat" function.

(d) Let the availability or supply of "boats" or inputs be infinitely elastic at price w per unit. The specialized form becomes wE.

Given these specializations, we have a dynamic system of the Lotka–Volterra form:

$$\dot{Z} = aZ - bEZ, \tag{A.1}$$

$$\dot{E} = -wE + pbEZ. \tag{A.2}$$

Eq. (A.1) is the growth–harvest dynamics and eq. (A.2) is the entry–exit dynamics. This simultaneous equation system has a nontrivial equilibrium point:

$$Z_0 = \frac{w}{bp}, \qquad E_0 = \frac{a}{b},$$

and there is a family of solutions which cycle about this point. (See, for example, Clark, 1976, 194–95, or May, 1973, 188–193.) One cycle serves as an attractive model of the cyclical collapse and regrowth of fishery exploitation. However, the system is not structurally stable and thus, though the cyclical behavior seems realistic, the model is unsatisfactory because the cyclical behavior is unstable. Samuelson (1972, ch. 170) has introduced some nonlinearities into the Lotka–Volterra model which results in a stable cycle, but this latter version is not a natural specialization of our model in the body of the chapter.

References

Clark, C. (1976) *Mathematical Bioeconomics: The Optimal Management of Renewable Resources* (John Wiley, New York).

Dasgupta, P.S. and G. M. Heal (1979) *Economic Theory and Exhaustible Resources* (Cambridge University Press).

Gordon, H.S. (1954) "Economic Theory of a Common-Property Resource: The Fishery", *Journal of Political Economy*, 62, 124–142.

Khalatbari, F. (1977) "Market Imperfections and Optimal Rate of Depletion of an Exhaustible Resource", *Economica*, 44, 409–414.

May, R.M. (1973) *Stability and Complexity in Model Ecosystems*, (Princeton University Press, Princeton, N.J.).

Plourde, C.G. (1971) "Exploitation of Common-Property Replenishable Resources", *Western Economic Journal*, 9, 256–266.

Samuelson, P.A. (1972) "A Universal Cycle?", in: R. Merton, ed. *Collected Scientific Papers of Paul A. Samuelson*, Vol. III (MIT Press, Cambridge, MA) ch. 170.

Smith, V.L. (1968) "Economics of Production from Natural Resources", *American Economic Review*, 58, 409–431.

Smith, V. L. (1975) "The Primitive Hunter Culture, Pleistocene Extinction, and the Rise of Agriculture", *Journal of Political Economy*, 83, 727–755.

Weitzman, M. (1974) "Free Access vs. Private Ownership as Alternative Systems for Managing Common Property", *Journal of Economic Theory*, 8, 225–234.

CHAPTER 9

Dynamic programming models of fishing: Monopoly

DAVID LEVHARI, RON MICHENER and LEONARD J. MIRMAN

1. Introduction

In this chapter we provide a simple mathematical model to describe the exploitation of renewable resources by a monopolist. In particular we analyze the interaction between markets and the natural biological dynamics of the renewable resource. Throughout the chapter, as a matter of convenience, the self-renewing resource will be referred to as "fish". However, it should be clear that the analysis is perfectly general in that it can be applied to any self-renewing resource.

In a previous paper (Levhari, Michener and Mirman, 1981) (LMM) we discussed and analyzed the exploitation of fish under competitive conditions. Two distinct competitive regimes were analyzed. In the first, free entry competition, there are no barriers to entry and no property rights. Under this market regime overfishing usually occurs. Potential benefits from restricting the current harvest, such as reduced costs or increased future availability of the resource, are not internalized by firms. In the second regime analyzed, "perfect competition" (hereafter simply "competition") property rights for the resource do exist. Under this market regime the potential benefits from restricting the current harvest *are* internalized by firms. The resulting paths of price and output are optimal, in the sense that they are identical to those which result from a central planner maximizing discounted consumer surplus. For both regimes the dynamic evolution of

*Research support from the NSF under Grants SOC 77-27340 and SOC 79-05900 and the U.S.–Israel BSF under Grant 1828-79 is gratefully acknowledged.

Essays in the economics of renewable resources, edited by L.J. Mirman and D.F. Spulber
© North-Holland Publishing Company, 1982

the resource was explored. It was shown that the characterization of steady states, the uniqueness of steady states, and even the existence of nonzero steady states often depend on the market regime. It is our intention in this paper to extend this analysis to cover monopoly. The results are both provocative, e.g. monopoly can save a species which would be depleted under both types of competitive markets, and surprising, e.g. a monopolist does not always supply less than a competitive market would supply.

Readers of our previous paper will recognize much that is familiar. In particular, the interpretation of an optimizing policy as one that equates financial and biological interest rates serves to clarify the monopolist's decision problem much as it clarifies that of the competitive firm. Furthermore, we will follow the pattern set in our previous paper by dealing first with the case in which the cost of harvesting is independent of the size of the stock. This has the benefit of isolating the intertemporal allocation problem from the problems associated with crowding costs, which are more familiar. Derivations and proofs which consist of little more than a restatement of results in (LMM) have frequently been omitted.

2. The dynamics of the fish population

Following most of the renewable resources literature, fish are assumed to follow a growth rule of the form $N_t = f(N_{t-1}) - Q_t$, where N_t is the population size at time t, Q_t is the size of the harvest or output and f is the natural biological growth function. It is assumed that f has the following properties:

$$f' > 0; \qquad f'' < 0; \qquad f(0) = 0; \qquad f'(0) \leq \infty; \qquad f'(\infty) = 0.$$

The function f, then, has all the properties usually associated with a production function in a neoclassical growth model, with the exception that $f'(0)$ may be finite. Consequently, the graphical depiction is quite familiar (fig. 9.1).

With respect to the market, it will be assumed that the demand function for fish as well as the cost function are the same in each period. However, in the section 3 we shall assume that costs do not depend on the size of the stock of fish. In section 4 we shall take into account the fact that costs may also be a function of the stock of fish.

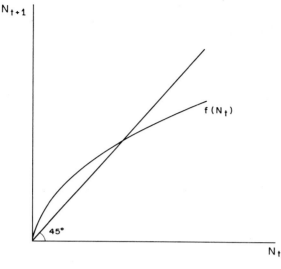

Figure 9.1

3. Costs do not depend on the size of the stock of fish

One peculiarity of renewable resource problems when costs are independent of resource stocks is that, even under monopoly, the resource may not have any scarcity value, i.e. it may have a shadow price of zero. Suppose we consider the elementary diagram shown in fig. 9.2. Here MC is the marginal harvesting cost function. If a monopolist (competitive industry) can maintain $\overline{Q}_m(\overline{Q})$ indefinitely, then there is no intertemporal allocation problem since the resource is not scarce. Given the dynamics of the fish population and $\overline{Q}_m(\overline{Q})$, the initial levels of the fish stock for which it is possible to maintain $\overline{Q}_m(\overline{Q})$ can be quickly settled by graphing $f(N) - \overline{Q}_m$ ($f(N) - \overline{Q}$) as is done in fig. 9.3. For example, consider the case depicted in fig. 9.3. Clearly for initial values $N > N^*$, the resource is not scarce to the monopolist and it is possible to maintain $\overline{Q}_m$. The existence of such an N^* clearly requires that $\overline{Q}_m$ be less than the maximum sustainable output which is $f(\overline{N}) - \overline{N}$, where $f'(\overline{N}) = 1$. If this condition is met, the dynamics to the right of N^* constitute optimal behavior for the monopolist. However, if the initial amount of fish is less than N^*, supplying $\overline{Q}_m$ will eventually deplete the stock of fish and profits would not be maximized for the monopoly. To

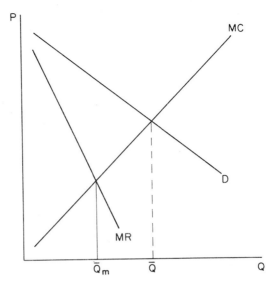

Figure 9.2

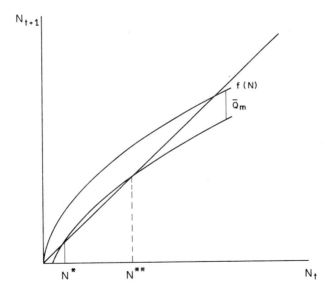

Figure 9.3

find the optimal catch in this case for the monopolist let $R[Q_t] = D[Q_t]Q_t \equiv$ revenue. Then the monopolist's problem is to maximize the discounted sum of profits subject to the biological constraints. The Lagrangian for this problem is

$$L = \sum_{t=0}^{\infty} \beta^t \{ [R(Q_t) - C(Q_t)] + \lambda_t [f(N_{t-1}) - N_t - Q_t] \},$$

where $\beta = 1/(1+r)$ is the discount factor and r the rate of interest. The first-order conditions are

$$\frac{\partial L}{\partial Q_t} : \beta^t [R'(Q_t) - C'(Q_t)] = \beta^t \lambda_t, \qquad t = 0, 1, \ldots,$$

$$\frac{\partial L}{\partial N_t} : \lambda_{t+1} \beta f'(N_t) = \lambda_t, \qquad t = 0, 1, \ldots.$$

Combining these equations yields

$$R'(Q_{t+1}) - C'(Q_{t+1}) = \frac{1}{\beta f'(N_t)} [R'(Q_t) - C'(Q_t)]. \tag{1}$$

This condition simply states that the divergence between marginal revenue and marginal cost, i.e. marginal profits, grows or shrinks depending upon whether or not $1/\beta f'(N_t) > 1$ or $1/\beta f'(N_t) < 1$. Eq. (1) can best be motivated from fig. 9.4. The line AB represents marginal revenue minus marginal cost. It is a geometric measure of the shadow price, or scarcity value, of fish to the monopolist. Whenever $\beta f'(N_t) > 1$, $f'(N_t) > 1 + r$. The "biological" rate of interest exceeds the market rate, and it is optimal to accumulate the resource. As the stock grows, so does output, and the line AB shrinks. The converse is true when $f'(N_t) < 1 + r$. Extinction in this case depends on $\beta f'(0)$. If $\beta f'(0) > 1$, extinction will not occur. If $\beta f'(0) < 1$, extinction will occur. Note that extinction occurs in finite time if and only if the marginal revenue schedule intersects the $Q = 0$ axis. A marginal revenue schedule which approaches $Q = 0$ asymptotically implies asymptotic extinction. If $\beta f'(0) = 1$, N_t will converge to zero. The nature of the convergence in this case would depend on properties of both the demand and production functions.

The analysis for competition given in (LMM) parallels that given here for monopoly. However, the simple fact that $\overline{Q} > Q_m$ creates some interesting contrasts between monopoly and competition. No attempt will be made to cover all possible cases, but a few special cases are given here for illustration.

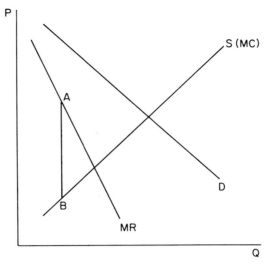

Figure 9.4

3.1. Example I

In the example illustrated in fig. 9.5, the competitor has a steady state at N^*, N^{**} and $\hat{N}$, where $\hat{N}$ is defined by the equation $\beta f'(\hat{N}) = 1$. For the steady states at N^* and N^{**}, fish are not scarce (in the dynamic sense) for the competitive solution. At $\hat{N}$ fish are scarce for the competitive solution. The monopolist does not have a steady state at $\hat{N}$, since fish are not scarce to the right of N_m^*, and hence have a zero shadow price. For the monopolist the steady state N_m^* is stable from the right and N_m^{**} is stable, while for the competitor there are stable steady states at $\hat{N}$ and N^{**}, with $N_m^* < \hat{N} < N^{**} < N_m^{**}$. Consequently, even if one knew the dynamics, it would be impossible to predict under which regime there would be a larger steady-state stock of fish without knowing the initial conditions.

3.2. Example II

In this example, $\beta f'(0) < 1$ and $\overline{Q}$ exceeds the maximum sustainable output, while $\overline{Q}_m$ does not. An initial stock to the right of N_m^*, cf. fig. 9.6, results in radically different outcomes under the two regimes. The monopolist allows the fish stock to grow to N_m^{**}, whereas the competitor eventually harvests all of the fish.

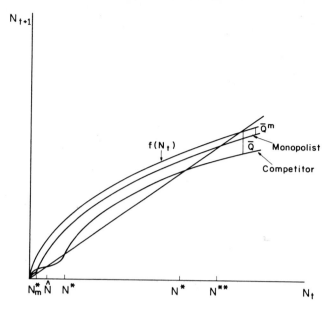

Figure 9.5

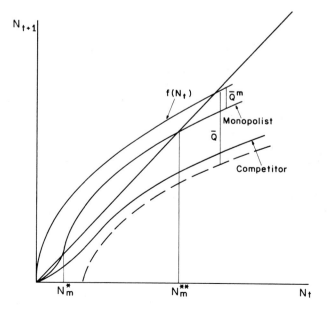

Figure 9.6

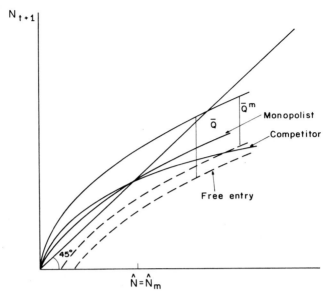

Figure 9.7

3.3. Example III

Here $\beta f'(0) > 1$ and both $\bar{Q}$ and $\bar{Q}_m$ exceed the maximum sustainable output. The interesting phenomenon, as illustrated in fig. 9.7, is that the competitor and monopolist both converge to the same steady state, $\hat{N}$, regardless of initial conditions. The condition for this positive shadow price steady state is the same in both cases, namely $f'(\hat{N}) = 1 + r$. No particular significance should be attached to the ordering of the curves here. As drawn, for example, the competitor sells less and saves more than the monopolist below the steady state. This may in fact be the case, but it depends on fairly nonintuitive considerations – for example, if costs are zero, on whether the elasticity increases or decreases along the demand curve or, in general, on the behavior of the elasticity of the average profit function in both cases. (See, for example, Stiglitz, 1976.)

4. Costs depend upon the stock of fish

In this section it is assumed that costs depend upon both the quantity of fish caught as well as the size of the stock of fish available. In particular, it is assumed that the profit function for the firm is

$$\pi(Q_t, f(N_{t-1})) \equiv D(Q_t)Q_t - C(Q_t, f(N_{t-1})),$$

and that $C_1 > 0, C_2 < 0$, and $C_{12} < 0$. The condition on the cross partial simply requires that marginal costs fall with an increase in stock size. It is also assumed that π is a strictly concave function of Q. In this case the optimum path must obey the condition

$$\left(1 + \frac{\Delta\lambda_t}{\lambda_t}\right)\left(1 + \frac{\pi_2^m(Q_{t+1}^m, f(N_t))}{\pi_1^m(Q_{t+1}^m, f(N_t))}\right)f'(N_t) = 1 + r, \tag{2}$$

and the nonzero steady states must satisfy,

$$\left(1 + \frac{\pi_2^m(Q^m, f(N))}{\pi_1^m(Q^m, f(N))}\right)f'(N) = 1 + r, \tag{3}$$

provided that one exists. Note that the derivation of these conditions from a Lagrange multiplier argument is similar to the one alluded to above and discussed in detail in (LMM) and will not be repeated.

Here

Q^m is the output of the monopolist,

$\pi_1^m(Q^m, f(N))$ is the marginal profit from selling a fish for the monopolist,

$\pi_2^m(Q^m, f(N))$ is the marginal profit (due to lower costs) from a fish in the sea for the monopolist.

Condition (2), of course, equates rates of return. The factor unique to this case is the term

$$\left(1 + \frac{\pi_2^m}{\pi_1^m}\right),$$

which is a rate of return in terms of lowered costs. If a monopolist forgoes harvesting he sacrifices π_1^m, his marginal profit from an additional unit sold. The benefit is π_2^m, the increase in profits from lowered costs. This term measures one of the factors in the "biological rate of return" on the left-hand side of (2), the others being appreciation and the marginal growth rate of the fish stock, respectively. As before, the stock and output will grow if

$$\left(1 + \frac{\pi_2^m}{\pi_1^m}\right)f'(N_t) > 1 + r,$$

i.e. fish are a good investment, and shrink if

$$\left(1+\frac{\pi_2^m}{\pi_1^m}\right)f'(N_t)<1+r,$$

i.e. if fish are a bad investment.

Superficially, this situation resembles the case in which costs do not depend upon the size of the stock, where, provided the steady states were nonzero, if the steady states involved a nonzero shadow price for fishing rights then both the optimum and the monopoly paths will have identical steady states at $\hat{N}$, where $f'(\hat{N})=1+r$. The situation here is more subtle. As is seen in eq. (3), the profit function enters into the steady-state condition. The monopolist and the competitor have different profit functions and thus different steady states. Indeed, one can show that, in the steady state, the monopolist always keeps a larger stock of fish, provided only that the solution of either the monopolist or the perfect competitor has a nonzero steady state. There is a simple and intuitive reason for this. In making the "investment" of leaving an additional fish uncaught the monopolist must only sacrifice marginal revenue minus marginal cost, whereas the competitor (or planner) must sacrifice *price* minus marginal cost; however, both achieve the same return in terms of lower cost. Since the monopolist achieves a higher rate of return from uncaught fish than the competitor, the monopolist always invests in a larger steady-state stock.

This can be shown mathematically. Let Q^c be the output of the competitors, $\pi_1^c(Q^c, f(N))$ is the marginal profit from selling a fish for the competitors, $\pi_2^c(Q^c, f(N))$ is the marginal profit (due to lower costs) from a fish in the sea for the competitors.

Consider a competitive steady state, $\overline{N}$, where from (LMM) it follows that

$$\left[1+\frac{\pi_2^c}{\pi_1^c}\right]f'(\overline{N})=1+r. \tag{4}$$

Suppose that $Q^m(\overline{N})\geqslant Q^c(\overline{N})$. Since

$$\frac{\partial(\pi_2^c/\pi_1^c)}{\partial Q}>0,[1] \qquad \frac{\pi_2^c(Q^m,\overline{N})}{\pi_1^c(Q^m,\overline{N})}\geqslant\frac{\pi_2^c(Q^c,\overline{N})}{\pi_1^c(Q^c,\overline{N})}. \tag{5}$$

Since, for identical output and stock, price exceeds marginal revenue,

$$\frac{\pi_2^m(Q^m,\overline{N})}{\pi_1^m(Q^m,\overline{N})}>\frac{\pi_2^c(Q^m,\overline{N})}{\pi_1^c(Q^m,\overline{N})}. \tag{6}$$

---

[1]Note here that $\pi_1^c=\lambda>0$, where λ is the value of fish in the competitive case, $\pi_2=-C_2>0$, and $\pi_{12}=-C_{12}>0$.

So that, combining (5) and (6), the steady-state condition (4) implies that

$$\left[1+\frac{\pi_2^m}{\pi_1^m}\right]f'(\overline{N})>1+r.$$

This means that at $\overline{N}$ the stock is growing for the monopolist, and hence at $\overline{N}$ the monopolist invests more than the competitors. This is a contradiction, which proves that $Q^m(\overline{N})<Q^c(\overline{N})$. Similarly, at a monopoly steady state, $\overline{\overline{N}}$,

$$\left(1+\frac{\pi_2^m}{\pi_1^m}\right)f'(\overline{\overline{N}})=1+r.$$

It then follows, assuming $Q^c(\overline{\overline{N}})\leqslant Q^m(\overline{\overline{N}})$, that

$$\left[1+\frac{\pi_2^m\left(Q^m,\overline{\overline{N}}\right)}{\pi_1^m\left(Q^m,\overline{\overline{N}}\right)}\right]\geqslant\left[1+\frac{\pi_2^m\left(Q^c,\overline{\overline{N}}\right)}{\pi_1^m\left(Q^c,\overline{\overline{N}}\right)}\right]>\left[1+\frac{\pi_2^c\left(Q^c,\overline{\overline{N}}\right)}{\pi_1^c\left(Q^c,\overline{\overline{N}}\right)}\right],$$

which in turn implies that $Q^c(\overline{\overline{N}})>Q^m(\overline{\overline{N}})$.

Consequently, any time the competitive dynamics lie above the 45° line, the monopoly dynamics must also lie above the 45° line. Furthermore, any time the monopoly dynamics lie below the 45° line, so do the competitive dynamics. As a consequence, the steady state for the monopolist, for any arbitrary nonzero starting point, must lie to the right of the competitive steady state for the same starting point. Curiously, this need not be true in the case when costs are independent of the size of the stock, as illustrated by example I. A few examples illustrate that this result has no obvious implications for *output*.

Case A. This is perhaps the most intuitively appealing case. If harvesting costs are sufficiently sensitive to the stock, i.e., if

$$\frac{\pi_2^c(Q^c(N),N)}{\pi_1^c(Q^c(N),N)}>r,$$

for every N, see (LMM, p. 659), then there is a unique steady state, for both the competitor and the monopolist, to the right of $f'=1$. In this case the monopoly steady state has a larger stock and smaller output than the competitive steady state.

Case B. In this case both steady states are to the left of $f'=1$, so that the steady-state monopoly output exceeds that of the competitive steady state. This is the curious case alluded to in the introduction.

References

Levhari, David, Ronald Michener and Leonard J. Mirman (1981) "Dynamic Programming Models of Fishing: Competition", *American Economic Review*, 71, 4, 649–661.
Stiglitz, J.E. (1976) "Monopoly and the Rate of Extraction of Exhaustible Resources", *American Economic Review*, 66, 4, 655–661.

CHAPTER 10

Bilateral monopoly in fisheries and optimal management policy

GORDON R. MUNRO*

1. Introduction

Traditional economic models of the fishery have tended either to push the processing sector into the background or to ignore it entirely.[1] In response to a shared suspicion that such an exclusion was unwarranted, Clark and Munro (1980) set out in a recent paper to incorporate explicitly the processing sector into the standard dynamic fishery model. Our object was to determine what implications for management policy, if any, would arise from such an extension of the basic model. We were soon convinced that if one can safely assume that the processing sector is characterized by atomistic competition, incorporation of the processing sector into the traditional model yields negligible analytical insights.

It is clear, however, even on the basis of casual observation, that highly competitive processing sectors are not the norm. (See, for example, Capalbo, 1976.) Indeed, Crutchfield and Pontecorvo (1969) in their book on the Pacific salmon go so far as to argue that throughout the non-Communist

---

*I am indebted to Colin W. Clark for his advice and assistance. Needless to say, I take full responsibilty for all remaining errors. I also gratefully acknowledge support from the University of British Columbia, Department of Economics Programme in Natural Resource Economics.

[1] There are exceptions. Crutchfield and Pontecorvo (1969), who will be cited at later points in the paper, do consider the processing sector. They have no explicit model which incorporates the sector, however. The processing sector is modelled explicitly in Cassidy (1973), and Rothschild, Gates and Carlson (1977). In both of these papers, however, the traditional static analysis is used. In this paper we choose to employ dynamic analysis

---

Essays in the economics of renewable resources, edited by *L.J. Mirman and D.F. Spulber*
© *North-Holland Publishing Company, 1982*

world fishing industries typically consist of highly competitive harvesting sectors confronting oligopsonistic processing sectors.

Important implications follow from this fact. Crutchfield and Pontecorvo assert that if a processing sector was not merely oligopsonistic but exercised full monopsony powers, the fishery would be managed in a socially optimal manner, even if the processing and harvesting sectors were unintegrated. The fact that many fisheries with oligopsonistic processing sectors are manifestly not run in a socially optimal manner can be ascribed to the fact that the oligopsonies are, contrary to appearances, weak.

If these assertions are correct, then obvious policy questions arise. Limited entry programs designed to prevent the dissipation of resource rent, which have been aimed at the harvesting sectors alone, have been less than unqualified successes.[2] Attempts to control as many as several thousand independent harvesting units have created near insoluble policing problems. Might it not be sensible, therefore, to direct limited entry programs at the processing sector with the object of transforming weak oligopsonies into strong monopsonies?[3] If this were so, we could view such monopsonies as "natural monopsonies".

In the aforementioned paper (Clark and Munro, 1980) the question of whether a monopsonized processing sector would lead to the fishery being exploited in a socially optimal manner was addressed. We did not, at that early stage, worry about how society might go about extracting rent from the processor. In the paper we considered the case in which the monopsonist was faced with a fully competitive harvesting sector. We concluded that monopsony would lead to a social optimum only under special circumstances. Moreover, we argued that backward integration could not be relied upon to correct deviations from the social optimum. Indeed, integration could well make matters worse. We also concluded, however, that, in principle at least, deviations from the social optimum could be corrected by the judicious use of taxes.

At the end of the paper we acknowledged that it was unrealistic to assume that the harvesters could always be relied upon tamely to accept monopsony in the processing sector. Properly we ought to allow for the possibility that the harvesters would react to a monopsony by forming a raw fish monopoly, either through a union or cooperative. This paper, then, is designed to fill that gap. First we review the results of the earlier paper.

---

[2] Detailed discussions of limited entry programs in Canada and the United States can be found in a series of articles appearing in the *Journal of the Fisheries Research Board of Canada*, vol. 36 (July 1979).
[3] This possibility was first raised in Cassidy (1973).

2. Monopsony and a competitive harvesting sector

We assume that the fishery is focused upon a single stock and that the fishery can be modelled with the well-known Schaefer model. Thus, we have

$$\frac{dx}{dt} = F(x) - h(t), \tag{1}$$

$$h(t) = qE(t)x(t), \tag{2}$$

where

$x(t)$ = biomass at time t,
$F(x)$ = natural growth rate,
$h(t)$ = harvest rate at time t,
$E(t)$ = fishing effort at time t, and
q = catchability coefficient.

It is assumed that $x(0) = x_0$ is known. Thus, any chosen fishing effort policy $E(t)$, $t > 0$, or alternatively harvest policy $h(t)$, $t > 0$, determines the future biomass levels $x(t)$ for $t > 0$. There are, of course, feasibility constraints:

$$x(t) \geq 0; \quad h(t) \geq 0; \quad E(t) \geq 0. \tag{3}$$

In modelling the harvesting sector we assume a cost function for fishing effort $C = C_1(E)$ satisfying

$$C_1'(E) > 0; \quad C_1''(E) \geq 0. \tag{4}$$

The net revenue flow to the harvesting sector at any point in time is given by

$$\pi_1(x, E) = p_1 qEx - C_1(E) \tag{5}$$

or, alternatively, by

$$\pi_1(x, h) = p_1 h - C_1(h/qx) \tag{5a}$$

where p_1 is the ex-vessel price of fish (see eq. (2) above).

In modelling the processing sector we first assume constant returns to scale. Secondly, we assume, in a rather ad hoc manner, that the average size of fish declines as the biomass is reduced and assume further that the size of fish affects the net revenue flow in the processing sector in several ways. We anticipate that the proportion of recoverable fish and unit processing costs may be affected by the average size of fish.[4]

---

[4] It is also possible, of course, that the price of the finished product will be affected by the size of harvested fish.

Let the net revenue per unit of raw fish received, processed and sold be denoted by $p_2(x)$. We have

$$p_2(x) = \alpha(x)p_m - c_2(x), \qquad (6)$$

where $c_2(x)$ denotes unit processing costs and where $\alpha(x)$ denotes the "recovery factor". We have

$$\alpha(x) \leqslant 1; \qquad \alpha'(x) > 0. \qquad (7)$$

Finally p_m denotes the price of the finished product. We assume initially that the demand for the processed fish products is perfectly elastic.

The net revenue flow for the processing sector can thus be expressed as

$$\pi_2(x, h) = [p_2(x) - p_1]h. \qquad (8)$$

The ex-vessel price, p_1, is determined by the processor in his capacity as monopsonist.

It is assumed that the harvesting sector will be in equilibrium when $\partial \pi_1 / \partial E = 0$, i.e. when

$$p_1 qx = C_1'(E), \qquad (9)$$

which can be expressed as

$$p_1 = \frac{1}{qx} C_1'\left(\frac{h}{qx}\right). \qquad (10)$$

It is supposed that this equation holds as p_1, $C_1(E)$, or x vary over time, and further that the level of fishing effort responds to changes in $\partial \pi_1 / \partial E$ without delays.

By controlling p_1, the monopsonist is thus able to control the harvesting sector. This is easiest to see when $C_1''(E) > 0$. Then eq. (10) defines for each x a one-to-one relationship between p_1 and h.[5] Thus, eq. (8) can be re-expressed as

$$\pi_2(x, h) = \left[p_2(x) - \frac{1}{qx} C_1'\left(\frac{h}{qx}\right)\right]h. \qquad (11)$$

It is assumed that the monopsonist will have the objective of maximizing the present value of profits from the fishery as perceived by itself. Thus, the

---

[5] If $C''(E) = 0$, eq. (10) merely specifies a biomass equilibrium, $x = c/p_1 q$, where c is the unit cost of fishing effort. To complete the model, one might assume that $h = 0$ for $x < c/p_1 q$ and $h = h_{max}$ for $x > c/p_1 q$, where h_{max} denotes a pre-assigned maximum harvest rate.

monopsonist's objective functional can be expressed as

$$P.V._2 = \int_0^\infty e^{-\delta_2 t} \pi_2(x(t), h(t)) dt,$$ (12)

where δ_2 denotes the monopsonist's discount rate.

It can be shown that the monopsonist's target or optimal biomass level, x_2^*, will be given by the equilibrium equation

$$F'(x_2^*) + \frac{\partial \pi_2 / \partial x_2^*}{\partial \pi_2 / \partial h} = \delta_2.$$ (13)

This is the familiar modified golden rule equation which states that it is optimal to invest in (disinvest with respect to) the resource up to the point that the own rate of interest of the resource is equal to the discount rate (see Clark and Munro, 1975). The optimal approach path to x_2^* will be either asymptotic or rapid depending upon whether $C_1''(E)$ is or is not positive.[6]

The monopsonist's optimal policy is compared with the social optimum. We abstract from second-best considerations and assume that p_m adequately measures social gross marginal benefit from fish products and assume that processing and harvesting costs adequately reflect social costs. The social net benefit flow and objective functionals are given respectively by

$$\pi_s(x, h) = p_2(x)h - C_1(h/qx)$$ (14)

and

$$P.V._s = \int_0^\infty e^{-\delta_s t} \pi_s(x(t), h(t)) dt,$$ (15)

where δ_s is the social discount rate. The socially optimal biomass level, x_s^*, is given by

$$F'(x_s^*) + \frac{\partial \pi_s / \partial x_s^*}{\partial \pi_s / \partial h} = \delta_s.$$ (16)

The monopsonist's optimal harvest policy can obviously deviate from the social optimum if $\delta_2 \neq \delta_s$. If, for example, $\delta_2 > \delta_s$, then ceteris paribus, one would expect that the monopsonist would overexploit the resource, i.e. $x_2^* < x_s^*$. It will also deviate, however, even if $\delta_2 = \delta_s$, so long as $C_1''(E) > 0$. Since the monopsonist pays the same price for each unit of fish regardless of the cost of harvesting it, the cost to the monopsonist of h will exceed the true social cost.

---

[6] If $C''(E) = 0$, the optimal approach path is the most rapid or "bang-bang" one.

We use the term "marginal stock effect" to describe the second term on the L.H.S. of the equilibrium equations (13) and (16), $(\partial \pi / \partial x)/(\partial \pi / \partial h)$. It is essentially a measure of the marginal impact of stock abundance upon net revenue flows from the fishery. For example, it is usually true that the greater the stock abundance the lower will be harvesting costs.

The fact that when $C_1''(E) > 0$ the monopsonist's perception of the cost of acquiring raw fish will exceed the true social cost will lead to a distortion in the monopsonist's perception of the marginal stock effect. The monopsonist's perception of the marginal stock effect will exceed that perceived by what we might term the social manager, i.e.

$$\frac{\partial \pi_2 / \partial x}{\partial \pi_2 / \partial h} > \frac{\partial \pi_s / \partial x}{\partial \pi_s / \partial h}.$$

Consequently, if $\delta_2 = \delta_s$, the monopsonist will be excessively conservationist in the sense that $x_2^* > x_s^*$.

We consider also cases in which the demand for the finished product exhibits a finite price elasticity. We argue that, if the entire output went into the export market (which is only a slight exaggeration for most Canadian fishing companies), demand considerations alone would not lead to divergences between the harvest policies of the social manager and what we might now refer to as the monopolist/monopsonist. If, on the other hand, the entire output were consumed domestically, then demand considerations could lead to divergent optimal harvest policies. Somewhat to our surprise we find that we cannot predict, a priori, whether the monopolist/monopsonist would over or underinvest in the resource in relation to x_s^*. Nor can we predict whether the long-run price of fish products under a monopolist/monopsonist's regime would be higher or lower than it would be under the regime of a social manager.

Finally, we investigate the possibility of correcting deviant monopsonist or monopolist/monopsonist behavior by the use of taxes. We conclude that, in most of the cases considered, we can with the aid of taxes correct deviant behavior, at least to the extent that the processor will be driven to the target biomass x_s^*. The taxes considered are unit landings taxes or alternatively unit taxes on the finished product.

Thus, for example, if the deviation in optimal harvest policies is a result of the processor's overestimate of harvesting costs, this can be corrected by introducing a negative landings tax. If the deviation arises because $\delta_2 \neq \delta_s$, we do not claim that one can alter the processor's perception of the discount rate. What we do claim is that with the aid of taxes it is possible to alter the processor's perception of the own rate of interest of the resource. The optimum tax will be one in which the own rate of interest of the resource, as perceived by the processor, will be equal to δ_2 at x_s^*. Denote the tax by τ. The optimal tax will be one which satisfies the following equation:

$$\frac{\partial \pi_{2,\tau}/\partial x_s^*}{\partial \pi_{2,\tau}/\partial h} = \frac{\partial \pi_s/\partial x_s^*}{\partial \pi_s/\partial h} + (\delta_2 - \delta_s). \tag{17}$$

In effect we correct for one "distortion", $\delta_2 \neq \delta_s$, by inducing a counter distortion.

An important drawback to our tax program is that the taxes, positive or negative, perform their corrective function by influencing the processor's perception of the marginal stock effect. It is known that there are likely to be cases in which the marginal stock effect will prove to be negligible. In such cases taxes will prove to be an ineffective corrective device.

3. A monopolized harvesting sector

We now suppose that the participants in the harvesting sector respond to a monopsony in the processing sector by uniting to establish a raw fish monopoly. Thus, the fishery is now characterized by bilateral monopoly.

James Crutchfield recognized the possibility of a bilateral monopoly emerging in a fishery over twenty years ago. He maintained, however, that the outcome of the struggle between the two sides over the division of the returns from the fishery would be indeterminate (Crutchfield, 1956, p. 297). We, on the other hand, shall argue that, if the problem is analyzed within a game-theoretic framework, a determinate solution can be obtained.

We commence with the observation that both sides will have an incentive to cooperate, since failure to cooperate bears with it the promise of losses for both. We shall suppose, therefore, that both harvesters and processors are prepared to contemplate cooperation. Since we continue to operate in a deterministic world, we shall also suppose that each side is prepared, if cooperation appears attractive, to enter into a *binding* agreement through time. There is, moreover, no reason why a time limit should be imposed on such an agreement.

The analytic framework which is required is obviously that provided by a model of a two-person cooperative game. We turn to the well-known and robust model developed by Nash (1953). In so doing, we shall assume that there exists a unique outcome or "threat point" if the two sides are unable to reach an agreement. Finally, for the sake of simplicity, we assume that $C_1''(E)=0$.[7]

While the bargaining will ostensibly be over the ex-vessel price, p_1, it would seem sensible to suppose that both sides will in fact focus upon the stream of net returns or "rent" from the fishery as a whole. Viewed in this way, the cooperative game which emerges is similar to a Nash cooperative game involving union-management wage negotiations, as described by Bacharach (1976, pp. 105–111). In such a game, both sides strive to maximize the economic profit of the firm or industry, with the "cost" of labor being set equal to its opportunity cost. Bargaining then takes place over the division of the economic profit.

If the two sides are uniform in their view of the appropriate rate at which to discount the future, then the cooperative game does in fact become as simple as the aforementioned union-management wage settlement game. If such uniformity does not prevail, however, additional complications arise.

The net return or revenue function for the fishery as a whole will be

$$\pi(x, h) = [p_2(x) - c_1(x)]h, \tag{18}$$

where $c_1(x) = c/qx$, and where c, a constant, denotes unit economic cost of fishing effort.[8] Let $\phi(t)$ denote the share of the total net return or "rent" accruing to the harvesting sector at each moment in time, where $0 \leqslant \phi(t) \leqslant 1$. The objective functionals of the monopolist (harvester) and monopsonist, respectively, can then be expressed as follows:

$$P.V._1 = \int_0^\infty e^{-\delta_1 t}\phi(t)\pi(x, h)\mathrm{d}t,[9] \tag{19}$$

$$P.V._2 = \int_0^\infty e^{-\delta_2 t}(1 - \phi(t))\pi(x, h)\mathrm{d}t. \tag{20}$$

It is customary in the theory of two-person cooperative games to make a distinction between games in which side payments can be made (i.e.

---

[7] In the case in which the processing sector was monopsonized and the harvesting sector was competitive, life was made much simpler for us by assuming that $C_1''(E) > 0$. Here the reverse is the case.

[8] That is, the cost of fishing effort is evaluated in terms of the opportunity cost of labor and capital generating fishing effort.

[9] It is more common to think of the monopolist's net return from the fishery at any point in time t as being equal to the harvest rate multiplied by the ex-vessel price, $p_1(t)$, less harvesting costs. It is easy to show that, given $\phi(t)$, $p_1(t)$ will be given by

$$p_1(t) = \phi(t)p_2(x) + (1 - \phi(t))c_1(x).$$

pay-offs are transferable) and those in which side payments cannot be made. We shall suppose initially that, for whatever reason one cares to choose, side payments cannot be made.

Let us also suppose initially that the harvester monopolist and processor monopsonist discount the future at the same rate, i.e. $\delta_1 = \delta_2$. Then, as promised, the bargaining problem becomes relatively simple. In particular, no difficulties arise by virtue of the fact that the two sides take differing views on what constitutes the optimal harvest policy.

Let is first be noted that, since both sides discount the future at the same rate, it is pointless to have ϕ vary over time, i.e. for the prospective partners to trade future against present proceed shares. Now observe that neither side's perception of the optimal biomass level will be influenced by the size of ϕ, given only that $0 < \phi < 1$. Let the harvester monopolist's perceived optimal biomass level by denoted by x_1^*. This biomass level will be given by the equation

$$F'(x_1^*) + \frac{\phi \partial \pi / \partial x_1^*}{\phi \partial \pi / \partial h} = \delta_1. \tag{21}$$

Obviously the ϕ's cancel out. The biomass level perceived as optimal by the processor monopsonist, x_2^*, will similarly be unaffected by the size of ϕ. Given that $\delta_1 = \delta_2$, we have $x_1^* = x_2^*$.

Since our model is, by assumption, linear, the optimal approach path as perceived by both partners will be the "bang-bang" approach path. Hence, the two sides will have identical views as to the optimal harvest policy which in turn will be to set $h(t)$ such as to maximize

$$P.V. = \int_0^\infty e^{-\delta t} \pi(x, h) \, dt, \tag{22}$$

where $\delta_1 = \delta_2 = \delta$.

Such bargaining as must take place will be over the size of ϕ, i.e. over the division of the present value obtained by maximizing Eq. (22). Here we turn to Nash's theory of two-person cooperative games. Define the pay-off to a prospective partner as the present value of the stream of its returns from the fishery given the implementation of a specific harvest policy. Denote the pay-offs for player 1 (harvester monopolist) as π and for player 2 (processor monopsonist) as θ. Let π^0, θ^0 and π^*, θ^* denote the "threat point" and solution pay-offs, respectively.

Nash proves that if six appealing assumptions are satisfied,[10] the solution to the game will be given by maximizing the expression

$$\text{maximize}(\pi^* - \pi^0)(\theta^* - \theta^0), \tag{23}$$

which can be rewritten as

$$\text{maximize}(\pi^* - \pi^0)(\omega - \pi^* - \theta^0), \tag{23a}$$

where ω denotes the present value obtained in maximizing eq. (22). Maximizing (23a) leads to the well-known result

$$\pi^* = (\omega - \theta^0 + \pi^0)/2, \tag{24}$$

$$\theta^* = (\omega - \pi^0 + \theta^0)/2. \tag{24a}$$

In obtaining a solution to the game, the size of ϕ is determined.

The results obtained are indeed simple and, as promised, are virtually indistinguishable from those which would be obtained in applying Nash's cooperative game model to wage bargaining. The simplicity of the results vanish, however, if for any reason the assumption that $\delta_1 = \delta_2$ proves to be invalid. For then bargaining will have to take place, not only over the division of the rent from the fishery, but over the management policy as well.

Let it be supposed that $\delta_1 > \delta_2$. Then it can easily be demonstrated that the high discount rate partner, the harvester monopolist, will have less desire to invest in the resource than its low discount rate partner, i.e. $x_1^* < x_2^*$.

In formulating this second bargaining problem, we turn to a recent paper by the author (Munro, 1979) on the optimal management of transboundary renewable resources. Of the several cases dealt with in that paper, one is very similar to the problem now before us (Munro, 1979, pp. 359–364).

We note first that with $\delta_1 \neq \delta_2$ we are no longer justified in arguing that it is needless to allow ϕ to be time variant. Hence, $\phi = \phi(t)$ will now be deemed to be a function of time.

In following the aforementioned paper, a *potential* agreement is characterized as a harvesting policy designed to maximize the weighted sum of the present values of the net returns from the fishery to the two prospective partners. Thus, we have (from eqs. (19) and (20)):

$$P.V.(\gamma) = \gamma \int_0^\infty e^{-\delta_1 t} \phi(t) \pi(x,h)\,dt$$

$$+ (1-\gamma) \int_0^\infty e^{-\delta_2 t}(1 - \phi(t)) \pi(x,h)\,dt, \tag{25}$$

---

[10] See Munro (1979, p. 361). For a discussion of the Nash competitive game see Luce and Raiffa (1967).

where γ $(0 \leqslant \gamma \leqslant 1)$ can be viewed as a bargaining parameter. The object of the game is to determine γ. Once γ is determined the compromise harvest policy will be determined as will the optimal time path of the harvest shares.

By varying γ between 0 and 1 and determining for each γ the harvest policy which will maximize P.V.(γ), the Pareto-efficient frontier in the space of realized outcomes or payoffs can be obtained (see Munro, 1979, for further discussion). A solution to the game is obtained in the same manner described before, i.e.,

$$\text{maximize}(\pi^* - \pi^0)(\theta^* - \theta^0). \tag{26}$$

The solution payoffs will be associated with a particular γ, i.e. γ^*. Thus, if we had $\gamma^* = \frac{1}{2}$, this would indicate that successful bargaining between the two partners had led to equal weight being given to the preferences of the two partners.

We now suppose that bargaining leads to $0 < \gamma^* < 1$[11] and consider the nature of the optimal harvest policy. The objective functional is given by eq. (25). The corresponding Hamiltonian is

$$H = \phi(t)\{\gamma e^{-\delta_1 t} - (1 - \gamma)e^{-\delta_2 t}\}\pi(x, h)$$
$$+ (1 - \gamma)e^{-\delta_2 t}\pi(x, h) + \lambda(t)(F(x) - h), \tag{27}$$

where $\lambda(t)$ is the adjoint variable discounted back to $t = 0$.

Both $h(t)$ and $\phi(t)$ are control variables. Hence, by the maximum principle the Hamiltonian must be maximized with respect to $\phi(t)$ (as well as with respect to $h(t)$) at each point in time. Given the reasonable assumption that no harvesting will take place if $\pi(x, h) \leqslant 0$, the maximum principle implies that

$$\phi(t) = \begin{cases} 1, & \text{if } \{\gamma e^{-\delta_1 t} - (1 - \gamma)e^{-\delta_2 t}\} > 0, \\ 0, & \text{otherwise.} \end{cases} \tag{28}$$

The expression

$$\sigma(t) = \gamma e^{-\delta_1 t} - (1 - \gamma)e^{-\delta_2 t} \tag{29}$$

is thus a switching function for $\phi(t)$.

If it is recalled that by assumption $\delta_1 > \delta_2$, it can be seen that, if $\gamma \leqslant \frac{1}{2}$, then $\sigma(t) < 0$ and $\phi(t) = 0$ for all t, i.e. all of the net return from the fishery would be enjoyed by the low discount rate partner forever. While this outcome cannot be ruled out entirely (Munro, 1979, pp. 363–364), we shall

---

[11] If $\gamma^* = 1$ or $\gamma^* = 0$, one partner's preferences would be fully dominant and the problem would lack interest.

suppose that the outcome is such that both players enjoy a positive return from the resource.

Such an outcome would be one in which $\gamma^* < 1$, but in which γ^* exceeds $\frac{1}{2}$ to the extent that $\sigma(t) > 0$ at the commencement of the management program. Since $\phi(t) = 1$, partner 1 will enjoy the entire net proceeds from the fishery. Upon inspecting (28), however, it can be seen that there must be a point in time T, $0 < T < \infty$, at which a switch will occur, i.e. $\phi(t) = 0$ for $t > T$. From that point on, all of the net proceeds from the fishery will be enjoyed by the low discount rate partner, the processor monopsonist. When the switch will occur, given δ_1 and δ_2, will, of course, depend upon the size of γ^*.

The nature of the solution appears to be extreme. However, the solution's extreme nature should not be exaggerated. It is worth emphasizing that at no point in the management program, when fish are actually being caught and processed, are labor and capital in either sector expected to receive less than their respective opportunity costs.[12]

The optimal harvest policy implied by this solution to the game can easily be described. The policy will be to approach x_1^* as rapidly as possible at the beginning of the program, and then to maintain the biomass level at x_1^* until $t = T$. At $t = T$ the optimal biomass level will switch to x_2^*.[13]

Up to this point we have not allowed for the possibility of side payments. Once these are introduced, the solution becomes particularly simple. It can be shown (see Munro, 1979) that it will be optimal to set $\phi(t) = 0$ for all $t > 0$. In other words, the resource should be exploited as if it were owned outright by the low discount rate partner, who in turn will make a side payment to its high discount rate partner. Furthermore, it can be shown that this should take the form of a lump-sum payment to be made at the commencement of the program (Munro, 1979, p. 364).

4. Taxation policy

There is, of course, no guarantee that the harvest policy arising from a successful cooperative game would be socially optimal. While no difficulties

[12] If one returns to footnote 9, it can be seen that if, for example, $\phi(t) = 0$, this will imply that $p_1(t) = c_1(x)$. Unit harvesting costs, of course, reflect the opportunity costs of labor and capital employed in the harvesting sector.
[13] One complication which is almost certain to arise is that the biomass level cannot be switched instantly at $t = T$ from x_1^*, to the higher level x_2^*. There is a lower bound on the control variable $h(t)$, i.e. $h(t) \geqslant 0$. This in turn can given rise to so-called blocked interval problems. For a discussion of such problems see Clark and Munro (1975).

would arise via harvesting costs even if $C_1''(E)>0$, there is the obvious possibility that $\delta_s < \delta_2 \leqslant \delta_1$.

If $\delta_1 = \delta_2$, no new difficulties arise. Then the partners can be driven to follow the socially optimal path by the use of a landings or processing tax. The tax policy would be the same as that described above in the case of a monopsonistic processor confronting a competitive harvesting sector where $C_1''(E)=0$ and $\delta_2 > \delta_s$ (see eq. (17)).

If, on the other hand, $\delta_1 \neq \delta_2$ and if side payments are not possible, then clearly the resource management policy resulting from bargaining between the two partners will be nonoptimal from a social standpoint. Unfortunately, there is no obvious way of inducing a socially optimal policy through the use of taxes. The tax policy required before and after $t = T$ will be quite different. The two players would, of course, anticipate the tax change and react accordingly. Indeed, one could foresee a complex three-person game emerging.

If side payments can be introduced, then it would appear that our problems would vanish, since the resource would be managed as if it were subject to sole ownership. Unfortunately, however, the "players", upon recognizing that the tax authorities would be stymied by a nonside payments game, may well conclude that it is to their mutual advantage to avoid side payments.

Thus, it may not be feasible to use taxes as a means of driving the industry to a socially optimal policy. Other devices, i.e. quantitative controls, would have to be contemplated. Whether quantitative controls would be effective, given their uncertain history in fisheries management, is not at all certain.

5. An example

It must be admitted that it would be difficult to find an example of a North American fishery in which the authorities fostered either a monopsonistic processing sector alone or a bilateral monopoly. Nonetheless, examples do exist elsewhere. One such example, which has been reported upon in detail, is provided by a fishery in Western Australia. The evidence on this example has been reported by T.F. Meany of the Economic Research section of the Australian Department of Primary Industry (Meany, 1979).

The existence of prawns off the Western Australian coast was discovered in commercially exploitable quantities in the early 1950s. No serious attempts were undertaken to develop the fisheries, however, for a decade. Then in order to encourage investment, the Western Australian government provided rights to processing to a strictly limited number of companies at each of the locations.

The first development at the isolated locality of Shark Bay, roughly 400 miles north of Fremantle, was a case in point. The government of Western Australia offered two companies exclusive processing rights in 1963. The two companies later turned into a monopsony when one of the companies absorbed its rival.

In addition, the authorities imposed limits upon the number of fishing licenses. While some of the licences were given to the processors, not all were. The processors (later processor) did not attempt to buy up licences held by independent fishermen. It was suggested the monopsonist feared that this would arouse governmental displeasure. As of 1977, 45 percent were held by parties other than the processor (Meany, 1979, p. 796).

Within the part of the harvesting sector not controlled by the processors, there has been a clear tendency for the licences to be acquired by non-processing companies, which causes Meany to comment on the "monopolistic tendencies" in the harvesting sector (p. 706). Hence countervailing power has emerged within the harvesting sector. Thus, if there has not been a move towards monopoly within the "independent" segment of the harvesting sector, there has been at the very least a move towards oligopoly.

While Meany does not have any data on returns on capital in the processing sector, he does have data on returns to vessel capital in the "independent" segment of the harvesting sector. From this he makes inferences on the returns on processor-owned vessel capital. Meany presents estimates for 1966–1977. Over this period the return never fell below 11 percent and has been as high as 50 percent. The yearly average was 28.4 percent (Meany, 1979, p. 796).

Meany's evidence permits us to draw two important conclusions. The first is that substantial rents have been and are being generated within the fishery. There is no perceptible trend in Meany's series. Hence, there is no evidence of rent dissipation. The second is that the independent harvesting sector has had sufficient bargaining power to obtain a not insubstantial share of the rents.

6. Conclusions

In this chapter an attempt has been made to analyze the implications for management policy of permitting, and indeed encouraging, monopsony in the processing sector and countervailing monopoly in the harvesting sector of a fishery. We concluded that, if the two sides bargained in a rational manner, a determinate solution could be obtained in the sense that the two sides could determine both a division of the proceeds from the fishery and a mutually acceptable resource management policy. Indeed, it appeared to be virtually inevitable in each instance discussed that at least de facto integration of the two sectors would occur.

We also concluded, however, that there was no reason to believe that a resource management plan devised by the two partners would be socially optimal. Moreover, there seemed to be no assurance that the authorities could always correct socially deviant management policies through the use of taxes. That corrective measures could be successfully implemented through the application of quantitative controls was by no means obvious.

The bilateral monopoly case thus differs from that of a monopsonist processing sector facing a competitive harvesting sector. In the latter case, there was reason to believe that in most instances taxes could be used effectively to produce socially optimal harvest strategies.

Having said this, however, two further comments are in order. First, even though socially nonoptimal management policies are not always easily correctible when bilateral monopoly prevails, the results which these policies are likely to produce will almost certainly be far superior to those produced by a fully competitive fishery. Secondly, while a fishery in which the processing sector is monopsonized, but in which the harvesting sector is compelled to remain competitive, may be easier to regulate, it is most unlikely that such an arrangement would prove to be feasible politically. Hence, the choice may well be between a fishery characterized by bilateral monopoly, a fully competitive fishery, or a fishery in which controls and restrictions are directed solely at the harvesting sector. Given the disastrous history of the second option and the disappointing history of the third, it can be argued that the bilateral monopoly option is at the very least worthy of further study and consideration.

References

Bacharach, Michael (1976) *Economics and the Theory of Games* (Macmillan, London).

Capalbo, M.C. (1976) "An Analysis of the Market Structure of the Food Fish Processing Sector of the United States Fishing Industry", unpublished M.Sc. thesis, Department of Resource Economics, University of Rhode Island, Kingston.

Cassidy, P.A. (1973) "Commonality, Fishery Resources, Potential and Policy: Comment", *American Journal of Agricultural Economics*, 55, August, 526–529.

Clark, Colin W. and Gordon R. Munro (1975) "The Economics of Fishing and Modern Capital Theory: A Simplified Approach", *Journal of Environmental Economics and Management*, 2, December, 92–106.

Clark, Colin W. and Gordon R. Munro (1980) "Fisheries and the Processing Sector: Some Implications for Management Policy", *The Bell Journal of Economics*, 11, Autumn, 603–616.

Crutchfield, J.A. (1956) "Common Property Resources and Factor Allocation", *Canadian Journal of Economics and Political Science*, 22, August, 292–300.

Crutchfield, J.A. and G. Pontecorvo (1969) *The Pacific Salmon Fisheries: A Study of Irrational Conservation* (The Johns Hopkins University Press, Baltimore).

Luce, R.D. and H. Raiffa (1967) *Games and Decisions* (Wiley, New York).

Meany, T.F. (1979) "Limited Entry in the Western Australia Rock Lobster and Prawn Fisheries: An Economic Evaluation", *Journal of the Fisheries Research Board of Canada*, 36, 7, July, 789–798.

Munro, Gordon R. (1979) "The Optimal Management of Transboundary Renewable Resources", *Canadian Journal of Economics*, 12, August, 355–376.

Nash, J.F. (1953) "Two-Person Cooperative Games", *Econometrica*, 21, January, 128–140.

Rothschild, B.J., J.M. Gates and A.M. Carlson (1977) "Management of Marine Recreational Fisheries", in: H. Clepper, ed., *Marine Recreational Fisheries* (Sports Fishing Institute, Washington) pp. 149–172.

CHAPTER 11

The economics of multi-purpose fleet behavior

LEE G. ANDERSON*

1. Introduction

The seminal work on fisheries economics by Gordon (1954) dealt with a single fleet exploiting a single independent fish stock. Papers that followed expanded the analysis to consider the exploitation of biologically and technologically interdependent species (see Anderson, 1975, 1977, and Clark, 1973, 1976). However, with the exception of Huppert (1979) there has been no analysis of a fleet that can spread its effort among various species that are completely independent. This phenomenon, which, following Huppert, will be called multi-purpose fleets, is very prevalent in most modern fisheries. Off the west coast of the United States, the same fleet will harvest groundfish at one season and then switch its effort to crustacea at other periods. Similarly, the trawler fleet off the coast of New England can exploit a variety of different types of fish. With respect to the first case, the change is due to seasonal availability; however, in the second the switching behavior may be motivated by changes in relative output prices, as well as changes in availability. Huppert's paper was a very stimulating introduction to this subject. However, because he assumed a constant catch per unit of effort and a predetermined quota, his analysis was not as complete as it might be.

The purpose of this chapter is to provide a detailed discussion of multi-purpose fleet behavior using several static models. The goal will be to

*Revised draft 11 January 1980. Paper presented at Conference on the Economics of Renewable Resource Management, Brown University, 19–20 October 1979. I would like to acknowledge the very useful comments of Kevin Cain and financial support from the National Science Foundation through grant 75-11205.

Essays in the economics of renewable resources, edited by L.J. Mirman and D.F. Spulber
© *North-Holland Publishing Company, 1982*

the describe open-access equilibrium and maximum economic yield in a manner that is analogous to previous models of independent and interdependent fish stocks.

The basic assumptions for the models to be presented are as follows. Two independent species of fish, S_1 and S_2, are exploited by a multi-purpose fleet. The number of vessels actively fishing, N, is determined by the profitability of the individual vessels. There is a constant price for each unit of the two species, P_1 and P_2, respectively. Similarly there is a constant operating cost per day fished for the two types of fish, C_1 and C_2, respectively. Each vessel has an annual capital cost of I. The number of days fished for species S_1 and S_2 by *each* of the boats are t_1 and t_2, respectively. The catch per day fished, for each species, will be assumed to be a function of total effort applied to the stock. Biological parameters will be assumed to be fixed. Days fished will be used as a proxy for effort. The *sustainable* catch rate equations will be represented as X_1 and X_2 as follows:

$$X_1 = X_1(Nt_1); \qquad X_2 = X_2(Nt_2).$$

The first derivative of these functions will be assumed negative to show diminishing marginal productivity. The net return per day fished for species S_1 and S_2 will be represented as r_1 and r_2, respectively, where

$$r_1 = (P_1 X_1 - C_1); \qquad r_2 = (P_2 X_2 - C_2).$$

In an open-access fishery, where each boat produces a small fraction of the total output of the fishery as a whole, the return per day fished for each of the species can be considered a parameter as far as each vessel is concerned. That is to say, r_1 and r_2 are functions of the total number of boats in the fishery and the number of days fished by each for the particular species. The number of days fished by any one boat will not appreciably affect it.

Two different models, both using these basic assumptions, will be discussed. The difference between them is the constraints on fishing behavior. Model 1 is the most general case where T is the maximum possible days fished per year for each boat as determined by weather conditions, repair time, etc. It will be assumed that this time can be allocated in any combination to fishing for S_1 or S_2. The only constraint on fishing behavior is that $t_1 + t_2$ must be less than or equal to T. In many instances, of course, seasonal availability will prevent such complete flexibility. Model 2 will describe these situations by using an assumption that is extreme in the other direction. T_1 will be the maximum days available for fishing species S_1, and T_2 the maximum days available for fishing S_2. There will be no possible trade-offs between these two types of fishing. The constraint is that t_1 must be less than or equal to T_1, and t_2 must be less than or equal to T_2. The remainder of the chapter will describe, for each of the models, the behavior of individual vessels and of the fleet under conditions of free and open access to the fishery and will compare them to the optimal vessel and fleet behavior necessary to achieve a static maximum economic yield.

2. Model 1

The annual profit for an individual vessel is the sum of total net returns earned from both species minus the annual capital costs. Assuming profit maximization to be the only goal for the individual operator, he faces the following constrained maximization problem where, as mentioned above, r_1 and r_2 are parameters to the firm:

maximize

$$\pi = r_1 t_1 + r_2 t_2 - I = (P_1 X_1 - C_1)t_1 + (P_2 X_2 - C_2)t_2 - I$$

subject to

$$T - t_1 - t_2 \geq 0,$$
$$t_1 \geq 0,$$
$$t_2 \geq 0.$$

The Lagrangian expression for this is as follows:

$$L = \pi + \lambda(T - t_1 - t_2).$$

The first-order Kuhn–Tucker conditions are as follows (see Baumol, 1977, p. 162):

$$\frac{\partial L}{\partial t_1} = r_1(Nt_1) - \lambda \leq 0, \tag{1a}$$

$$\frac{\partial L}{\partial t_2} = r_2(Nt_2) - \lambda \leq 0, \tag{2a}$$

$$t_1(r_1 - \lambda) = 0, \tag{3a}$$

$$t_2(r_2 - \lambda) = 0, \tag{4a}$$

$$T - t_1 - t_2 \geq 0, \tag{5a}$$

$$\lambda(T - t_1 - t_2) = 0, \tag{6a}$$

$$t_1 \geq 0, \tag{7a}$$

$$t_2 \geq 0, \tag{8a}$$

$$\lambda \geq 0. \tag{9a}$$

Entry to or exit from the fishery will cease when the annual profit rate per vessel is equal to zero. Therefore, by adding condition (10a) below to the above nine Kuhn–Tucker conditions for individual profit maximization, it will be possible to solve for the open-access number of boats as well as the number of days fished for each species by each boat:

$$r_1 t_1 + r_2 t_2 - I = 0. \tag{10a}$$

These ten conditions can be interpreted by analyzing the hypothetical examples pictured in figs. 11.1, 11.2 and 11.3. Figure 11.1 contains the information from conditions (1a) and (2a), and it can be used to determine the number of days fished by each vessel for each species. The return per unit of effort as a function of the number of days fished *per boat*, is dependent upon the number of vessels in the fleet, and so fleet size must be directly considered. Each of the three diagrams in fig. 11.1 contains a return per unit of effort curve for the two types of fishing for a different fleet size. These curves show how the return per unit of effort will change as the number of days fished by every boat in the fleet increases for a given fleet size. In each diagram, the maximum possible days fished per boat, T, is represented on the length of the horizontal axis. The return per unit of effort on species 1 is plotted in the normal way from the left-hand vertical axis. The return per unit of effort on species 2 is plotted in a right to left direction from the left vertical axis.

In fig. 11.1(a), it can be seen that for this fleet size, the optimal allocation of days fished for each boat in an open-access situation will be to spend all of the time available fishing for species 2 because the return per unit of effort is always higher than the return for species 1. This means that λ, the opportunity cost of the first constraint, is as indicated on the graph, equal to r_2 when t_2 is equal to T.

If the number of vessels in the fleet increases, the r curves will rotate on their vertical axis in a downward direction. Figure 11.1(b) represents a situation in the same fishery where the number of vessels has increased. In this case, the curves intersect in the relevant range, and the proper allocation of effort to each species, as far as the individual profit-maximizing vessel is concerned, is determined by their intersection. At this point, the marginal return per unit of effort is the same for both species and there will be no inducement to shift from one to the other. At any other distribution of effort, it would be possible to increase profits by shifting from the species with the lower return per day fished to the one with the higher return. At this equilibrium λ is equal to the rate of return in both species.

Figure 11.1(c) represents a case where the fleet size has increased to such an extent that the two curves do not intersect above the horizontal axis.

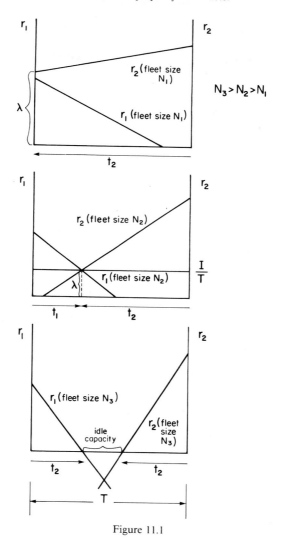

Figure 11.1

Therefore the optimal allocation of days fished will occur at the points where the two curves cross the horizontal axis, as indicated. There will be idle capacity. That is to say, each boat will only operate a portion of the T days available to it. This idle capacity is represented by the distance between the two intersection points. Since the first constraint is not binding, which is to say that the inequality holds in condition (5a), then from condition (6a) we know that λ must equal zero. As will be pointed out below, the interpretation of this situation can be hazardous because of the open-access assumption. This interpretation will suffice for the present however.

Figure 11.2(a) presents this same information but from a different perspective. The horizontal axis measures the number of vessels in the fleet, N. The distribution of the T days available for fishing by each vessel is plotted on the vertical axis, with t_1 being measured in an upward direction and t_2

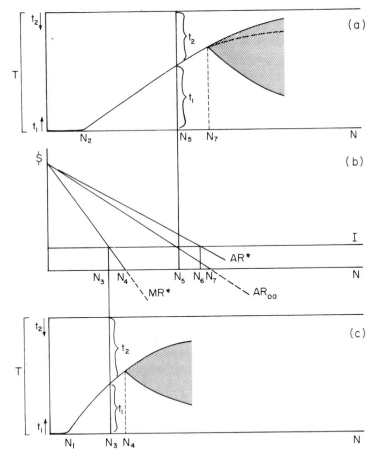

Figure 11.2

being measured in a downward direction. The purpose of this diagram is to show how each vessel in the fishery will allocate its effort among the two species given the fleet size indicated on the horizontal axis. How fleet size is determined is described below. Corresponding to the analysis in fig. 11.1, at small fleet sizes (i.e. less than N_2) t_2 will equal T. Beyond that, however, t_1 will become positive. After N reaches N_7, the r curves do not intersect before they cross the horizontal axis and therefore there must be excess capacity on each vessel in the range of fleet size. The idle time is represented by the hatched area in the graph.

Figure 11.2(b) allows for an analysis of vessel entry and exit and for the determination of open-access equilibrium fleet size. The curve labelled AR_{oa} shows the average revenue per vessel given the effort allocation as determined in the *open-access* situation. That is, the AR_{oa} curve in fig. 11.2(b) shows the revenue per vessel for a particular fleet size and the distribution of the T days among the two species, as shown in fig. 11.2(a). Ignore the other negative-sloped curve for the moment. The straight line labelled I represents the annual capital cost per vessel. At the intersection of the AR_{oa} and the I curve, the equality represented by condition (10a) holds. At this point, revenue, net of operating costs, is equal to the annual capital cost and so the profit for the average vessel is zero. Therefore entry into the fishery will cease. As fig. 11.2, is drawn here, the open-access levels of vessels in the fishery will be N_5. Note that the open-access equilibrium level of vessels, N_5, is to the left of N_7, the point where "idle capacity" begins. Close observation of the diagrams will show that this must always be the case. Consider fig. 11.1(b). At the fleet size represented here, there is no idle capacity and there is a positive net return per day fished. That is to say, after paying the variable costs associated with each day of fishing, there will be excess earnings which can be thought of as a return to capital.

Assume that the rate of return earned in the equilibrium pictured in fig. 11.1(b) is I/T, where I is the annual capital cost and T is the total days available to the vessel. Therefore, the net earnings of this vessel will be $T(I/T)$ or I. That is, at this particular fleet size and effort allocation, each vessel will just be making enough over its variable costs to cover its annual capital cost, which is to say that economic profit is zero. If the fleet size where smaller, the two r curves would shift up and the return per day fished earned in both species, as determined by the new intersection point, would be higher than I/T. Therefore an economic profit would be earned. On the other hand, if the number of vessels in the fishery were to increase, the intersection of the r curves would be at a lower net return per day than I/T and so there would not be enough extra earnings to cover all of the annual capital costs. However, as long as the net return per day is positive, some of the annual capital costs are being covered, and so in the short run the vessel would continue to fish. In the long run, however, some boats will leave the fishery.

To go one step farther, if the number of vessels is increased until the two r curves intersect at the horizontal axis, the equilibrium net return per day is zero. Here even if the fisherman operate full time, their annual loss will be the same as if they were to shut down. If the fleet size increases even more, it moves into the range of idle capacity, as described above. This idle capacity can be explained in more detail given this discussion. Given the fact that the two r curves intersect below the horizontal axis, the only way the fleet can keep the equilibrium return per day non-negative is for each vessel to cease fishing at the points where the two curves cross the axis. Note that at N_7 in fig. 11.2 the numbers of days fished for each species when the entire fleet is operating at full capacity is enough to push the net return per day to zero. As more boats enter, all will have to cut back on their days fished so that the same total number of days fished is produced. If the fleet does in fact operate this way, then beyond N_7 the average revenue per boat will not become negative but will remain at zero. It is fair to say, however, that given open access, this sort of behavior is not very likely. Each boat will try to maximize its own profits by fishing as much as possible. Therefore, there will probably not be as much idle capacity as indicated in the graph, if indeed there will be any at all. Since the range of idle capacity lies in the area where, at best, long-run profits are equal to $-I$ (i.e. net returns over variable costs are zero) there will not be a long-run equilibrium here anyway, and so the area is of little importance to this static analysis.

Figure 11.2(b) can be related to fig. 11.1 in the following way. The fleet size, where the equilibrium return is equal to I/T and hence economic profit is equal to zero, must be N_5 in fig. 11.2(b) because at this point AR_{oa} equals I. Similarly, the fleet size where the two r curves intersect at the horizontal axis must be N_7 in fig. 11.2(b), because at this point net average return per day is just equal to zero. It has thus been shown that N_5, the open-access equilibrium fleet size, is less than N_7, the fleet size that marks the beginning of the "idle capacity" range.

It is now possible to use figs. 11.2(a) and 11.2(b) to interpret the open-access operation of a multi-purpose fleet. A complete description of the open-access situation (and indeed any other operation point) must include the fleet size and the allocation of vessel effort towards the two species. And, from what has been said above, the fleet size at open access can be determined from fig. 11.2(b) (the point of intersection of the AR_{ao} and the I curve). Effort distribution can be determined by reading fig. 11.2(a) at the appropriate fleet size. The effort distribution under open access at N_5 is noted in the diagram.

Note that if the fleet size ever gets above N_5, the equilibrium level of earnings to all vessels will be such that there will be an exit of vessels. If the fleet size were ever to go beyond N_7, the losses will at best continue at the same level as at N_7 if the fleet adopts an idle capacity rule or, as is more likely, the losses will increase as the pressure of the extra boats push the net return per day into the negative range.

Consider now the problem of determining the static maximum economic yield for a multi-purpose fleet harvesting two independent species in the context of this model. Here again it will be necessary to specify both fleet size and effort allocation. Under the assumption of a constant price (such that there is no consumer surplus), maximum economic yield occurs when the profit to the fishery as a whole is maximized. Therefore, in order to find a maximum economic yield it is necessary to solve the following constrained maximum problem:

maximize $\pi^* = N\pi$,

where N and π, as defined above, are the number of vessels and the profit per boat, respectively.

subject to

$$T - t_1 - t_2 \geq 0,$$
$$t_1 \geq 0,$$
$$t_2 \geq 0.$$

There are two main differences between this analysis and the previous one. First, the size of the fleet is directly addressed in the problem. Secondly, because a fishery-wide approach is being used, the return per days fished for the various species cannot be considered a parameter for the individual boat as they could be in the individual profit maximization. The Lagrangian for this problem is

$$L^* = \pi^* + \lambda'(T - t_1 - t_2).$$

The first-order Kuhn–Tucker conditions for a solution to the above maximization problem are as follows:

$$\frac{\partial L^*}{\partial t_1} = \left(r_1 + P_1 t_1 \frac{\partial X_1}{\partial t_1} \right) - \frac{\lambda'}{N} \leqslant 0, \tag{1b}$$

$$\frac{\partial L^*}{\partial t_2} = \left(r_2 + P_2 t_2 \frac{\partial X_2}{\partial t_2} \right) - \frac{\lambda'}{N} \leqslant 0, \tag{2b}$$

$$t_1 \left(\frac{\partial L^*}{\partial t_1} \right) = 0, \tag{3b}$$

$$t_2 \left(\frac{\partial L^*}{\partial t_2} \right) = 0, \tag{4b}$$

$$T - t_1 - t_2 \geqslant 0, \tag{5b}$$

$$\lambda'(T - t_1 - t_2) = 0, \tag{6b}$$

$$t_1 \geqslant 0, \tag{7b}$$

$$t_2 \geqslant 0, \tag{8b}$$

$$\lambda' \geqslant 0, \tag{9b}$$

$$\frac{\partial L^*}{\partial N} = (r_1 t_1 + r_2 t_2 - I) + N \left(P_1 t_1 \frac{\partial X_1}{\partial N} + P_2 t_2 \frac{\partial X_2}{\partial N} \right) \leqslant 0, \tag{10b}$$

$$N \left(\frac{\partial L^*}{\partial N} \right) = 0. \tag{11b}$$

Using these conditions it is possible to solve for the static MEY fleet size and also for the effort allocation of the individual vessels. By comparing the open access with MEY conditions, it is possible to show the important differences. It can be seen from (1a) and (2a) and (1b) and (2b) that in order to have a maximum economic yield, decisions to expand t_1 or t_2, the amount of effort applied to species 1 and species 2, must consider the effect that this will have on every other boat. This is the meaning of the second term in the parentheses in (1b) and (2b). The term λ'/N in the second set of equations is analogous, but not equal, to λ in the first set. The term λ' is the opportunity cost of the constraint as far as the entire fleet is concerned. It is divided by N to get the value of the constraint expressed in terms of one vessel. Comparing condition (10a) with condition (10b) it can be seen that in order to get an optimal fleet size it is necessary to take into consideration the effect that the introduction of an additional boat will have on the profit of the remaining boats, rather than just the profit level of the last boat.

Figure 11.3 is analogous to fig. 11.1. The r_1 and r_2 curves are graphical representations of conditions (1a) and (2a), as before. The curves below

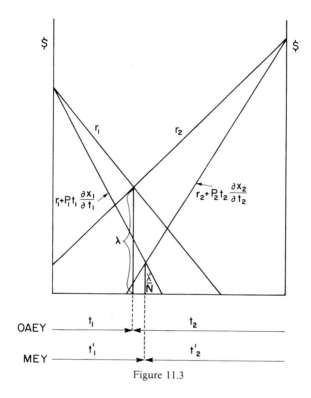

Figure 11.3

them, however, are graphical representations of conditions (1b) and (2b). Since $\partial X_i / \partial t_i$ is negative, the curves representing (1b) and (2b) will always be below (1a) and (2a), respectively. All four are drawn assuming a given fleet size. Unless there is a peculiar situation where the MEY curves intersect at the same point as the open-access curves, the optimal allocation of days fished at any given fleet size will be different from the open-access allocations. As it is graphed here, the amount of effort extended toward species 1, the relatively less productive one, is expanded in the optimal situation for any given fleet size. As described in the appendix, this is what will occur in this instance if both species have Schaeffer-type sustainable yield curves. There it is shown that if the vertical intercept of the r_2 curve is higher than the vertical intercept of the r_1 curve, then t_1 will increase relative to t_2 at MEY.

Similar to the open-access situation, note that at small fleet sizes optimality may call for all effort to go toward one species. As the fleet size expands, the optimal r curves will intersect and so optimality will require fishing for both species. Finally, at large fleet sizes, the optimal r curves may intersect below the horizontal axis, in which case optimality will require some effort directed at both species, but also some idle capacity. As will be pointed out below, the interpretation of idle capacity in this case is straightforward.

Using this information, it is possible to create a diagram analogous to fig. 11.2(a) which shows the optimal vessel behavior at different fleet sizes for the MEY situation. This is done in Fig. 11.2(c). Note that in Fig. 11.2(c) t_1 is higher for every level of N than in fig. 11.2(a).

If the vessels do distribute their effort, as is indicated in fig. 11.2(c), average revenue per boat will be higher than that earned under open access. By taking into account the harmful effects of an extra boat or an extra day fished, directed at any one of the species by all existing vessels, it is possible to reallocate effort such that total revenue for the fishery, and hence average revenue per vessel, increases. This higher level of vessel average revenue is plotted as AR^* in fig. 11.2(b). The reason this higher average revenue per boat is not earned in open access is the individualistic decision-making in a common property situation described above. To review this, consider the fleet size depicted in fig. 11.3. The optimal allocation of effort given this fleet size is t_1' and t_2' for species 1 and species 2, respectively. Note at this point, however, the average return per day fished for species 2 is greater than for species 1. Each individual fisherman will see it to his advantage to shift from species 1 to species 2. As each of them do this, all will suffer.

To return to the main argument, the marginal revenue curve that is associated with the AR^* curve is labelled MR^* in fig. 11.2(b). The intersection of MR^* and the I curve provides a solution to eq. (10b) in the same way that the intersection of AR_{ao} and the I curve provided a solution to eq. (10a). This is because the MR^* curve shows the marginal revenue to the fishery as a whole when taking into account how an additional boat will decrease the average catch per unit of effort for all boats.

To obtain a complete description of the maximum economic yield position it is necessary to go to fig. 11.2(b), determine the optimal number of boats, N_3, and then to fig. 11.2(c) to determine the optimal effort distribution. Note that both of these are different at MEY than at the open-access equilibrium. In fact, one conclusion that can be made from this analysis is that under open access not only will there be an excess number of vessels, but for whatever number of vessels used, the effort allocation will be incorrect.

As drawn in fig. 11.2(c), the maximum economic yield fleet size is less than N_4, the fleet size where the "optimum idle capacity" range begins. The logic behind this is similar to the above discussion concerning the open-access situation. The range of "optimum idle capacity" will begin where the MR^* curve crosses the horizontal axis. At that point the marginal revenue to the fishery for adding another boat is zero, which is to say that the optimal r curves, as pictured in fig. 11.3, must just intersect at the horizontal axis. Therefore, since the idle capacity range starts where the MR^* curve equals zero and the MEY point is where the MR^* curve intersects the I curve, then the MEY point is to the left of the "optimum idle capacity" range.

It can now be seen that the "optimum idle capacity" range can be interpreted as follows. For fleet sizes in this range, given the constraint that all vessels must be used in an identical manner, it will be optimal to use each boat at a point less than its full capacity.

The policy recommendations that fall out of this discussion are as follows. Regulation in a multi-purpose fleet will require specification of fleet size and of effort distribution. If only fleet size is controlled, the vessels will determine their effort allocation according to fig. 11.2(a) rather than 11.2(b) and a suboptimal allocation will result.

Another important point is that if it is difficult to control for fleet size, at least in the short run, a useful first step would be to set a moratorium on entry and then control the effort allocation among the various species for the existing fleet. This will allow for some improvement. Note that at N_5, the open-access equilibrium, a change to the optimal effort distribution will increase the average revenue per boat by the distance between the AR^* curve and the AR_{oa} curve. The moratorium will be necessary to prevent this increase in revenue from attracting new vessels to the fishery. While regulating a multi-purpose fleet should prove to be more complicated than regulating a single independent fishery, and perhaps just as complicated as regulating a fleet harvesting interdependent species, the fact that some gains can be made without reducing the fleet size is certainly a bonus. It provides the potential for relatively fast gains to all fisherman in the fishery and hence should increase the acceptability of regulation. In addition, it provides a base from which further gains can be made. For example, the rent earned at this point could be taxed away and used for the beginnings of a buy-back fund to reduce the number of vessels.

3. Model 2

For purposes of comparison, the above model will be modified by assuming that the two species can be harvested only at different times of the year. Let T_1 and T_2, respectively, represent the possible number of days that the two species are available for harvest. Letting t_1 and t_2 again represent the

The economics of renewable resources

number of days actually spent fishing for species 1 and 2, respectively, the constraints on the individual vessels can be represented as follows:

$$T_1 - t_1 \geqslant 0,$$
$$t_1 \geqslant 0,$$
$$T_2 - t_2 \geqslant 0,$$
$$t_2 \geqslant 0.$$

The individual vessel operator under open access will therefore attempt to maximize his profit subject to this set of constraints. The Lagrangian for this maximization problem is as follows:

$$L_1 = \pi + \theta_1(T_1 - t_2) + \theta_2(T_2 - t_2),$$

where π is as defined above.

The first-order Kuhn–Tucker conditions for an individual profit maximum will be very similar to the set described for the model in the previous section. Nevertheless, for completeness they are listed below, along with condition (10c) which states that the profit level for the individual vessel is zero. Using these conditions it is possible to describe the open-access fleet size and individual vessel operating behavior:

$$\frac{\partial L}{\partial t_1} = r_1(Nt_1) - \theta_1 \leqslant 0, \tag{1c}$$

$$\frac{\partial L}{\partial t_2} = r_2(Nt_2) - \theta_2 \leqslant 0, \tag{2c}$$

$$t_1(r_1 - \theta_1) = 0, \tag{3c}$$
$$t_2(r_2 - \theta_2) = 0, \tag{4c}$$
$$T_1 - t_1 \geqslant 0, \tag{5c}$$
$$T_2 - t_2 \geqslant 0, \tag{5'c}$$
$$\theta_1(T_1 - t_1) = 0, \tag{6c}$$
$$\theta_2(T_2 - t_2) = 0, \tag{6'c}$$
$$t_1 \geqslant 0, \tag{7c}$$
$$t_2 \geqslant 0, \tag{8c}$$
$$\theta_1 \geqslant 0, \tag{9c}$$
$$\theta_2 \geqslant 0, \tag{9'c}$$
$$r_1 t_1 + r_2 t_2 - I = 0. \tag{10c}$$

Static maximum economic yield, as before, will occur when the profit to the fishery as a whole is maximized, assuming that the final output prices are fixed. In formal terms the problem is:

maximize $\pi^* = N\pi$

subject to

$T_1 - t_1 \geqslant 0,$

$t_1 \geqslant 0,$

$T_2 - t_2 \geqslant 0,$

$t_2 \geqslant 0.$

The Lagrangian for this problem is

$L^* = N\pi + \theta_1'(T_1 - t_1) + \theta_2'(T_2 - t_2).$

The first-order Kuhn–Tucker conditions for the MEY are again similar to those of the previous model, but are included below for completeness.

$$\frac{\partial L^*}{\partial t_1} = \left(r_1 + P_1 t_1 \frac{\partial x_1}{\partial t_1} \right) - \frac{\theta_1'}{N} \leqslant 0, \tag{1d}$$

$$\frac{\partial L^*}{\partial t_2} = \left(r_2 + P_2 t_2 \frac{\partial x_2}{\partial t_2} \right) - \frac{\theta_2'}{N} \leqslant 0, \tag{2d}$$

$$t_1 \left(\frac{\partial L^*}{\partial t_1} \right) = 0, \tag{3d}$$

$$t_2 \left(\frac{\partial L^*}{\partial t_2} \right) = 0, \tag{4d}$$

$$T_1 - t_1 \geqslant 0, \tag{5d}$$

$$T_2 - t_2 \geqslant 0, \tag{5'd}$$

$$\theta_1'(T_1 - t_1) = 0, \tag{6d}$$

$$\theta_2'(T_2 - t_2) = 0, \tag{6'd}$$

$$t_1 \geqslant 0, \tag{7d}$$

$$t_2 \geqslant 0, \tag{8d}$$

$$\theta_1' \geqslant 0, \tag{9d}$$

$$\theta_2' \geqslant 0, \tag{9'd}$$

$$\frac{\partial L^*}{\partial N} = (r_1 t_1 + r_2 t_2 - I) + N \left(P_1 t_1 \frac{\partial X_1}{\partial N} + P_2 t_2 \frac{\partial X_2}{\partial N} \right) \leqslant 0, \tag{10d}$$

$$N \left(\frac{\partial L^*}{\partial N} \right) = 0. \tag{11d}$$

Since each of these sets of conditions are so similar to those in the previous section, the analysis of their meaning can proceed rapidly.

The basics of individual vessel behavior can be explained using the hypothetical example pictured in fig. 11.4. Since the harvest of the two species is completely independent, and it is not possible to switch a day fishing in one to a day fishing in the other, vessel behavior must be graphed in two separate diagrams. Figs. 11.4(a) and 11.4(b) describe the determination of the profit-maximizing level of t_1 and t_2, respectively. Again there will be a family of r curves, one for each different fleet size, which show the return per unit of effort assuming all vessels operate at the same level of effort. These curves are representations of conditions (1c) and (2c). As N

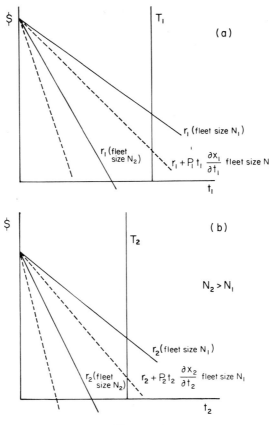

Figure 11.4

increases, the curves will shift down by rotating around the intersection point on the vertical axis. As drawn here, when fleet size is equal to N_1, the constraints on fishing time will be binding in both species and so t_1 will equal T_1 and t_2 will equal T_2. However, as the fleet size increases, the curves shift down and eventually one and/or both of the constraints will become nonbinding. For these fleet sizes there will be "idle capacity" for each vessel in one or both of the fishing seasons.

Vessel operation can be described in somewhat more detail by fig. 11.5(a), which is analogous to fig. 11.2(a). The fleet size is plotted on the horizontal

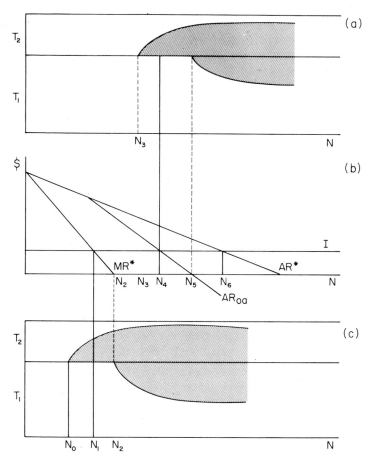

Figure 11.5

axis and the two constraints are plotted on the vertical axis. For low levels
of N both t_1 and t_2 will be at their maximum allowable level. However, as
the fleet size expands, first one and then the other will fall below the
maximum amounts. As depicted here, all vessels will be operating at full
capacity until fleet size equals N_3, at which time there will be "idle
capacity" during the season for species 2. Similarly, with fleet sizes beyond
N_5 there will be idle capacity during the season for species 1 as well. Again,
the hatched area represents the "idle capacity" for each individual vessel.
As discussed below, idle capacity is possible in one season with open-access
in this model. It is not possible in both, however.

Since conditions (10a) and (10c) and conditions (10b) and (10d) are
identical, the analysis of the determination of the open-access fleet size and
the MEY fleet size is not changed. Fig. 11.5(b) is identical to fig. 11.2(b).
The AR_{oa} curve plots the equilibrium average net return per boat that will
be earned using the open-access distribution of effort described in fig.
11.5(a). The open-access equilibrium will occur at a fleet size of N_4, where
this average annual net revenue per vessel is equal to annual capital costs.

As drawn here, there will be "idle capacity" in the season for species 2.
This is a distinct possibility in multi-purpose fleets with nonoverlapping
seasons. Consider this in more detail. In order for a vessel to break even, the
sum of the net returns from each season must be enough to cover the annual
capital costs. Depending upon the nature of the population dynamics for
each stock, this can happen in two ways. Recall that as more and more
vessels enter a fishery, the catch per unit of effort, and hence net return, will
decrease. If the fleet is directed at two different species, the net return of
both will fall; but, excepting the peculiar situation where the two stocks of
fish are identical, the net returns will be different and will fall at different
rates. Consider fig. 11.6(a) which shows the r curves for a hypothetical set of
two species at a particular fleet size. Note that if all boats in the fishery
work to full capacity in both seasons, the average net variable return for the
two species will be k_1 and k_2, respectively. This means that this will be an
equilibrium fleet size if

$$T_1 k_1 + T_2 k_2 = I,$$

i.e. if earnings over and above variable costs are just enough to cover the
annual capital costs but no more. Boats will have no tendency to enter the
fishery, but at the same time there will be no incentive for exit either. If
the left-hand side of the above equation is greater than the right-hand side
there will be entry into the fishery. Likewise, there will be exit if the
opposite is true.

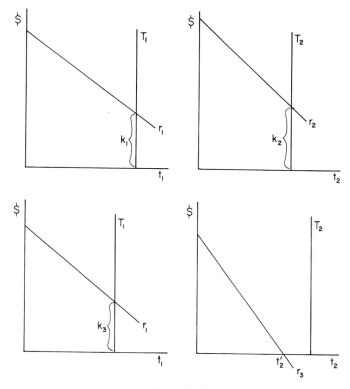

Figure 11.6

Consider now fig. 11.6(b) which contains a different set of r curves for a particular fleet size for a different hypothetical fishery. In this case the r curve for species 1 intersects the constraint line. If all of the boats in the fleet work to full capacity in the first fishing season, the net return will be equal to k_3. The r curve for species 2 intersects the horizontal axis indicating that the net return for fishing in this season will fall to zero at a level of activity less than full capacity. This can also be an equilibrium fleet size if

$$T_1 k_3 = I.$$

Essentially, this means that the fishery for species 1 is profitable enough to carry the fleet by itself. However, once the fleet is there, it will make sense to fish for species 2 as long as variable costs (including a normal profit) are being covered. Just how much effort will be applied to the second stock under open access and hence the meaning of idle capacity, is hard to determine. In fig. 11.6(b) it can be seen that as long as the amount of effort allocated to species 2 is less than t'_2 there will be some positive net returns over variable costs. But since at its equilibrium size the fleet has the potential to exert T_2 units of effort during the season for species 2, under open access there will probably be something approaching pulse-fishing for species 2. That is, all vessels will fish until the long-run return becomes negative and then many or all will cease. As a result of the decreased effort the stock will rebuild and the net return will also increase. This will encourage fishing again, and the cycle will start over. If the assumption of a homogeneous fleet is used, it is very difficult to specify any other hypothesis concerning individual firm behavior which makes sense. If its appears profitable for one vessel to fish, it will appear profitable for all to fish. All boats acting in concert will reduce the return during this season such that it will appear profitable to none. In the real world, however, the fleet will more than likely not be homogeneous. Owing to specific characteristics of management, home port, other opportunities during the season for stock 2, etc. it is possible that only part of the fleet will fish for stock 2 in such a way that an equilibrium can be reached.

To sum up this discussion of open access, note that in model 1, where there is complete freedom to switch from species to species, it was shown that the open-access equilibrium could not occur in the range of fleet size where there is "idle capacity". In this model, however, open-access equilibrium can occur where there is "idle capacity" in one of the seasons.

The analyses of vessel and fleet behavior under maximum economic yield in this case are very similar to that of model 1. In order to determine the optimal level of effort in each of the fishing seasons for a given fleet it is necessary to consider eqs. (1d) and (2d). The graphs of these equations for two fleet sizes are the dotted curves in fig. 11.4(a). Each one corresponds to an open-access r curve for a given fleet size, and will always be below it because the sign of $\partial X_i / \partial t_i$ is negative. It can be seen that at lower fleet sizes the optimal amount of t_1 and t_2 at MEY will be equal to that produced under open-access conditions because the relevant curve will intersect the seasonal constraint line in both situations. As the fleet expands, however, a point will be reached where the optimal level of t_1 and t_2 will be less than that supplied under open access. The effect of increases in the fleet on optimal vessel behavior are indicated in fig. 11.5(c).

As before, the maximum economic yield occurs at a point where the marginal net revenue for the fleet as a whole intersects the I curve. At this point condition (10d) will hold. The optimal vessel behavior at this fleet size can be determined from fig. 11.5(c). As drawn here, the optimal fleet size will be N_1, and at this fleet size there will be idle capacity during the season for species 2. Idle capacity could not exist at MEY in the previous model, but it is quite possible here because of the restrictions on switching days fished between the various species. The main condition for a maximum economic yield is that the value of the extra output to the fleet as a whole caused by entry of the marginal boat be equal to the opportunity cost of that boat. The fact that there is idle capacity for part of one of the seasons has no relevance. Marginal benefits are at least equal to marginal costs and if the vessels expand effort beyond the designated amount during the slack season, there would actually be a decrease in the value of output.

By definition, MEY is a nonequilibrium situation which can be achieved only with regulation. Given the nature of the yield curves of the two stocks, optimal regulation during the season for species 2 will call for less effort than the optimal fleet can physically produce. (The optimal fleet size is determined primarily by revenue and cost conditions for species 1.) The optimal point will be where the net revenue just covers variable cost, which is to say it is at that point where the r curve crosses the horizontal axis. This amount of effort can be produced by having part of the fleet fish full time or all of the fleet fish part time.

Aside from the conclusion about the possibility of "idle capacity" during one season at the open-access point and at the MEY point (and the special interpretation that must be placed on each) the basic conclusions of this model are the same as those for model 1.

4. Summary, conclusions, and suggestions for further work

The main conclusions of the paper are as follows.

(1) In order to achieve a static maximum economic yield of stocks that are exploited by multi-purpose vessels, it is necessary to specify the optimal number of boats and the optimal distribution of effort for each of the boats.

(2) In an open-access fishery with multi-purpose vessels, there will be an incorrect number of vessels and, in addition, there will be an improper allocation of effort by each vessel for any given fleet size.

(3) An interesting peculiarity of multi-purpose fleets is that some gains, both to society as a whole and to individual fisherman, can be obtained by influencing vessel behavior but without reducing fleet size. However, to obtain full benefits possible, both fleet size and vessel behavior must be regulated.

The stated purpose of this chapter was to present a model which could describe the open-access utilization and the conditions necessary to achieve the maximum economic yield with multi-purpose fleets in a manner that is comparable to earlier models dealing with interdependent and independent fisheries. This has been accomplished, but there is much more work to be done. For one thing, the model is static, whereas to get a complete picture of optimal utilization a dynamic analysis is necessary. In addition, the current model looks at switching behavior only from an annual point of view. The analysis would be much more robust and much more useful for policy analysis if it could consider switching on a week-to-week or even a day-to-day basis. Mathematical programming may be one way of attacking this aspect of the problem.

Appendix

The purpose of this appendix is to show the relationship between the allocation of a fixed number of fishing days by an individual vessel among two distinct fish stocks in an open-access situation and the static MEY situation in those instances where both fish stocks have a Schaeffer-type sustainable yield function. The equation for the basic Schaeffer sustainable yield curve (see Schaeffer, 1954, 1957, and 1959) is

$$\text{yield} = AE - bE^2, \tag{A.1}$$

where E represents fishing effort. By changing the notation to utilize the definition of effort used above, it follows that the catch per unit of effort, or catch rate, X_i, for a particular fish stock is

$$X_i = a_i - b_i N t_i. \tag{A.2}$$

The open-access operation point of individual vessels when the time constraint is binding occurs at the intersection of the r curves represented by eqs. (1a) and (2a) above. Substituting in the appropriate notation for X_i in the two stocks, this becomes

$$P_1(a_1 - b_1 N t_1) - C_1 - \lambda = P_2(a_2 - b_2 N t_2) - C_2 - \lambda. \tag{A.3}$$

By letting $t_2 = T - t_1$, as it must when the constraint is binding, it is possible to solve the above for t_1. The result is

$$t_1 = \left(\frac{P_1 a_1 - C_1 - P_2 a_2 - C_2}{N(P_1 b_1 + P_2 b_2)} \right) + \frac{P_2 b_2 T_2}{P_1 b_1 + P_2 b_2}. \tag{A.4}$$

The optimal individual vessel operation point occurs at the intersection of the curves represented by eqs. (1b) and (2b) above. Note from eq. (A.2) that

$$\frac{\partial X_i}{\partial t_i} = -b_i N. \tag{A.5}$$

By referring to the optimal amounts allocated to each stock as t_1^* and t_2^*, and by making the appropriate substitutions from eqs. (A.2) and (A.5), this interception can be represented by the following equation:

$$P_1(a_1 - b_1 N t_1^*) - P_1 t_1^* b_1 N - c_1 - \lambda$$
$$= P_2(a_2 - b_2 N t_2^*) - P_2 t_2^* b_2 N - C_2 - \lambda. \tag{A.6}$$

Again by letting $t_2^* = (T - t_1^*)$ it is possible to solve for t_1^*. The result is

$$t_1^* = \frac{(P_1 a_1 - C_1) - (P_2 a_2 - C_2)}{2N(P_1 b_1 + P_2 b_2)} + \frac{P_2 b_2 T}{P_1 b_1 + P_2 b_2}. \tag{A.7}$$

This is identical to eq. (A.4) except for the inclusion of the "2" in the denominator of the first term in each. It follows then that if

$$(P_1 a_1 - C_1) > (P_2 a_2 - C_2), \tag{A.8}$$

then

$$t_1^* < t_1. \tag{A.9}$$

Also, since $t_1^* + t_2^* = T$, then given (A.9) it must be true that in this case

$$t_2^* > t_2. \tag{A.10}$$

The reverse is also true. Note that the terms being compared in condition (A.8) are the vertical intercepts of eqs. (1a) and (2a). The economic interpretation of the two terms is the initial value of the marginal product of a day's fishing on the two stocks. Therefore, the conclusions surrounding conditions (A.8), (A.9) and (A.10) can be stated as follows. If a multi-purpose fleet is harvesting two stocks, then for any given fleet size, under open access, there will be an excess of effort applied to the one that is initially more productive.

References

Anderson, Lee G. (1975) "Analysis of Commercial Exploitation and Maximum Economic Yield in Biologically and Technologically Interdependent Fisheries, *Journal of the Fisheries Research Board of Canada*, 32, November, 1825–1942.
Anderson, Lee G. (1977) *The Economics of Fisheries Management* (Johns Hopkins University Press, Baltimore).

Baumol, William J. (1977) *Economic Theory and Operations Analysis*, 4th edn. (Prentice-Hall, Englewood Cliffs, New Jersey).

Clark, Colin W. (1973) "Economic Theory of the Multi-Species Fishery," Dept. of Mathematics, University of British Columbia, unpublished manuscript.

Clark, Colin W. (1976) *Mathematical Bioeconomics* (John Wiley and Sons, New York).

Gordon, H.S. (1954) "Economic Theory of a Common-Property Resource: The Fishery", *Journal of Political Economy*, 62, 124–142.

Huppert, Daniel D. (1979) "Implications for Multipurpose Fleets and Mixed Stocks for Control Policies," *Journal of the Fisheries Research Board of Canada*, 36, July, 845–854.

Shaeffer, M.B. (1954) "Some Aspects of the Dynamics of Populations Important to the Management of Commercial Marine Fisheries, *Inter-American Tropical Tuna Commission Bulletin*, 1, 25–56.

Schaeffer, M.B. (1957) "Some Considerations of Population Dynamics and Economics in Relation to the Management of the Commercial Marine Fisheries", *Journal of the Fisheries Research Board of Canada*, 14, May, 669–681.

Schaeffer, M.B. (1959) "Biological and Economic Aspects of the Management of Commercial Marine Fisheries", *Transactions of the American Fisheries Society*, 99, April, 100–104.

CHAPTER 12

Using the household production function in bioeconomic models

KENNETH E. McCONNELL and JON G. SUTINEN*

1. Introduction

Research in the economics of renewable resources has been primarily devoted to the study of the exploitation of these resources for commercial purposes. For example, in his estimable book, Clark (1976) is solely concerned with commercial resources. Yet renewable resource stocks can be exploited for profit or fun. Both the models and the implications of the models differ, depending on whether one addresses the commercial exploitation of renewable resources or the harvesting of these resources for recreational purposes.

A generation ago the one-sided research into commercial ventures would have been appropriate, particularly in the marine environment, because the commercial exploitation of species, measured by any yardstick, was vastly more important than the recreational exploitation. However, the growth in incomes and leisure time have continued to increase substantially the demand for recreational use of renewable resources, particularly marine fish stocks. Currently there are several important commercial stocks which are heavily harvested by recreational anglers. For example, cod in the north-west Atlantic, Pacific salmon, and striped bass up and down the East coast are species where there is considerable competition between the commercial and recreational harvestors.

*Paper presented at the conference on the Economics of Renewable Resource Management, 19–20 October, 1979, Brown University, Providence, Rhode Island.

Essays in the economics of renewable resources, edited by L.J. Mirman and D.F. Spulber
© *North-Holland Publishing Company, 1982*

There has been some work on the modelling of the bioeconomic recreational sector (for example, see Anderson, 1978; Conrad and Storey, n.d; McConnell and Sutinen, 1979). The results of these efforts suggest that the structure of recreational models is similar to commercial models. Models developed in the past have relied on the assumption that anglers respond passively to changes in fish stocks and do not directly vary the rate at which they catch fish. In this chapter we develop a bioeconomic framework using the household production function which allows recreational anglers to directly vary their catch rate and the number of fishing trips taken.

2. The household production functions and consumer's surplus

Our environment for modelling recreational fishing is simple. We assume that there are n identical anglers exploiting a single species. These anglers get utility from x, the number of trips they fish per period of time, and q, the number of fish they catch per trip. Neither q nor x is purchased directly on the market. Each is produced in the individual angler's household using inputs, some of which are purchased on the market. (The household production function model developed here is based on Bockstael and McConnell, 1978.) The household production functions for x and q are given by

$$x = x(w_1),$$ (1)

where w_1 is the vector of inputs used in producing days fishing. For example, inputs are miles travelled and days away from work or other opportunities. For fish caught per trip the production function is

$$q = q(w_2, S).$$ (2)

Here w_2 is the set of inputs which can be purchased to change the trip catch rate, for example bait, services of a boat, etc. S is an index of biomass density and clearly influences the daily catch rate. In our exposition, we assume for simplicity that the catch rate is the same for each trip. (In empirical applications, this assumption can be relaxed.)

Modelling the anglers' behavior can best be appreciated by assuming a two-step optimization approach. In the first step, the angler minimizes

$$p_1 w_1 + (p_2 w_2) \cdot x$$ (3)

subject to

$$x = x(w_1),$$
$$q = q(w_2, S),$$

where p_i are the vectors of prices for inputs w_i. The result of this minimization is a cost function

$$C = C(x, q, S, p_1, p_2),$$ (4)

where

$$C_x, C_q, C_{p_i} > 0,$$
$$C_S < 0.$$

Even though we have defined the catch rate so that it does not vary with trips, hence avoiding joint production, it is not possible to have an annual cost function such that $\partial^2 C / \partial x \partial q = 0$ (see Bockstael and McConnell, 1981, for details).[1]

In the second step, the angler maximizes consumer's surplus by choosing the optimal x and q. Consumer's surplus can be given by the line integral:

$$G(x, q, S, p_i)$$

$$= \int_R \left[f_x(x, q) - C_x(x, q, S) \right] dx + \left[f_q(x, q) - C_q(x, q, S) \right] dq$$

$$= \int_R \left[f_x(x, q) dx + f_q(x, q) dq \right] - C(x, q, S),$$ (5)

where

$f_x(x, q)$ = marginal value for trips function,
$f_q(x, q)$ = marginal value for catch rate function
R = path of integration
$\quad = (0,0)$ to (x^*, q^*), the optimal values of the choice variables.

The biological side is very simple. We suppose that the fish stock reproduces according to the growth function

$$\dot{S} = g(S),$$ (6)

where $g(S)$ is concave with a single maximum. In any period t, each angler takes $x(t)$ trips and catches $q(t)$ fish per trip. Thus, individual anglers take $q(t)x(t)$ per t and the change in the biomass for n anglers is

$$\dot{S} = g(S) - nx(t)q(t).$$ (7)

---

[1] A reasonable form of this annual cost function is

$$C(x, q, S, p_i) = a(S, p_2)q^\alpha x + t(p_1)x^\beta,$$

where $\alpha > 0$, $\beta > 0$, $a(\cdot)q^\alpha x$ is the annual cost of catching qx fish and $t(p_1)x^\beta$ is the annual cost of x trips. Here, the marginal cost of q is $\alpha a(\cdot)xq^{\alpha-1}$ and the marginal cost of x is $a(\cdot)q^\alpha + \beta t(\cdot)x^{\beta-1}$. Below, some of our results are derived for this specific cost function.

3. A behavioral model of recreational fishing

Since we are dealing with a realm of economic activity that involves nonmarket goods, it is instructive to attempt to explain economic behavior in such a setting. To do this we assume there exist n identical anglers, each choosing a number of trips and a catch rate to maximize his net benefits, given by (5).

The first-order conditions for the angler's problem are

$$G_x = f_x(x, q) - C_x(x, q, S, p_1, p_2) = 0,$$ (8)

$$G_q = f_q(x, q) - C_q(x, q, S, p_2) = 0,$$ (9)

and the second-order conditions are

$$(f_{xx} - C_{xx}) < 0,$$ (10)

$$(f_{qq} - C_{qq}) < 0,$$ (11)

$$A = \begin{vmatrix} (f_{xx} - C_{xx}) & (f_{xq} - C_{xq}) \\ (f_{xq} - C_{xq}) & (f_{qq} - C_{qq}) \end{vmatrix} > 0.$$ (12)

We assume further that under open access anglers enter and exit the fishery according to

$$\dot{n} = h(B(S, p_i)),$$ (13)

where

$$B(S, p_i) = G(x^*, q^*, S, p_i),$$
$$h' > 0, \qquad B_S > 0, \qquad B_{p_i} < 0.$$

This specification assumes either that $B(\cdot)$ includes the opportunity cost of forgone recreational alternatives, or that in $h(\cdot)$ there is a parameter representing the value of forgone recreational alternatives.

In its steady state, the fishery is represented by the following system of equations:

$$f_x(x, q) - C_x(x, q, S, p_1, p_2) = 0,$$ (14)

$$f_q(x, q) - C_q(x, q, S, p_2) = 0,$$ (15)

$$g(S) - nxq = 0,$$ (16)

$$h(B) = 0.$$ (17)

We now examine this system to derive some behavioral properties of the model.

3.1. Effects of an increase in p_1

The prices p_1 and p_2 are for the inputs used to produce trips and catch per trip, respectively. For example, p_1 may represent the price of gasoline or other transportation inputs, and p_2 may represent the price of fishing gear or bait. To determine how x, q, S and n respond to an increase in p_1, we totally differentiate (14)–(17) with respect to p_1. This yields

$$
\begin{bmatrix}
(f_{xx} - C_{xx}) & (f_{xq} - C_{xq}) & -C_{xS} & 0 \\
(f_{qx} - C_{qx}) & (f_{qq} - C_{qq}) & -C_{qS} & 0 \\
-nq & -nx & g' & -xq \\
0 & 0 & C_S & 0
\end{bmatrix}
\begin{bmatrix}
dx \\
dq \\
dS \\
dn
\end{bmatrix}
=
\begin{bmatrix}
C_{xp_1} dp_1 \\
0 \\
0 \\
-C_{p_1} dp_1
\end{bmatrix}.
$$

(18)

Using Cramer's rule to solve (18) for dS/dp_1 we obtain:

$$
\frac{dS}{dp_1} = \frac{-xqC_{p_1}
\begin{vmatrix}
(f_{xx} - C_{xx}) & (f_{xq} - C_{xq}) \\
(f_{qx} - C_{qx}) & (f_{qq} - C_{qq})
\end{vmatrix}}
{\begin{vmatrix}
(f_{xx} - C_{xx}) & (f_{xq} - C_{xq}) & -C_{xS} & 0 \\
(f_{qx} - C_{qx}) & (f_{qq} - C_{qq}) & -C_{qS} & 0 \\
-nq & -nx & g' & -xq \\
0 & 0 & C_S & 0
\end{vmatrix}}
$$

(19)

Call the determinant in the denominator of (19) D. From (12) we know the determinant in the numerator is positive, and it is easily shown that $D < 0$. Therefore, since $C_{p_1} > 0$,

$$
\frac{dS}{dp_1} = \frac{(-)(+)}{(-)} > 0.
$$

A rise in, say, the price of gasoline induces a larger stock size in the steady state. And the larger stock size will allow for a larger or smaller total catch depending on whether the stock is heavily exploited ($g' > 0$) or lightly exploited ($g' < 0$). The total catch, of course, is equal to nxq, and we now examine the effects of this price rise on each of these three factors.

$$
\frac{dx}{dp_1} = -xq\left[\overset{+}{C_{xp_1}} \overset{+}{B_S}\left(f_{qq} \overset{-}{-} C_{qq} \right) \right.
$$

$$
\left. + \overset{-}{B_{p_1}} \overset{-}{C_{qS}}\left(f_{qx} - C_{qx} \right) - \overset{-}{C_{xS}}\left(f_{qq} \overset{-}{-} C_{qq} \right) \right] / \overset{-}{D},
$$

(20)

where the sign of each term except $(f_{qx} - C_{qx})$ is indicated above the respective term. A sufficient condition for (20) to be negative is for $(f_{qx} - C_{qx}) < 0$, which holds if

$$\frac{dx}{dq} < 0. \tag{21}$$

Differentiating the angler's first-order conditions (8) and (9), holding S and p_i constant, yields:

$$\frac{dx}{dq} = \frac{-(f_{xq} - C_{xq})}{(f_{xx} - C_{xx})} .$$

It can be argued that $dx/dq < 0$ holds locally with utility held constant. Since $(f_{xx} - C_{xx}) < 0$ and $(f_{qq} - C_{qq}) < 0$ from the second-order conditions, (10) and (11), then $dx/dq < 0$, iff $(f_{xq} - C_{xq}) < 0$. For the remainder of this chapter we assume $(f_{xq} - C_{xq}) < 0$, though it may have some counterintuitive implications.[2]

Solving (18) for dq/dp_1 we find that a sufficient condition for $dq/dp_1 > 0$ is

$$\frac{C_{p_1}}{C_{xp_1}} - \frac{C_S}{C_{xS}} < 0; \tag{22}$$

otherwise the sign of dq/dp_1 is ambiguous.[3] That is, a rise in the price of gasoline will insure a rise in the catch if the "relative stock effect", $-C_S/C_{xs} < 0$, dominates the "relative price effect", $C_{p_1}/C_{xp_1} > 0$. If not, the catch rate could fall even though the stock size becomes (unambiguously) larger. Furthermore, observe that this result is independent of whether $g'(S)$ is positive or negative.

Solving (18) for dn/dp_1, and after considerable manipulation, we obtain:

$$\frac{dn}{dp_1} = -\left\{ nq[1-\varepsilon]\left\{ C_{p_1}\left[C_{qS}(f_{xq} - C_{xq}) \right.\right.\right.$$

$$\left.\left. + C_{xS}(f_{qq} - C_{qq}) \right] + C_S C_{xp_1}(f_{qq} - C_{qq}) \right\}$$

$$\left. + C_{p_1} g'(S)\cdot A \right\}/D, \tag{23}$$

[2] Namely, that a rise in the catch rate per trip reduces the marginal net benefits of a trip.
[3]
$$\frac{dq}{dp_1} = xq\left\{ (f_{xq} - C_{xq})C_{xS}C_{xp_1}\left[\frac{C_{p_1}}{C_{xp_1}} - \frac{C_S}{C_{xS}} \right] - C_{qS}C_{p_1}(f_{xx} - C_{xx}) \right\}/D.$$

where $\varepsilon = -xdq/qdx$, the elasticity of substitution in consumption between q and x. If $\varepsilon = 1$, as estimated by Stevens (1966) for salmon, then the sign of dn/dp_1 depends solely on whether the fishery is heavily exploited or lightly exploited. If heavily exploited, $g'(S) > 0$ and $dn/dp_1 > 0$; if lightly exploited, $g'(S) < 0$ and $dn/dp_1 < 0$. If $\varepsilon < 1$, as estimated by Goodreau (1977) for striped bass, then $dn/dp_1 > 0$ unambiguously if the fishery is heavily exploited, $g'(S) > 0$. If $\varepsilon > 1$, then $dn/dp_1 < 0$ unambiguously if the fishery is lightly exploited, $g'(S) < 0$.

If sign $(1-\varepsilon) = $ sign $g'(S)$, then

$$\text{sign} \frac{dn}{dp_1} = \text{sign}(1-\varepsilon),$$

otherwise sign (dn/dp_1) is ambiguous.

Further insight into the changes of x, q and n may be obtained by recalling that in the steady state $g(S) = nxq$. Therefore

$$g'(S)dS = nxdq + nqdx + xqdn,$$

or rearranging terms,

$$\frac{dn}{n} = \frac{g'(S)}{g(S)} dS - \frac{dx}{x}[1-\varepsilon]. \tag{24}$$

Eq. (24) shows clearly the roles of $g'(S)$ and ε in determining the change in the number of anglers, n.

3.2. Effects of an increase in p_2

To determine how x, q, S and n respond to an increase in p_2, we totally differentiate (14)–(17) with respect to p_2. This yields:

$$\begin{bmatrix} (f_{xx} - C_{xx}) & (f_{xq} - C_{xq}) & -C_{xS} & 0 \\ (f_{qx} - C_{qx}) & (f_{qq} - C_{qq}) & -C_{qS} & 0 \\ -nq & -nx & g' & -xq \\ 0 & 0 & C_S & 0 \end{bmatrix} \begin{bmatrix} dx \\ dq \\ dS \\ dn \end{bmatrix} = \begin{bmatrix} C_{xp_2}dp_2 \\ C_{qp_2}dp_2 \\ 0 \\ -C_{p_2}dp_2 \end{bmatrix}. \tag{25}$$

Solving (25) for dS/dp_2 yields:

$$\frac{dS}{dp_2} = \frac{-xqC_{p_2} \cdot A}{D} > 0.$$

As with p_1, an increase in p_2 also induces a larger stock size in the steady state.

The remaining comparative statics results for this case are as follows:

$$\frac{\mathrm{d}x}{\mathrm{d}p_2} = \frac{-xqC_SC_{p_2}}{D}\left\{(f_{xq}-C_{xq})\left[\frac{C_{qp_2}}{C_{p_2}}-\frac{C_{qS}}{C_S}\right]\right.$$
$$\left.-(f_{qq}-C_{qq})\left[\frac{C_{xp_2}}{C_{p_2}}-\frac{C_{xS}}{C_S}\right]\right\}, \tag{26}$$

$$\frac{\mathrm{d}q}{\mathrm{d}p_2} = \frac{xqC_SC_{p_2}}{D}\left\{(f_{xx}-C_{xx})\left[\frac{C_{qp_2}}{C_{p_2}}-\frac{C_{qS}}{C_S}\right]\right.$$
$$\left.-(f_{xq}-C_{xq})\left[\frac{C_{xp_2}}{C_{p_2}}-\frac{C_{xS}}{C_S}\right]\right\}, \tag{27}$$

$$\frac{\mathrm{d}n}{\mathrm{d}p_2} = \frac{nC_{p_2}C_S(f_{xq}-C_{xq})}{D}$$
$$\times\left\{x\left[1-\frac{1}{\varepsilon}\right]\left[\frac{C_{xp_2}}{C_{p_2}}-\frac{C_{xS}}{C_S}\right]+q[1-\varepsilon]\left[\frac{C_{qp_2}}{C_{p_2}}-\frac{C_{xS}}{C_S}\right]\right\}$$
$$\times\frac{-C_{p_2}g'(S)\cdot A}{D}. \tag{28}$$

Since (26), (27) and (28) are difficult, if not impossible, to sign without additional information, assume that the cost function takes the following specific form:

$$C(x,q,S,p_1,p_2)=a(S,p_2)q^\alpha x+t(p_1)x^\beta, \tag{29}$$

where $\alpha>0$, $\beta>0$, $a_S<0$, $a_{p_2}>0$, $t_{p_1}>0$. Here, costs are comprised of fishing costs per trip, $a(S,p_2)q^\alpha$, times the number of trips per period, plus trip costs in the period, $t(p_1)x^\beta$. This empirically plausible form of the cost function results in

$$\left[\frac{C_{qp_2}}{C_{p_2}}-\frac{C_{qS}}{C_S}\right]=\left[\frac{C_{xp_2}}{C_{p_2}}-\frac{C_{xS}}{C_S}\right]=0. \tag{30}$$

When (30) is substituted into (26)–(28), we find that

$$\frac{dx}{dp_2} = 0, \tag{31}$$

$$\frac{dq}{dp_2} = 0, \tag{32}$$

$$\frac{dn}{dp_2} = \frac{-C_{p_2}g'(S)\cdot A}{D}, \tag{33}$$

or

$$\text{sign}\frac{dn}{dp_2} = \text{sign } g'(S). \tag{34}$$

These results mean that an increase in, say, the price of fishing gear has no effect on the catch rate nor on the number of trips anglers take. The only effect is on the number of anglers. If the fishery is lightly exploited, $g'(S)<0$, and the number of anglers decreases; if heavily exploited, $g'(S)>0$, and the number of anglers increases. Such effects are not immediately intuitively obvious.

The highly conditional nature of the comparative statics results are disturbing indeed. The results clearly demonstrate the difficulty of explaining economic behavior in recreational fisheries.

4. Optimal management of recreational fishing

A central management authority, we assume, would maximize the discounted value of the stream of net benefits from the recreational harvest. This discounted value of net benefits is given by

$$\int_0^\infty e^{-\delta t} n\left\{ \int_R \left[f_x(x,q)dx + f_q(x,q)dq \right] - C(x,q,S) \right\}, \tag{35}$$

where δ is the instantaneous social discount rate and $\int_R$ is the line integral with the path of integration going from $(0,0)$ to (x^*,q^*). The authority's problem is to maximize (35) subject to (7), the resource constraint. The current value Hamiltonian for this problem is

$$H = n\int_R \left[f_x(x,q)dx + f_q(x,q)dq \right] - nC(x,q,S) + \lambda[g(S) - nxq]. \tag{36}$$

The necessary conditions for an interior maximum include:

$$f_x(x, q) - C_x(x, q, S) - \lambda q = 0, \tag{37}$$

$$f_q(x, q) - C_q(x, q, S) - \lambda x = 0, \tag{38}$$

$$G(x, q, S) - \lambda xq = 0, \tag{39}$$

$$\dot{\lambda} = \delta\lambda + nC_S(x, q, S) - \lambda g'(S), \tag{40}$$

$$\dot{S} = g(S) - nxq \tag{41}$$

Since conditions analogous to these have been interpreted extensively in the commercial fisheries literature we will not examine them in detail here. For present purposes we solve for the imputed marginal social value of the fish stock, λ, in the steady state:

$$\lambda = \frac{nC_S(x, q, S)}{g'(S) - \delta}. \tag{42}$$

To determine the optimal allocation between commercial and recreational users of the fishery we modify the above model as follows. Let $F(Q)$ be the inverse demand function for commercially harvested fish, where Q is the quantity of the commercial harvest per period. Total costs of the commercial harvest are represented by $K(Q, S)$. The sum of producers' and consumers' surplus in the commercial sector, therefore, is given by

$$\int_0^{Q^*} \left[F(Q) - K_Q(Q, S) \right] dQ,$$

where Q^* is the optimal commercial catch rate.

The problem for the central management authority is to maximize the total surplus from both the commercial and recreational sectors. That is, the problem is to maximize

$$\int_0^\infty e^{-\delta t} \left\{ n \int_R \left[f_x dx + f_q dq \right] - nC(x, q, S) \right.$$

$$\left. + \int_0^{Q^*} \left[F(Q) - K_Q(Q, S) \right] dQ \right\}$$

subject to

$$\dot{S} = g(S) - nxq - Q.$$

The steady-state marginal value of the fish stock is now

$$\lambda = \frac{nC_S(x, q, S) + K_S(Q, S)}{g' - \delta}.$$ (43)

As pointed out in an earlier paper (McConnell and Sutinen, 1979), any optimal management program would require an estimate of the marginal value of the fish stock. Eqs. (42) and (43) indicate that the estimation problems for λ are not further complicated by incorporating household production functions in the model.

5. Implications for research and management

The household production function approach lets us describe more realistically anglers' behavior. However, the superior description comes at a cost of increasing the empirical problem of the estimated household demand function for fishing. While we can live with the incomplete conceptual complexity, it is questionable whether we can adequately handle the econometric implications (for a description of these complexities, see Bockstael and McConnell, 1981). Hence, it seems desirable to test whether it is possible to estimate the model implied by the household production function approach. Such a test will be equivalent to testing whether catch rate is endogenous.

The comparative statics results for the household production function model are so ambiguous that they provide little guidance for policy. It seems likely that the costs of enforcing the regulatory scheme which can discriminate between exogenous and endogenous catch rates would far outweigh the benefits of the scheme. Such a conclusion should not be taken as pessimistic. It is simply that the household production function is not yet ready to leave the academic womb.

References

Anderson, L. (1978) "Common Property and Non-existant Markets for Output: An Integration of the Economic Theory of Recreational and Commercial Fisheries", Department of Economics, University of Delaware, mimeo.

Bockstael, N.E. and K.E. McConnell (1981) "Theory and Estimation of the Household Production Function for Wildlife Recreation", *Journal of Environmental Economics and Management*, 8, 199–214.

Clark, C.W. (1976) *Mathematical Bioeconomics: The Optimal Management of Renewable Resources* (Wiley–Interscience, New York).

Conrad, J.M., and D.A. Storey (n.d.) "Allocation of a Renewable Resource Between Recreational and Commercial Users", Department of Food and Resource Economics, University of Massachusetts, mimeo.

Goodreau, L.J. (1977) "Willingness to Pay for Striped Bass Sportfishing in Rhode Island", M.A. Thesis, University of Rhode Island.

McConnell, K.E. and J.G. Sutinen (1979) "Bioeconomic Models of Marine Recreational Fishing", *Journal of Environmental Economics and Management*, 6, 127–139.

Stevens, J.B. (1966) "Angler Success as a Quality Determinant of Sport Fishing Recreational Values", *Transactions of the American Fishing Society*, 95, 357–362.

PART VI

GAME THEORY AND THE FREE-ACCESS FISHERY

Introduction to Part VI

An important aspect of the theory of renewable resources is the interaction between a small number of "competitors", for example countries competing for fish in international waters or fish species competing among themselves, e.g. predator–prey relationships. In modelling the economics of the exploitation of any natural resource, the effect of this type of competition should play a central role. In particular, when these relationships are taken into account the model must incorporate strategic behavior explicitly. A natural way to model this strategic behavior is through the theory of games, and the Nash equilibrium concept. Hence, the natural extension of the dynamic optimization technique in the theory of renewable resources is the use of dynamic games and stochastic games. These techniques are the main focus of the chapters that make up Part VI.

The "Great Fish War", by Levhari and Mirman, considers competition between two countries for the use of natural resources in international waters. This is particularly interesting in view of the developments of the last several years which have witnessed the universal adoption of the two hundred mile fishing limit. Moreover, there have been several near serious altercations between several countries, e.g. England and Iceland or the United States and Canada. Levhari and Mirman emphasize the strategic aspects of the behavior of the participants, and obtain, in an example, explicit optimal harvesting policies. The chapter demonstrates that strategic competition increases the total catch for each level of the stock over the level it would have been if the countries had cooperated. This leads to a lower-steady level of the stock, which implies a steady state with less fish and less consumption of fish under the cooperative solution. Moreover, this type of strategic behavior may lead to a depletion of the stock in situations in which cooperative behavior does not. This example shows that profound changes in behavior occur due to strategic behavior.

Strategic behavior is also important when there are several species of fish and the dynamics of each species depends upon the interactions of these stocks both for predator–prey models or competition for prey models. Moreover, if the dynamic behavior of the stock is stochastic then a stochastic games formulation of the problem, using the Nash equilibrium concept, is applicable. Such a model is studied by Sobel in Chapter 14, "Stochastic Fishery Games with Myopic Equilibrium". The focus of Sobel's chapter is the existence of an equilibrium. The main result is the existence of a myopic equilibrium under rather weak conditions, one of which is the assumption that there is a separate sub-industry harvesting each species. The existence result is valid in the case of pure strategies. However, it is also shown that it can be extended to the case of random strategies. Finally, it is shown that a repeated static equilibrium is also an equilibrium for the dynamic game.

CHAPTER 13

The great fish war: An example using a dynamic Cournot–Nash solution*

DAVID LEVHARI and LEONARD J. MIRMAN[†]

1. Introduction

In recent years we have witnessed numerous international conflicts about fishing rights in various seas and water zones. The most well-known conflict is the "Cod War" between Iceland and the United Kingdom. These conflicts have much wider scope and motives than those which are captured by our simple model. Yet the model sheds some light on the economic implications inherent in the fishing conflicts and also in other duopolistic or oligopolistic situations in which the decisions of the participants have an effect on the evolution of the underlying population of interest, which in our model is fish.

Our model has two basic features. First, there is the strategic aspect: each of the participants must take account of the actions of the other participant. The second feature is that the underlying population is changing, so that the actions of both participants affect the future size or rate of growth of the fish population. In effect, these two features together create a dynamic externality which is the essence of the problem being studied. Although there are many areas of economics to which this type of model is applicable,

*The Bell Journal of Economics, vol. 11, no. 1, Spring 1980, pp. 322–334, Copyright 1980, The American Telephone and Telegraph Company. Reprinted with permission from The Bell Journal of Economics.

†Research support from National Science Foundation under grant SOC 76-11583 and U.S.–Israel BSF 1828-79 is gratefully acknowledged.

Essays in the economics of renewable resources, edited by L.J. Mirman and D.F. Spulber
© North-Holland Publishing Company, 1982

e.g. imperfect competition among firms or macroeconomic stabilization, the fishing context will be used for expository reasons.

The dynamics of the fish population is a natural phenomenon governed by the "law of growth" for fish.[1] The economics of natural resources, and fishing, in particular, has been studied quite extensively during the last several years. In particular, the pioneering works of Gordon (1954), Scott (1955), and Smith (1968) have been especially important. These papers use the natural dynamics of the fish population to study the economic implications of fishing for the population of fish. While these authors develop positive models, the more recent literature, which is concerned with normative models, uses dynamic optimization techniques to study the optimal rate of extraction of fish and its long-run implications. The papers of Clark (1971), Clark and Munro (1975), Long (1977), and Levhari, Michener and Mirman (1978) study various aspects of optimal fishing policies and their effect on the size or possible depletion of the fish population.[2] There are, then, several ways to study dynamic models of fishing.

The point of view of this chapter is that the object of each country is to maximize the sum of discounted utilities.[3] The maximization technique used is essentially discrete-time dynamic programming, which in this context is a discrete time analogue of a differential game. Differential games are useful for modelling many economic problems which involve both dynamics and strategic behavior and have been recently surveyed by Clemhout and Wan (1978).[4]

To capture the strategic aspects in our model, we assume that each of the participants acts as a Cournot duopolist in a dynamic framework and takes the policy of the other participant as given, while trying to maximize his own discounted sum of utilities. The two players may have different subjective discount factors. It is quite possible, of course, that one of the major elements in the fishing conflict is the different time preferences of the participants. However, as we show, in the present model, this difference in

---

[1] For a discussion of the laws of biological growth see Lotka (1956).

[2] Much, although not all of this literature, is discussed in Clark (1976) or the surveys of Smith (1977) and Fisher and Peterson (1976).

[3] Discounted profit maximization is another criterion which is often used; unfortunately, in the present context, *a second externality is introduced by this criterion*. If profit maximization were the objective, then each country would have to consider the effect of the other countries' catch on the current market price, the "market" externality, as well as on the future fish population, the dynamic externality. These two externalities combined make the analysis very difficult.

[4] Moreover several recent papers have used dynamic dominant player models to study the economics of imperfect competition; see, for example, Kydland (1977a).

subjective time preferences is quite consistent with the existence of a stable equilibrium.

To study the dynamic duopoly problem in its most simplified form we shall make several assumptions. In particular, we assume that only economic considerations count. Moreover, threats are not allowed, so that actions based on retaliation for behavior in the past will not be considered. Finally, each country is interested in the maximization of the welfare of its own citizens: the catch cannot be used for resale or for profit.

The structure of the dynamic Cournot equilibrium used in this chapter is similar to the simple duopoly problem first studied by Cournot in the static context. Although it may be interpreted in a dynamic context, the original Cournot solution is static in nature, as is made clear by the Nash analysis in the theory of games. In the context of the fishing model, however, there is a true dynamic structure to the problem. In particular, the fish population responds in a natural way to the quantity of fish extracted by both countries. Hence, although each period's equilibrium is a Cournot–Nash solution, there may be a change in the size of the fish population. Moreover, the sequence of decisions by both countries is in fact itself a Cournot–Nash equilibrium, even though the fish population need not be in equilibrium. In this framework it is natural to ask whether or not the size of the fish population eventually settles down to an equilibrium in the dynamic sense. This equilibrium will be referred to as a steady-state equilibrium. It is desirable to keep the two notions of equilibrium separate. The system which will be studied in this chapter is always in equilibrium in the Cournot–Nash sense, while it may or may not be in a steady state equilibrium.

We derive the infinite horizon Cournot–Nash policies by finding finite horizon Cournot–Nash policies and letting the horizon tend to infinity. The size of the fish population under the influence of these infinite horizon Cournot–Nash policies is also studied. We show in the context of an example, that a positive finite steady state is eventually attained. Moreover, we derive for this example a closed-form solution for both the Cournot–Nash policy functions and the steady-state quantity of fish. These Cournot–Nash policy functions and the steady-state quantity of fish are then compared with the optimal policy functions and the optimal steady-state quantity of fish when both countries form a cooperative venture and pool their resources. We find, not surprisingly since it is utility that is maximized, that the Cournot–Nash policies imply a greater harvest of fish, and therefore, a smaller steady state.

Finally, we apply these same techniques to several special cases. For example, we study the von Stackelberg case with a leader–follower structure. This example is especially interesting since it is applicable to areas of government policy-making (Kydland and Prescott, 1977) and to imperfect competition among firms (Kydland, 1977a, 1977b; Brock, 1975). We also give a linear example which shows that it is possible for the stock to grow infinitely large under a cooperative solution, while under a Cournot–Nash solution the stock tends to zero.

2. The model

Let x_t be the quantity of fish at time t. Suppose that, if uninterrupted, the quantity of fish would grow according to the biological rule

$$x_{t+1} = x_t^\alpha, \qquad 0 < \alpha < 1. \tag{1}$$

Thus, one easily observes that $x_t = = x_{t+1} = 1,$[5] is a stable steady state of the fish population (See fig. 13.1). Suppose, however, that two countries fish the waters. Each country has a utility for the fish it catches in each period and thus an interest in the long-run effect of its present catch. Moreover, each country must take the catch of the other country into consideration when deciding on its own catch. The former consideration is accounted for by using a dynamic programming argument, and the latter by using the concept of a Cournot–Nash equilibrium. To be more precise, suppose that country i has a utility function u_i for present consumption. Let c_i be the present consumption of country i and suppose that the utility function of country i is logarithmic, i.e. $u_i(c_i) = \log c_i$. Let $0 < \beta_i < 1$ be the discount factor for country i. Suppose, moreover, that the objective of each country is to maximize the sum of the discounted utility of fish.

Consider the problem in the context of a finite horizon. Assume that if there were no future period, each country would get[6] an equal share (or any other prescribed share) of all the remaining fish. The initial level of fish is given by x. If there is a *one-period horizon*[7] and if country 1 takes country 2's actions as given, the optimal response for country 1 is found from the maximization problem

$$\max_{0 \le c_1 \le x - c_2} \left\{ \log c_1 + \beta_1 \log \tfrac{1}{2}(x - c_1 - c_2)^\alpha \right\}$$
$$= \max_{0 \le c_1 \le x - c_2} \left\{ \log c_1 + \alpha\beta_1 \log(x - c_1 - c_2) + \beta_1 \log \tfrac{1}{2} \right\}, \tag{2}$$

---

[5] A normalization of the fish population is employed for expositional purposes.
[6] This assumption actually plays no role in the derivation of the Cournot–Nash policies, as will become clear below.
[7] Note that here horizon refers to the number of future periods. Hence, a one-period horizon problem is in fact a two-period maximization problem.

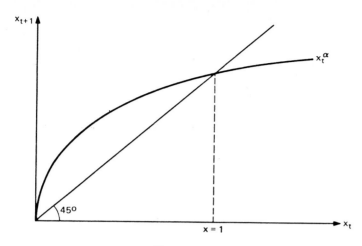

Figure 13.1

where c_1 is the optimal present consumption of country 1, given the consumption c_2 of country 2. The value $x - c_1 - c_2$ is the remaining stock of fish which becomes $(x - c_1 - c_2)^\alpha$ in the next period. The first-order condition for this problem is

$$(1 + \alpha\beta_1)c_1 + c_2 = x. \tag{3}$$

Eq. (3) represents the reaction curve of country 1.

Using a similar argument for country 2, the optimal response is given by

$$c_1 + (1 + \alpha\beta_2)c_2 = x. \tag{4}$$

These policies are depicted in fig. 13.2, as the reaction functions for each of the countries. The Cournot–Nash $\bar{c}_1, \bar{c}_2$ is the intersection of these two reaction functions.

In this case, the Cournot–Nash equilibrium is given by the simultaneous solution of eqs. (3) and (4). The solution, as seen in fig. 13.2, is

$$\bar{c} = \frac{\alpha\beta_2}{\alpha^2\beta_1\beta_2 + \alpha\beta_1 + \alpha\beta_2} x, \tag{5}$$

and

$$\bar{c}_2 = \frac{\alpha\beta_1}{\alpha^2\beta_1\beta_2 + \alpha\beta_1 + \alpha\beta_2} x. \tag{6}$$

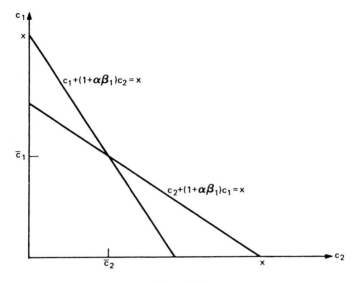

Figure 13.2

The remaining stock of fish is then given by

$$x - \bar{c}_1 - \bar{c}_2 = \frac{\alpha^2 \beta_1 \beta_2}{\alpha^2 \beta_1 \beta_2 + \alpha \beta_1 + \alpha \beta_2} x. \tag{7}$$

Next consider a two-period horizon problem with the first country again reacting to the second country in the present under the *assumption* that in the future the one-period horizon Cournot–Nash solution, given above, will prevail. To solve this problem we must find a one-period horizon Cournot–Nash "valuation" function. To find it, consider the one-period horizon objective function of country 1 under the Cournot–Nash equilibrium given above (or the one-period "valuation" function):

$$\log \bar{c}_1 + \beta_1 \log \tfrac{1}{2} + \alpha \beta_1 \log(\bar{x} - \bar{c}_1 - \bar{c}_2) = (1 + \alpha \beta_1) \log x + A_1,$$

where

$$A_1 = \log \frac{(\alpha \beta_2)(\alpha^2 \beta_1 \beta_2)^{\alpha \beta_1}}{(\alpha^2 \beta_1 \beta_2 + \alpha \beta_1 + \alpha \beta_2)^{1 + \alpha \beta_1}} + \beta_1 \log \tfrac{1}{2}.$$

Notice that A_1 is a constant (independent of x) and will have no effect on the optimal policy. Hence, the objective function for the two-period horizon problem is

$$\log c_1 + \alpha\beta_1(1+\alpha\beta_1)\log(x-c_1-c_2)+A_1.^8 \tag{8}$$

Again the optimal response c_1 of country 1 corresponding to the decision c_2 of country 2 satisfies the first-order condition

$$(1+\alpha\beta_1+\alpha^2\beta_1^2)c_1+c_2=x. \tag{9}$$

Similarly, the optimal response for country 2 is given by

$$c_1+(1+\alpha\beta_2+\alpha^2\beta_2^2)c_2=x. \tag{10}$$

Once again, by solving (9) and (10) as a simultaneous system, we can find the Cournot–Nash equilibrium for the two-period horizon case.

The process can be repeated for an n-period horizon yielding the Cournot–Nash policies,

$$\bar{c}_1 = \frac{\alpha\beta_2\left[\sum\limits_{j=0}^{n-1}(\alpha\beta_2)^j\right]x}{\left(\sum\limits_{j=0}^{n}(\alpha\beta_1)^j\right)\left(\sum\limits_{j=0}^{n}(\alpha\beta_2)^j\right)-1}, \tag{11}$$

$$\bar{c}_2 = \frac{\alpha\beta_1\left[\sum\limits_{j=0}^{n-1}(\alpha\beta_1)^j\right]x}{\left(\sum\limits_{j=0}^{n}(\alpha\beta_1)^j\right)\left(\sum\limits_{j=0}^{n}(\alpha\beta_2)^j\right)-1}, \tag{12}$$

and

$$x-\bar{c}_1-\bar{c}_2 = \frac{\alpha^2\beta_1\beta_2\left(\sum\limits_{j=0}^{n-1}(\alpha\beta_1)^j\right)\left(\sum\limits_{j=0}^{n-1}(\alpha\beta_2)^j\right)x}{\left(\sum\limits_{j=0}^{n}(\alpha\beta_1)^j\right)\left(\sum\limits_{j=0}^{n}(\alpha\beta_2)^j\right)-1}. \tag{13}$$

[8] Note we have let c_1 be the optimal reaction and $\bar{c}_1$ be the Cournot–Nash policy in the first period under both a one- and a two-period horizon. They will in fact be different, with the length of the horizon playing an essential role. However, the context should make clear which horizon is being used and no confusion should arise.

As the horizon tends to infinity, the limiting values of $\bar{c}_1$, $\bar{c}_2$ and $x - \bar{c}_1 - \bar{c}_2$ are:

$$\bar{c}_1 = \frac{\alpha\beta_2(1 - \alpha\beta_1)x}{1 - (1 - \alpha\beta_1)(1 - \alpha\beta_2)}, \tag{14}$$

$$\bar{c}_2 = \frac{\alpha\beta_1(1 - \alpha\beta_2)x}{1 - (1 - \alpha\beta_1)(1 - \alpha\beta_2)}, \tag{15}$$

and

$$x - \bar{c}_1 - \bar{c}_2 = \frac{\alpha^2\beta_1\beta_2 x}{\alpha\beta_1 + \alpha\beta_2 - \alpha^2\beta_1\beta_2}. \tag{16}$$

Equations (14) and (15) represent consumption policies for countries 1 and 2, respectively, when an infinite horizon is considered, while eq. (16) represents both countries' combined investment policy for fish. Note that these policies are applicable in each period and no longer depend upon the length of the horizon. Hence, these policies may be used in deriving the dynamic behavior of the stock of fish from which the steady-state solution may be found. Let $x_0 > 0$ be any initial stock of fish. Under a Cournot–Nash equilibrium the dynamic equation for fish becomes

$$x_{t+1} = [x_t - c_1(x_t) - c_2(x_t)]^\alpha. \tag{17}$$

In particular,

$$x_1 = [x_0 - c_1(x_0) - c_2(x_0)]^\alpha = \left(\frac{\alpha^2\beta_1\beta_2}{\alpha\beta_1 + \alpha\beta_2 - \alpha^2\beta_1\beta_2}\right)^\alpha x_0^\alpha,$$

---

[9]It can be shown that for the infinite-horizon maximization problem for both countries, the optimal policies satisfy the following functional equations.

$$\begin{array}{l} i, j = 1, 2 \\ i \neq j \end{array} \quad u_i'(g_i(x)) = \beta_i u_i'[g_i(f(x - g_1(x) - g_2(x)))]f'(x - g_1(x) - g_2(x))[1 - g_j'],$$

where u_i represents the one period utility of country i, $f(x)$ is the growth function, and $g_i(x)$ is the Cournot–Nash policy function for country i. In our example $u_i(x) = \log x$, $f(x) = x^\alpha$. Setting $g_1(x) = \lambda_1 x$ and $g_2(x) = \lambda_2 x$, we find the set of two linear equations:

$$\lambda_1 + (1 - \alpha\beta_1)\lambda_2 = 1 - \alpha\beta_1 \quad \text{and} \quad (1 - \alpha\beta_2)\lambda_1 + \lambda_2 = 1 - \alpha\beta_2.$$

Therefore,

$$\lambda_1 = \frac{(1 - \alpha\beta_1)\alpha\beta_2}{1 - (1 - \alpha\beta_1)(1 - \alpha\beta_2)} \quad \text{and} \quad \lambda_2 = \frac{(1 - \alpha\beta_2)\alpha\beta_1}{1 - (1 - \alpha\beta_1)(1 - \alpha\beta_2)}.$$

A different approach has been followed in the paper, since to justify, even intuitively, the functional equations would be a lengthy procedure.

and

$$x_2 = \left(\frac{\alpha^2 \beta_1 \beta_2}{\alpha\beta_1 + \alpha\beta_2 - \alpha^2\beta_1\beta_2} \right)^{\alpha + \alpha^2} x_0^{\alpha 2}.$$

In general,

$$x_t = \left[\frac{\alpha^2 \beta_1 \beta_2}{\alpha\beta_1 + \alpha\beta_2 - \alpha^2\beta_1\beta_2} \right]^{\sum_{j=1}^{t} \alpha^j} x_0^{\alpha t}. \tag{18}$$

Hence,

$$\lim_{t \to \infty} x_t = \left[\frac{\alpha^2 \beta_1 \beta_2}{\alpha\beta_1 + \alpha\beta_2 - \alpha^2\beta_1\beta_2} \right]^{\alpha/(1-\alpha)} = \bar{x}, \tag{19}$$

where $0 < \bar{x} < 1$ (notice that $0 < \alpha\beta_1, \alpha\beta_2 < 1$).

Thus the "volume" of fish x_t converges to a steady-state level $\bar{x}$. The steady-state level may be rewritten as

$$\bar{x} = \left(\frac{1}{\dfrac{1}{\alpha\beta_1} + \dfrac{1}{\alpha\beta_2} - 1} \right)^{\alpha/(1-\alpha)} \tag{20}$$

This dynamic behavior is illustrated in fig. 13.3. From (20) observe that the

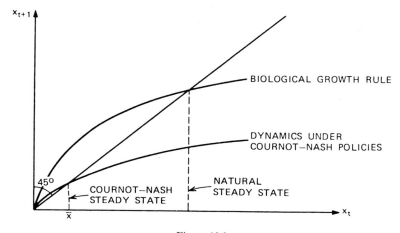

Figure 13.3

higher $\beta_i (i = 1,2)$ – that is, the higher the discount factor of either country – the higher the steady-state level of fish $\bar{x}$. If both countries have the same rate of time preference so that $\beta_1 = \beta_2 = \beta$, the steady state is

$$\bar{x} = \left(\frac{1}{\dfrac{2}{\alpha\beta} - 1} \right)^{\alpha/(1-\alpha)} = \left(\frac{\alpha\beta}{2 - \alpha\beta} \right)^{\alpha/(1-\alpha)}. \tag{21}$$

Let us compare the Nash–Cournot steady state with the steady-state solution to the problem when the countries combine their take so as to maximize the discounted sum of both countries' utilities. The identical rate of time preference serves as the common discounting factor.

If the countries plan for an infinite number of periods, then the optimal policy in any period can be found from the equation

$$x - 2c = \alpha\beta x.^{10} \tag{22}$$

Here the entire catch is $2c$, while c is the part of the catch consumed by each country. Under this policy the dynamic equation is

$$x_{t+1} = (\alpha\beta x_t)^\alpha \tag{23}$$

and the steady-state quantity of fish[11] is

$$\hat{x} = (\alpha\beta)^{\alpha/(1-\alpha)}. \tag{24}$$

---

[10] The objective function for this "cooperative" solution, assuming both countries are identical, is

$$\max_{\{c_0,\dots,c_t,\dots\}} \sum_{t=0}^{\infty} \beta^t \{2u(c_t)\}$$

subject to $x_t + 2c_t = f(x_{t-1})$, $t = 0,\dots$, and the initial output $x = f(x_{-1})$. For this problem the optimal policy must satisfy the equations

$$2u'(c_t) = \beta 2u'(c_{t+1})f'(x_t), \qquad t = 0,\dots.$$

Letting $u(c) = \log c$ and $f(x) = x^\alpha$, it follows that

$$\frac{1}{c_t} = \frac{\alpha\beta}{c_{t+1}} x_t^{\alpha-1}. \tag{i}$$

It is clear that if $f(x_{t-1}) = x$, then $c_t = \lambda x$, $c_{t+1} = \lambda(x - \lambda x)^\alpha = \lambda x^\alpha (1-\lambda)^\alpha$, and $x_t = (1-\lambda)x$. Eq. (22) follows from equation (i) by replacing c_t, c_{t+1}, x_t and solving for λ. Also, compare this with the discussion in footnote 9.

[11] The *steady-state level* under joint management is identical in the present example to that achieved when there is just one country with the aim of maximizing

$$\sum_{t=0}^{x} \beta^t \log c_t$$

Comparing the steady-state quantity of fish with that of the Cournot–Nash duopoly, one easily observes that

$$\hat{x} = (\alpha\beta)^{\alpha/(1-\alpha)} > \left(\frac{\alpha\beta}{2-\alpha\beta}\right)^{\alpha/(1-\alpha)} = \bar{x}. \tag{25}$$

Hence, as expected, a Cournot–Nash duopoly implies a smaller steady-state quantity of fish.

Note that in the steady state the constant level of fish consumed by each country in the Cournot–Nash case is

$$
\begin{aligned}
c_N &= \frac{\alpha\beta(1-\alpha\beta)}{1-(1-\alpha\beta)(1-\alpha\beta)} \left(\frac{\alpha\beta}{2-\alpha\beta}\right)^{\alpha/(1-\alpha)} \\
&= \left(\frac{1-\alpha\beta}{2-\alpha\beta}\right) \left(\frac{\alpha\beta}{2-\alpha\beta}\right)^{\alpha/(1-\alpha)}.
\end{aligned} \tag{26}
$$

Under joint exploitation of the seas' resources, the steady-state level of catch of each country is:

$$c_j = \left(\frac{1-\alpha\beta}{2}\right)(\alpha\beta)^{\alpha/(1-\alpha)}. \tag{27}$$

It is not difficult to verify that $c_J > c_N$; that is, by combined management the two countries will consume, for each level of the population of fish, smaller quantities of fish, but will be able to achieve a higher "permanent" catch. Hence, the conflict implicit in the duopoly problem leads both countries to overconsume, with less left for future generations.

3. Extensions

In section 2 we assumed that the two countries operate either as Cournot duopolists or as "good neighbors" exploiting jointly the "fruits of the sea". Another possibility which has been raised in the duopoly literature is that one of the countries is "sophisticated" while the other is "naive". This is a dynamic version of the von Stackelberg duopoly analysis. The "sophisticated" country takes into account its ability to manipulate the other

---

subject to $x_{t+1} = (x_t - c_t)^\alpha$. The steady-state catch of both countries (combined) is the same as that of a single country with the same utility function. This seems to stem from the logarithmic form of the utility function since the utility of twice the catch does not affect the optimal size of the catch. Moreover, doubling the utility has no effect on the optimal size of the catch. However, it is more generally true, since in the joint management case only technological consideration and the rate of discount determine the steady state.

country's output, while the "naive" country follows the same Cournot-type assumption as made above. For definiteness we assume that country 1 is the "leader", while country 2 is the "follower".

The aim of the follower with a one-period horizon (assuming that in the last period there is a given rule of division, possibly each receiving $x/2$) is

$$\max_{0 \leqslant c_2 \leqslant x - c_1} \{\log c_2 + \alpha\beta_2 \log(x - c_1 - c_2)\}. \tag{28}$$

Operating in Cournot fashion, taking c_1 as given, the first-order condition for country 2 is

$$c_2 = \frac{x - c_1}{1 + \alpha\beta_2}. \tag{29}$$

Country 1 takes the policy of the second country as given and thus its aim with a one-period horizon is

$$\max_{c_1} \left\{ \log c_1 + \alpha\beta_1 \log\left(x - c_1 - \frac{x - c_1}{1 + \alpha\beta_2}\right) \right\}. \tag{30}$$

Notice that the aim of country 1 is similar to that of a monopolist. The first-order condition is

$$c_1 = \frac{1}{1 + \alpha\beta_1} x. \tag{31}$$

Substituting the policy c_1 in country 2's policy, we find

$$c_2 = \frac{x - \dfrac{1}{1 + \alpha\beta_1} x}{1 + \alpha\beta_2} = \frac{\alpha\beta_1 x}{(1 + \alpha\beta_2)(1 + \alpha\beta_1)}. \tag{32}$$

The remaining quantity of fish is

$$x - c_1 - c_2 = \frac{\alpha^2 \beta_1 \beta_2 x}{(1 + \alpha\beta_1)(1 + \alpha\beta_2)}. \tag{33}$$

Hence, with a two-period horizon under a standard dynamic programming formulation, the aim of country 2 is

$$\max_{0 \leqslant c_2 \leqslant x - c_1} \{\log c_2 + \alpha\beta_2(1 + \alpha\beta_2) \log(x - c_1 - c_2) + \text{constant}\}. \tag{34}$$

Repeating this process, we find, in the limit,

$$c_1 = (1 - \alpha\beta_1)x, \qquad c_2 = \alpha\beta_1(1 - \alpha\beta_2)x$$

and

$$x - c_1 - c_2 = (\alpha\beta_1)(\alpha\beta_2)x.$$

Thus, using these "sophisticated–naive" policies, the quantity of fish x_t approaches the steady state

$$\hat{x} = [(\alpha\beta_1)(\alpha\beta_2)]^{\alpha/(1-\alpha)}.$$

Comparing this steady state with the Cournot–Nash steady-state solution $\bar{x}$, it is clear that $\bar{x} > \hat{x}$, since $0 < (1 - \alpha\beta_1)(1 - \alpha\beta_2) < 1$. Thus, the steady-state quantity of fish in the von Stackelberg solution is smaller than that in the Cournot–Nash solution. The "sophisticated" country enjoys the *short-run* catch while in the steady state comparisons are ambiguous.[12]

The growth function used in the previous example was of the form x^α, $0 < \alpha < 1$. This is a quite reasonable growth function possessing a natural steady state at $x = 1$ when there is no external interference. However, to show in a more pronounced fashion the difference between duopoly and combined exploitation of the sea, we shall use a linear growth function. Moreover, there are situations, e.g. resource depletion models, in which this model can be applied. It will be shown that it is quite possible in this case that if the countries operate jointly, the quantity of fish diverges to infinity, while if they operate in the Cournot–Nash mode, the quantity of fish converges to zero.

The growth function for fish is now assumed to be of the form

$$x_{t+1} = r(x_t - c_1(x_t) - c_2(x_t)), \quad \text{with } r > 1. \tag{35}$$

The infinite-horizon Cournot–Nash policies are

$$\bar{c}_1 = \frac{1(1-\beta_2)\beta_1}{1-(1-\beta_1)(1-\beta_2)}x, \qquad \bar{c}_2 = \frac{(1-\beta_1)\beta_2}{1-(1-\beta_1)(1-\beta_2)}x,^{13} \tag{36}$$

and

$$x - \bar{c}_1 - \bar{c}_2 = \frac{\beta_1\beta_2 x}{1-(1-\beta_1)(1-\beta_2)} = \frac{\beta_1\beta_2}{\beta_1+\beta_2-\beta_1\beta_2}x = \frac{x}{\dfrac{1}{\beta_1}+\dfrac{1}{\beta_2}-1}. \tag{37}$$

Hence, from eqs. (37) and (38), the dynamic equation is easily found to be

$$x_{t+1} = r\left(\frac{x}{\dfrac{1}{\beta_1}+\dfrac{1}{\beta_2}-1}\right) = \frac{r}{\dfrac{1}{\beta_1}+\dfrac{1}{\beta_2}-1}x_t.$$

[12] If both countries have $\beta_1 = \beta_2 = \beta$, then, as in the case of cooperative exploitation, $\hat{x} > \bar{x}$, hence a fortiori $\hat{x} > \hat{x}$, i.e. $((\alpha\beta)^{\alpha/(1-\alpha)} > (\alpha\beta)^{2\alpha/(1-\alpha)})$. Whether the "leader" country consumes more under cooperation depends on whether $(\alpha\beta)^{\alpha/(1-\alpha)} < \frac{1}{2}$.

[13] Note that the consumption policy is independent of the rate of return, r. This results from the logarithmic form of the utility function.

Assuming $0 < \beta_1 < 1, 0 < \beta_2 < 1$, it is clear that

$$\frac{1}{\dfrac{1}{\beta_1} + \dfrac{1}{\beta_2} - 1} < 1.$$

If

$$\frac{r}{\dfrac{1}{\beta_1} + \dfrac{1}{\beta_2} - 1} > 1, \quad \text{then } x_t \to \infty \tag{38}$$

for any $x_0 > 0$, while if

$$\frac{r}{\dfrac{1}{\beta_1} + \dfrac{1}{\beta_2} - 1} < 1, \quad \text{then } x_t \to 0$$

for any $x_0 > 0$. In the borderline case, i.e.

$$\frac{r}{\dfrac{1}{\beta_1} + \dfrac{1}{\beta_2} - 1} = 1,$$

x_t remains at a neutral steady state at the level of the initial stock of fish x_0.

If both countries have the same rate of time discount $\beta_1 = \beta_2 = \beta$, we have:

$$x_t \to \infty, \quad \text{if } \frac{r\beta}{2 - \beta} > 1, \quad \text{while } x_t \to 0, \quad \text{if } \frac{r\beta}{2 - \beta} < 1.$$

If both countries combine their resources to exploit the sea, the limiting policy is given by

$$c = \frac{1 - \beta}{2} x, \tag{39}$$

and the dynamics is given by

$$x_{t+1} = r[x_t - 2c] = r\beta x_t.$$

If $r\beta > 1$, then $x_t \to \beta$; if $r\beta < 1$, then $x_t \to 0$.[14]

Note that $(1 - \beta)/(2 - \beta) > (1 - \beta)/2$. Hence, the proportion consumed is smaller under joint maximization. It is, of course, conceivable that $r\beta > 1$, while $r\beta/(2 - \beta) < 1$. Thus, it is quite possible that when the countries

---

[14] If $r = 1$, then the stock of "fish" can be interpreted as an exhaustible resource in which case depletion occurs at a slower rate under joint maximization.

cooperate, the "quantity" of fish will diverge to infinity, while under the Cournot–Nash solution the number of fish tends to zero.

4. Summary and conclusion

In this chapter, we have studied a model incorporating both dynamic and strategic aspects. The dynamics enters through the natural biological dynamics of the fish population, and the strategic aspect enters since there are two countries competing for fish. The equilibrium concept used to study the strategic aspect is a Cournot–Nash equilibrium in which each country maximizes the sum of discounted utilities subject to the actions of the other country. We studied only responses in the form of the size of the catch which depend upon the size of the fish population. Therefore threat strategies are excluded. We derived closed-form expressions for the Cournot–Nash policies for an example and studied the dynamics of the fish population under the influence of these Cournot–Nash policies. We also obtained closed-form expressions for the long-run or steady-state properties of these dynamics for this example. Then we compared these expressions with the values which result when the countries combine their resources and maximize a convex combination of their discounted utilities. We showed that the Cournot–Nash equilibrium leads to greater consumption as a function of the size of the fish population and to a smaller steady-state consumption. In fact, for a linear model, it is possible for the stock of fish to tend to extinction in the Cournot–Nash equilibrium, while with a cooperative regime the stock of fish tends to infinity.

Although we have derived our results only for an example, we may use them to study many important economic problems which require strategic behavior of the participants in a dynamic framework, e.g., limit-pricing models. Moreover, in the fishing or natural resource area other aspects of the problem can be studied: for example, the effects of profit maximization, when costs of extraction depend upon the size of the fish stock, or the effects of fixed costs (or nonconvexities) on the optimal policies. However, it should be noted that one is not likely to be able to derive results as simple as those in our example when more general models are considered. In fact, even under the rather simplified assumptions made in this chapter, the Cournot–Nash equilibrium need not be unique, as is shown in Mirman (1978). But local properties for these nonunique equilibria should yield interesting results.

References

Brock, W. (1975) "Differential Games with Active and Passive Variables", University of Chicago.

Clark, C.W. (1971) "Economically Optimal Policies for the Utilization of Biologically Renewable Resources", *Mathematical Biosciences.*

Clark, C.W. (1976) *Mathematical Bioeconomics* (Wiley–Interscience, New York).

Clark, C.W. and G.R. Munro (1975) "The Economics of Fishing and Modern Capital Theory: A Simplified Approach", *Journal of Environmental Economics and Management,* 2, 92–106.

Clemhout, S. and H.Y. Wan (1978) "Interactive Economic Dynamics and Differential Games: A Survey", Cornell University.

Fisher, A. and F. Peterson (1976) "Natural Resources and the Environment in Economics", University of Maryland; published in part as: "The Environment in Economics: A Survey", *Journal of Economic Literature,* 14, 1–33.

Gordon, H.S. (1954) "The Economic Theory of a Common Property Resource: The Fishery", *Journal of Political Economy,* 62, 124–142.

Kydland, F. (1977a) "Equilibrium Solutions in Dynamic Dominant Player Models", *Journal of Economic Theory,* 15, 2.

Kydland, F. (1977b) "A Dynamic Dominant-Firm Model of Industry Structure", University of Minnesota.

Kydland, F. and E. Prescott (1977) "Rules rather than Discretion: The Inconsistency of Optimal Plans", *Journal of Political Economy,* 85, 473–491.

Levhari, D., R. Michener and L.J. Mirman (1978) "Dynamic Programming Models of Fishing", University of Illinois.

Long, N. (1977) "Optimal Exploitation and Replenishment of a Natural Resource", in: J. Pitchford and S. Turnovsky, eds., *Applications of Control Theory to Economic Analysis* (North-Holland, Amsterdam) pp. 81–106.

Lotka, A.J. (1956) *Elements of Mathematical Biology* (New York).

Mirman, L.J. (1979) "Dynamic Models of Fishing: A Heuristic Approach", in: P.T. Liu and J.G. Sutinen, eds., *Control Theory in Mathematical Economics* (Dekker, New York) pp. 39–73.

Scott, A. (1955) "The Fishery: The Objectives of Sole Ownership", *Journal of Political Economy,* 63, 16–124.

Smith, V.L. (1968) "Economics of Production from Natural Resources", *American Economic Review,* 58, 409–431.

Smith, V.L. (1977) "Control Theory Applied to Natural and Environmental Resources: An Exposition", *Journal of Environmental Economics Management,* 4, 1–24.

Takayama, T. (1977) "Dynamic Theory of Fisheries Economics – II; Differential Game Theoretic Approach", University of Illinois.

CHAPTER 14

Stochastic fishery games with myopic equilibria*

MATTHEW J. SOBEL

1. Introduction

Most implemented fishery models use a single pooled age class. If the model concerns more than one species, then the species are pooled too. The reasons given to justify such highly aggregated models are mathematical complexity, numerical complexity, and sparse data. Many scientists and regulatory agencies realize that less highly aggregated models are desirable planning tools.

Different species of fish may prey on one another or compete for common prey (fig. 14.1). For example, in New England, cod, pollock, and silver hake feed on herring; mackerel and silver hake feed on each other; and cod feed on mackerel. The age–class structure of a single species often exhibits marked fluctuations as time passes. These fluctuations should affect harvesting policies so there are biological reasons to build multi-species multi-age–class models.

The Fishery Conservation and Management Act of 1976 (P.L. 94-265) mandates a regional approach to fishery management. Therefore, the biological interactions mentioned above preclude disaggregation of the management task into independent tasks of managing each species separately. The Act creates Regional Councils so now there are institutional and legal reasons to build multi-species models.

*Presented at the University of Chicago, Georgia Institute of Technology, and Yale University in 1976 and 1977 and at a Conference on the Economics of Renewable Resource Management, Brown University, October 1979. Partially supported by NSF Grant SOC 78-05770.

Essays in the economics of renewable resources, edited by L.J. Mirman and D.F. Spulber
© *North-Holland Publishing Company, 1982*

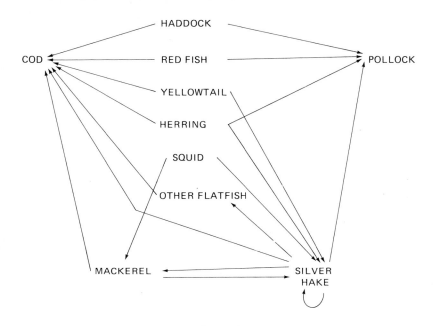

Figure 14.1

Some species of fish are caught commercially together with other species. This "bycatch" phenomenon is a technological reason to build multi-species models.

These technological and biological considerations provide economic incentives to coordinate the management of several species. From fig. 14.1, in New England we should not stipulate the mackerel catch without considering the effects on cod and silver hake.

The stochastic game in section 2 includes a general class of species and age–class interactions in the underlying population dynamics. The model is presented in section 2 and critiqued in section 4. The special case of linear returns leads to a simplification which is presented formally in section 3. The potential applications to fisheries are discussed in section 5. In this case, the stochastic game has a "myopic" equilibrium point which can be computed relatively easily.

There is a large and growing literature on the 1976 Act. Other writers have noted the multiplicity of objectives and "players" in a regional fishery (cf. Mendelssohn, 1977). Some writers have analyzed the international "game" in conflicts over fisheries resources (cf. Levhari and Mirman, 1980). This paper proposes that *sequential* game models be used to analyze dynamic interactions. Many others (cf. Clark, 1976) have advocated the use of sequential models to analyze the optimal operation of renewable resources where "optimal" refers to a single perspective (firm, agency, country, etc.).

2. A stochastic fishery game

Let I be the set of relevant species. The species identities are assumed to be equivalent to the various sub-industries that fish for the species. In year t, $t = 1, 2, \ldots$, the *state* is the vector s_t. The ith component of s_t is s_t^i which is the biomass of species i at the beginning of the fishing season. Let S denote the set of all possible states. If $s \in S$, then s^i denotes the ith component of s. This notation is consistent with a more general model that has several age–classes for each species. Then s_t^i and s^i become vectors with as many components as there are age–classes for species i. The same remark applies to the following notation.

Let a_t^i denote the biomass of species i at the end of the fishing season in year t, i.e. its "escapement", and let $a_t = (a_t^i, i \in I)$. The set of possible values of a_t depends, generally, on s_t. For example, $0 \leq a^i \leq s^i$ unless species i reproduces extraordinarily quickly. If the constraint is $0 \leq a_t^i \leq s_t^i$, we might interpret $s_t^i - a_t^i$ as the size of the catch of species i in year t. This interpretation is reasonable only if natural mortality and recruitment are negligible during the fishing season. Generally, let A_s^i denote the set of feasible values of a_t^i if $s_t = s$. Then $C_s = \mathsf{X}_{i \in I} A_s^i$ is the set of feasible values of a_t if $s_t = s$ and $a_t \in C_{s_t} \Leftrightarrow a_t^i \in A_{s_t}^i$ for all $i \in I$. Let $A = \cup_{s \in S} C_s$. If $a \in A$, then a^i denotes the ith component of a. For any t, $W = \{(s, a): a \in C_s, s \in S\}$ denotes the set of feasible (s_t, a_t) pairs. If $A_s^i = [0, s^i]$ for each i, then $W = \{(s, a): 0 \leq a \leq s, s \in S\}$. For computational and expository convenience, *assume that W is a set with only finitely many elements.*

The population dynamics are specified by transition probabilities. Assume that (i) the dynamics are Markovian so s_{t+1} has a distribution that depends on $s_1, a_1, \ldots, s_t, a_t$ only through s_t and a_t; (ii) the distribution of s_{t+1} does not depend on s_t. Assumption (i) is made throughout the stochastic game literature and is reasonable for a fishery. The biomasses in year $t + 1$ depend on the biomasses and catches in year t. Assumption (ii) is a characteristic of regional fisheries that significantly simplifies the analysis of their dynamics.

Assumptions (i) and (ii) together imply that there are numbers $p_j(a), j \in S$ and $a \in A$, such that

$$\begin{cases} p_j(a) = P\{s_{t+1} = j \mid a_t = a\} \\ \qquad = P\{s_{t+1} = j \mid s_1, a_1, \ldots, s_t, a_t = a\}, \end{cases} \tag{1}$$

for all t. Therefore, the biomasses at the start of the $t+1$st fishing season are assumed to depend only on the biomasses at the end of the tth season (and, possibly, on exogenous uncertainty). In fact, (1) is implicit in most theoretical and empirical fisheries research. It is a stochastic generalization of the ''metered model'' in Anderson (Chapter 11, this volume).

Let α_i, $0 \leq \alpha_i < 1$, denote the single-period discount factor for the sub-industry which harvests species i. Let $r_i(s, a)$ denote sub-industry i's (expected) profit in any year t where $s_t = s$ and $a_t = a$. For example, if (i) sub-industry i's profit depends only on the catch of species i, (ii) $s^i - a^i$ is the catch of species i, and (iii) if its profit is proportional to the size of the catch, then

$$r_i(s, a) = b_i \cdot (s^i - a^i), \tag{2}$$

where b_i is the unit profit. Let

$$V_i = \sum_{t=1}^{\infty} \alpha_i^{t-1} r_i(s_t, a_t) \tag{3}$$

denote sub-industry i's sum of discounted profits.

Let π^i denote the set of all nonanticipative decision rules (possibly history dependent and randomized) which player i could use to choose the sequence of actions $a_1^i, a_2^i, \ldots$. Let $\pi = \mathsf{X}_{i \in I} \pi^i$ be the product set of all players' possible rules and, for $\rho \in \pi$, write $\rho = (\rho^i, \rho^{-i})$, where $\rho^{-i} \in \prod_{j \neq i} \pi^j$.

For $\rho \in \pi$, the expectation $v_i(\rho \mid s) = E_\rho[V_i \mid s_1 = s]$ exists for all $i \in I, s \in S$, and $\rho \in \pi$.

Definition. A policy $\delta \in \pi$ is an *equilibrium point relative to* $X \subseteq S$ iff

$$v_i(\delta \mid s) = \sup\{v_i(\rho\delta^{-i}) \mid s): \rho \in \pi^i\}, \qquad s \in X, \quad i \in I. \tag{4}$$

Thus, an equilibrium point relative to X is noncollusively optimal for every player for each initial state in X.

There is a stationary policy which is an equilibrium point relative to S (Shapley, 1953; Fink, 1964; Rogers, 1969; Sobel, 1971). However, even a two-person zero sum stochastic game with $|W| < \infty$ and rational data may possess an irrational value. Therefore, a finitely convergent algorithm is not achievable in general.

3. Myopic equilibria

Assumption (1) and two others below lead to a relatively easily computable equilibrium point relative to a proper subset of S. Suppose

$$r_i(s, a) = K_i(a) + L_i(s), \qquad i \in I, \quad (s, a) \in W. \tag{5}$$

The case which is pertinent for fisheries is (2) where $K_i(a) = -b_i a^i$ and $L_i(s) = b_i s^i$. Under assumptions (1) and (5), let

$$G_i(a) = K_i(a) + \alpha_i \sum_{s \in S} p_s(a) L_i(s), \qquad a \in A, \quad i \in I. \tag{6}$$

When (5) is caused by (2),

$$G_i(a) = -b_i a^i + \alpha_i b_i \sum_{s \in S} p_s(a) s^i. \tag{7}$$

Let $S(a) = \{s: s \in S, a \in A_s\}$ denote the states in which action $a \in A$ is feasible. Let Γ denote the following noncooperative static (Nash) game among the players in I. Player $i \in I$ has available the set $A^i = \bigcup_{s \in S} A_s^i$ of alternative actions and $G_i(a)$ is player i's pay-off if the actions are $a = (a^i, i \in I)$. Since $|A^i| < \infty$ for each i and $|I| < \infty$, there is an equilibrium point of Γ. First, suppose that a_* is an unrandomized equilibrium point of Γ:

There exists $a_* \in A$ which is an equilibrium point of Γ. $\tag{8}$

Theorem. Assumptions (1), (5), (8), and

$$\sum_{j \in S(a_*)} p_j(a_*) = 0 \tag{9}$$

imply $a_t = a_*$ for all $t = 1, 2, \ldots$ is an equilibrium point relative to $S(a_*)$.

There is a more general version of this result where the equilibrium point may represent randomized strategies. The more general version is the corollary below. The significance of the theorem and corollary is that there are several finitely convergent algorithms to compute an equilibrium point of a game such as Γ (a Nash game). The algorithms are cited in Sobel (1981) which proves the theorem and corollary. A stochastic game that satisfies the conditions of the theorem or corollary is said to have a *myopic equilibrium* point. Ad infinitum repetition of the equilibrium point of a static game comprises an equilibrium point of the dynamic game.

For the corollary, let D_s^i denote the set of all probability vectors on A_s^i and $D = \mathbf{X}_{i \in I} \bigcup_{s \in S} D_s^i$ which is the randomization version of $A = \mathbf{X}_{i \in I} \bigcup_{s \in S} A_s^i$.

Let $d \in D$ denote an equilibrium point of Γ $\tag{10}$

which necessarily exists because $|A| < \infty$. In this notation,

$$\boldsymbol{d}(a) = \prod_{i \in I} P\{\text{in } \Gamma \text{ player } i \text{ chooses action } a^i \in A^i\}.$$

Let

$$A' = \{a : a \in A, \boldsymbol{d}(a) > 0\}$$

$$S' = \{s : s \in S, a \in A_s \text{ for all } a \in A'\} = \bigcup_{a \in A'} S(a).$$

Corollary. Assumptions (1), (5), and

$$\sum_{j \in S'} p_j(a) = 1, \quad \text{for all } a \in A' \tag{11}$$

imply $P\{a_t = a\} = \boldsymbol{d}(a)$, for all $t = 1, 2, \ldots$ is an equilibrium point relative to S'.

4. Critique of assumptions

The applicability of the theorem and corollary depends on the extent to which the assumptions are reasonable in fisheries. Assumption (2), $r_i(s, a) = b_i(s^i - a^i)$, and its consequences are discussed in section 2. It is implicit in (2) that $s^i - a^i$ is interpreted as the catch of species i. We have already observed that this interpretation is reasonable if natural mortality and recruitment are not too massive during the fishing season.

The stochastic game model in section 2 uses a_t^i, the biomass of species i in the fishery at the end of the tth fishing season, as the generic decision variable. In practice, often the estimates of such biomasses are crude. Actually one has only sample data from which to infer posterior distributions of s_t and a_t and these distributions may exhibit significant variation. Is catch size a more appropriate decision variable because it can be measured accurately? It is a Hobson's choice.

Let $\xi(a)$ denote a random variable with the distribution given in (1):

$$p_j(a) = P\{\xi(a) = j\}, \quad j \in S, \quad a \in A.$$

Then (1) asserts $s_{t+1} \sim \xi(a_t)$, where $X \sim Y$ indicates that random variables X and Y have the same distribution. The preceding paragraph admits that we have only sample data concerning s_t. Suppose X_t are the sample data and let z_t^i denote the catch size $s_t^i - a_t^i$. Then $s_{t+1} \sim \xi(s_t - z_t)$ but we have to settle for

$$s_{t+1} \sim \mathrm{E}\big[\xi(s-z_t)\mid X_t\big], \tag{12}$$

where the expectation is taken with respect to the conditional distribution of s_t given X_t. In words, even if the decision variable is catch size rather than residual biomass, (12) exhibits the same posterior distribution for s_{t+1}.

Assumption (9) has the following interpretation in a fishery model where $s_t^i - a_t^i$ indicates catch size:

$$P\big\{s_{t+1}^i \geqslant a_*^i\big\} = 1, \qquad i \in I, \quad t = 1, 2, \dots. \tag{13}$$

More generally, in the notation of the corollary let

$$a_0^i = \max\big\{a^i : a = (a^i, a^{-i}) \in A'\big\}$$

and $a_0 = (a_0^i, i \in I)$. In the notation of the preceding paragraph, assumption (11) is equivalent to

$$P_d\big\{\xi(a) \geqslant a_0\big\} = 1, \tag{14}$$

where a is the random action that will be taken using d.

In a fishery model, $\xi(\cdot)$ is usually stochastically nondecreasing (this ignores overpopulation, i.e. "overcompensation"), so

$$P\{\xi(a') \leqslant b\} \geqslant P\{\xi(a'') \leqslant b\}, \qquad a' \leqslant a'', \tag{15}$$

for every non-negative I-vector b. Let

$$a_+^i = \min\big\{a^i : a = (a^i, a^{-i}) \in A'\big\} \quad \text{and } a_+ = \big(a_+^i, i \in I\big).$$

Then (11) and (15) require

$$P\{\xi(a_+) \geqslant a_0\} = 0. \tag{16}$$

The general sense of (9), (11), (13), (14), or (16) is that, with probability one, recruitment minus natural mortality exceeds catch size. If any component of a_* (or a_+) is very low then the assumption is likely to be unreasonable ("overfishing").

It is implicit in section 2 that a separate sub-industry harvests each major commercial species. Without such an assumption, consider a dynamic model of equilibrium between sub-industries. Such a model would still be a stochastic game and an equilibrium point would necessarily exist. But computation and characterization would be more difficult (or impossible) because the theorem and corollary would be invalid.

The identification of sub-industries with species may be a reasonable first approximation in some contexts. Only empirical results can support a conclusion regarding whether or not the courseness of the approximation is an acceptable price to pay for relatively easy computations.

5. Fisheries applications of myopic equilibria

Linear returns (2) leads to (7) which may be written

$$G_i(a) = b_i \sum_{s \in S} p_s(a)(\alpha_i s^i - a^i). \tag{17}$$

It is apparent that the set of equilibrium points of Γ does not depend on $b = (b_i, i \in I)$. Also, $G_i(a)$ is proportional to a weighted average of the difference between the discounted biomass at the start of next year's season and the biomass at the end of this year's season.

The myopic equilibrium asserted in the theorem is closely related to a result in Mendelssohn and Sobel (1981). The model there is a (single player) version of the present one where there is exactly one species. Then linear returns (and some technical assumptions) yields a myopic optimum without the restriction (9), i.e. without requiring feasibility with probability one.

The decision rule in the theorem and corollary is part of a *stationary* policy. A policy $\rho \in \pi$ is said to be stationary if there is an element $\delta \in D$ such that $\delta(s_t) = P\{a_t = a\}$ for all $t = 1, 2, \ldots$. Thus, the actions are not necessarily the same for all t but the rule that determines the actions *is* the same. What are the ergodic consequences of using a stationary policy in a stochastic game? Section 6 in Mendelssohn and Sobel (1981) contributes to the literature (see also references therein) which answers this question for single species models. The primary tool used in Mendelssohn and Sobel is the general theory of discrete-time Markov processes. The same theory was used by Sanghvi (1978) to obtain some ergodic consequences of stationary policies in stochastic games. He focuses on probabilities of absorbtion. In most fisheries models the absorbing states connote "extinction", so Sanghvi's results may be useful here.

Consider a variant of the model in section 2 which stresses aggregate regional benefits. Instead of a game-like perspective, suppose that the objective is to maximize the expected discounted aggregate benefits:

$$\max E\left[\sum_{t=1}^{\infty} \sum_{i \in I} \alpha_i^{t-1} r_i(s_t, a_t) \right].$$

Let

$$G(a) = \sum_{i \in I} G_i(a) = \sum_{s \in S} p_s(a) \sum_{i \in I} b_i(\alpha_i s^i - a^i), \qquad a \in A, \tag{18}$$

and let a_* denote an element of A that maximizes $G(\cdot)$ on A. Such an element exists because A is a finite set. Suppose $C_s = [0, s]$ for $s \in S$. As a consequence of the theorem, assumptions (1), (2), and (9) imply $a_t = a_*$ for all $t = 1, 2, \ldots$ is optimal with respect to all initial states $s \geq a_*$. Such a policy is called a *myopic optimum*. This result can easily be extended to a more general model where (i) each species has an age structure, and (ii) sub-industries are not equivalent to species.

When $|I| = 1$ so species (and age–classes) are pooled, a myopic optimum in (18) is merely the familiar discounted version of maximum sustained yield. Suppress subscript i in (18) because $I = \{1\}$ and let $\mu(a)$ denote $\Sigma_{s \in S} p_s(a) s$. Then (18) is the familiar relationship

$$G(a) = b[\alpha\mu(a) - a].$$

If A were an (open) interval and $\mu(\cdot)$ were continuously differentiable, then a necessary condition for a_* would be $\alpha\mu'(a_*) - 1 = 0$ or $\mu'(a_*) = \alpha^{-1}$. This stochastic version of the usual maximum sustained yield condition occurs in the model (with $K = 0$) that Daniel F. Spulber presented in Chapter 6 of this volume.

Another example of a myopic optimum occurs in a stochastic version of the model that Lee G. Anderson presented in Chapter 11 of this volume. His model concerns fleet size and allocation of fishing effort between two species. The following model addresses only allocation of effort. For each n, s_n, a_n, and $\xi(a_n)$ are two-vectors with a component for each species. In fact, the objective in Spulber's chapter leads to (18) with $|I| = 2$. The distinguishing feature in Spulber is an upper bound on a linear combination of the catches of the two species:

$$w_1 \cdot (s_n^1 - a_n^1) + w_2 \cdot (s_n^2 - a_n^2) \leq u, \tag{19}$$

where u denotes the maximum feasible fishing effort. Suppose that $a_* = (a_*^1, a_*^2)$ maximizes (18). Then (19) implies that (9) is equivalent to

$$P\{\xi(a_*) \geq a_*, \quad w \cdot (\xi[a_*] - a_*) \leq u\} = 1,$$

where $w = (w_1, w_2)$.

Colin W. Clark's chapter (Chapter 15) in this volume includes a duopoly model that does *not* have a myopic equilibrium point. His model has two players: player 1 is the fishing fleet and player 2 is the processor. Let a^1 denote the escapement chosen by the fleet and let a^2 denote the unit price of fish that the processor will pay the fleet. Then the single-period rewards are

$$r_1(s, a) = (a^2 - c)(s - a^1); \qquad r_2(s, a) = (\rho - a^2)(s - a^1),$$

where s is the biomass at the beginning of the season, $a = (a^1, a^2)$, and ρ is the wholesale price (less processing cost) that the processor receives for processed fish. Therefore,

$$r_1(s, a) = a^2 s - cs + ca^1 - a^1 a^2$$

and

$$r_2(s, a) = -a^2 s + \rho s - \rho a^1 + a^2 a^1,$$

whose first terms lack the additive decomposition feature in (5).

References

Clark, C.W. (1976) *Mathematical Bioeconomics* (Wiley, New York).

Fink, A.M. (1964) "Equilibrium in a Stochastic n-Person Game", *Journal of Science*, Hiroshima Univ. Ser. A-I 28, 89–93.

Levhari, D. and L. Mirman (1980) "The Great Fish War: An Example Using a Cournot-Nash Equilibrium", *Bell Journal*, 8, 1, 322–334.

Mendelssohn, R. (1977) "Harvesting Policies and the Fishery Conservation and Management Act of 1976", unpublished manuscript.

Mendelssohn, R. and M.J. Sobel (1980) "Capital Accumulation and the Optimization of Renewable Resource Models," *Journal of Economic Theory*, 23, 243–260.

Parthesarthy, T. and M. Stern (1977) *On Markov Games*, Lecture Notes in Pure and Applied Mathematics, vol. 30 (Marcel Dekker Publishing Company, New York) pp. 1–46.

Rogers, P.D. (1969) "Nonzero-sum Stochastic Games", Report ORC 69-8 (Operations Research Center, University of California, Berkeley).

Sanghvi, A.P. (1978) "Sequential Games as Stochastic Processes", *Stochastic Processes and their Applications*, 6, 323–336.

Shapley, L. (1953) "Stochastic Games", in: *Proceedings of the National Academy of Sciences, USA*, 39, pp. 1095–1100.

Shubik, M. and M.J. Sobel (1981) "Stochastic Games, Oligopoly Theory, and Competitive Resource Allocation", in: P.T. Liu, ed., *Dynamic Optimization and Mathematical Economics*, vol. 19 in the series *Mathematical Concepts and Methods in Sciences and Engineering* (Plenum Press, New York).

Sobel, M.J. (1971) "Noncooperative Stochastic Games", *Annals of Mathematical Statistics*, 42, 1930–1935.

Sobel, M.J. (1981) "Myopic Solutions of Markov Decision Processes and Stochastic Games", *Operations Research*, 29, 995–1009.

Whitt, W. (1980) "Representation and Approximation of Noncooperative Stochastic Games", *Journal of SIAM Control*, 18, 33–48.

PART VII

MODELS OF FISHERY REGULATION

Introduction to Part VII

Owing to increased demand for marine resources and the significant problem of free access, the unwanted depletion of many resource stocks is a real possibility. Regulatory policies must be designed with careful attention to biological characteristics of the species harvested and the technology of harvesting. In addition, the regulatory authority must take into account industry structure and the behavioral responses of individual firms. The possibility of strategic interaction between harvesting firms, between harvesting firms and the processing sector and between harvesting firms and the regulatory authority itself are important determinants of the success of regulatory policy.

As a variety of regulatory policies are pursued in practice, a comparison of their effects on resource stocks is essential. In "Models of Fishery Regulation," Clark allows for continuous harvesting during each fishing season and examines the effect of regulatory policy on total catch and on the entry of individual vessels into the fishery. Alternative regulatory policies of total catch quotas, restricted access, allocated vessel quotas and landings taxes are examined and compared to the welfare-optimizing solution and to the free access outcome. By paying close attention to the number and size of firms under regulation, Clark presents an interesting framework for the evaluation of alternative regulatory policies under varying market structures.

CHAPTER 15

Models of fishery regulation

COLIN W. CLARK

1. Introduction

Since the publication of H. Scott Gordon's original analysis of the "common-property" fishery (Gordon, 1954), a number of increasingly sophisticated models of fishery economics have been developed (e.g. Crutchfield and Zellner, 1962; Smith, 1969; Scott, 1970; Clark and Munro, 1975; Reed, 1975; Anderson, 1977; Mendelssohn and Sobel, 1980; Clark et al., 1979). In the majority of these studies the economic performance of the unregulated common-property fishery is analyzed and compared to a social optimum. The analyses show how externalities in the unregulated (competitive) fishery result in an equilibrium that fails to be Pareto optimal. Beyond observing that the fishery could in theory be forced into the optimal mode by the use of appropriate taxes, however, these analyses have generally not addressed the problem of predicting the response of the fishery to various practical regulatory policies. This is the question that will occupy us here.

In addressing this question, we will at first employ a highly aggregated biological population model – essentially the Ricker stock-recruitment model (Ricker, 1954). Our model of fishing activity, however, is disaggregated to the level of individual vessel operation (cf. Anderson, 1977). On the hypothesis that each vessel is operated so as continuously to maximize revenue flow – subject to the particular regulations under consideration – we study the behavior of the fishery under a variety of regulatory policies, namely: (a) no regulation, (b) total catch quotas, (c) restricted access (i.e. vessel licenses), (d) allocated vessel quotas, and (e) taxes. A welfare-optimization analysis is also presented, and serves as a touchstone against which the results of the

Essays in the economics of renewable resources, edited by L.J. Mirman and D.F. Spulber
© *North-Holland Publishing Company, 1982*

various alternative policies can be evaluated. Currently, actual cases exist in which a fishery has been regulated by methods belonging to each regulatory category, except taxes.[1]

We will also discuss briefly the possibility of extending the model to deal with the multi-species fishery. All the models discussed here, however, are deterministic; the effects of uncertainty on fishery regulation have yet to be assessed in any detail.

2. The basic model[2]

Our biological fish population model is the following:

$$R_{k+1} = F(S_k); \qquad S_k = R_k - H_k, \tag{1}$$

where R_k denotes recruitment to the fishery in year k, S_k denotes spawning escapement, and H_k is the annual catch. The stock-recruitment function $F(\cdot)$ is assumed to satisfy

$$F(0) = 0; \qquad F'(s) > 0, \qquad F''(S) < 0.$$

The operation of the fishery during the kth season is modelled by the equations

$$\frac{dx}{dt} = -qx \sum_{i=1}^{N} E_i(t), \qquad 0 \leqslant t \leqslant T, \tag{3}$$

$$x(0) = R_k; \qquad x(T) = S_k, \tag{4}$$

where $x(t)$ denotes the size of the population at time t during the season, T is the length of the season (e.g. $T =$ one year), and $E_i(t)$ denotes the level of standardized fishing effort exerted by the ith vessel, $i = 1, 2, \ldots, N$. The constant $q > 0$ is the catchability coefficient. Eq. (3) is readily solved explicitly:

$$S_k = R_k \exp\left\{ -q \sum_1^N \int_0^T E_i(t)\,dt \right\}. \tag{5}$$

---

[1] Examples: skipjack tuna (unregulated); yellowfin tuna (total catch quota in the Eastern Tropical Pacific); Pacific salmon (vessel license system in British Columbia and in Alaska); Atlantic herring (allocated vessel quotas in the Bay of Fundy).
[2] This model is developed more fully in Clark (1980).

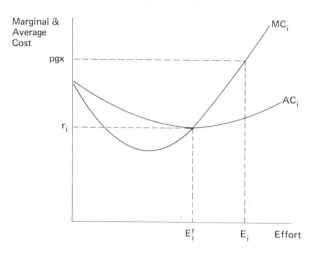

Figure 15.1

The flow of net revenue accruing to the ith vessel is

$$\pi_i(x, E_i) = pqxE_i - c_i(E_i) \tag{6}$$

Here $h_i(t) = qx(t)E_i(t)$ denotes the catch rate, p is the price of landed fish, and $c_i(E_i)$ denotes the cost of effort E_i for the ith vessel. The marginal cost curve $c_i'(E_i)$ is assumed to have the traditional U-shape (fig. 15.1).

We shall assume, unless otherwise specified, that the fishery is exploited *competitively*, with each vessel exerting a level of effort E_i so as to maximize the flow of net revenue π_i.[3] Below, additional constraints will be imposed, to reflect the influence of various regulations.

3. The unregulated fishery

Assume first that the fishery is completely unregulated and that access to the fishery is unrestricted. By our behavioral hypothesis we have (see fig. 15.1)

$$
\begin{aligned}
c_i'(E_i) &= pqx, && \text{if } pqx > r_i, \\
E_i &= 0, && \text{if } pqx < r_i,
\end{aligned}
\tag{7}
$$

---

[3] For an analysis of the oligopolistic fishery as a differential game see Clark (1979).

Thus, the ith vessel's effort level E_i is completely determined by the observed marginal return to effort, pqx, which is itself determined by the current fish stock $x = x(t)$. The evolution of $x(t)$ over a given season then follows eq. (3), i.e.

$$\frac{dx}{dt} = -qx \sum_{i=1}^{N} E_i, \qquad x(0) = R_k, \tag{8}$$

where the E_i are given by eq. (7). Total seasonal revenue for the ith vessel equals

$$\tilde{\pi}_i(R_k, N) = \int_0^T \pi_i(x(t), E_i(t)) \, dt. \tag{9}$$

If β_i denotes the ith vessel's "set-up" cost, associated with entering the fishery in a given season, the vessel will earn a net seasonal revenue given by

$$\tilde{\pi}_i(R_k, N) - \beta_i, \tag{10}$$

and the vessel will in fact enter the fishery in year k if and only if this expression is positive, where $N = N_k$ denotes the total number of vessels entering the fishery. (The vessel owner's decision to enter the fishery will depend of course on his *estimate* of N_k.) The marginal vessel will thus have $\tilde{\pi}_i - \beta_i = 0$.

   The above equations determine (from the assumed data) the number of vessels entering the fishery in year k, as well as the effort schedule for each vessel, and hence (via eq. (8)) the escapement population S_k. Thus, invoking the stock-recruitment relation of eq. (1), we are able to predict the dynamic evolution of the fishery from any given initial stock level R_1. The fishery will reach "bionomic equilibrium" when

$$R_{k+1} = R_k.$$

Of course, this equilibrium will shift if any of the parameters of the model change. The comparative statics are easily worked out (e.g. $\partial \bar{R}_k / \partial p < 0$), but we shall not pause to do so.

4. Welfare optimization

For comparison purposes, we now perform an optimization analysis based on our model. To avoid unnecessary, complicated side issues, we assume an infinitely elastic demand schedule so that price equals marginal utility, and we also suppose that effort costs $c_i(E_i)$ represent true social opportunity costs. Our optimization problem breaks down into two suboptimization problems.

The intraseasonal optimization problem is:

$$\max \int_0^T \sum_1^N \pi_i(x, E_i)\, dt \tag{11}$$

subject to the conditions

$$\frac{dx}{dt} = -qx \sum_1^N E_i(t), \qquad 0 \leqslant t \leqslant T, \tag{12}$$

$$x(0) = R, \qquad x(T) = S, \tag{13}$$

$$E_i(t) \geqslant 0, \tag{14}$$

where $R = R_k$, $S = S_k$, and $N = N_k$ refer to the year in question. This problem is readily solved by means of the maximum principle; we obtain

$$
\begin{aligned}
c_i'(E_i) &= (p - \lambda)qx, && \text{if } (p - \lambda)qx > r_i, \\
E_i &= 0, && \text{otherwise,}
\end{aligned}
\tag{15}
$$

where $\lambda = \lambda(t)$ is an adjoint variable satisfying

$$\frac{d\lambda}{dt} = -(p - \lambda)q \sum_1^N E_i. \tag{16}$$

Given that *some* fishing is optimal, it follows that $\lambda(t) \geqslant 0$ and $\lambda(t) \not\equiv 0$. Thus, comparing eq. (15) for the optimum and eq. (7) for the unregulated fishery, we see that each vessel in the unregulated fishery exerts an excessive effort level during the season. In fact, we have from eqs. (3) and (16):

$$\frac{d}{dt}\{(p - \lambda)x\} = 0, \tag{17}$$

so that, by (15), the optimal effort levels $E_i = E_i^*$ *remain constant throughout the fishing season.*[4] The unregulated fishery, on the other hand, exerts a decreasing level of effort as the season progresses and the fish stock is reduced. This behavior reflects the competitive "scramble" of each vessel to

---

[4] As noted by Phil Neher, this result (constancy of optimal effort over time) is a consequence of the special form of our harvest production functions, $h_i = qE_ix$. If a Cobb–Douglas form $h_i = qE_ix^\beta$ is assumed instead, then optimal effort $E_i^*(t)$ *decreases* over time (when $\beta < 1$). In other words, if the fish population becomes more catchable as its abundance decreases (i.e. $\beta < 1$), then optimal effort decreases as the stock is reduced.

catch fish at the beginning of the season, before they are caught by someone else.

How many vessels will actually be employed in the optimized fishery? It is easily shown that the optimum number will be the minimum number required to take the seasonal catch $R_k - S_k$ in the available time; there will never be any unused capacity. For the open-access fishery, however (even if escapement S_k is regulated), the zero-profit condition implies excessive entry of vessels.[5]

Next, let

$$W(R_k, S_k) = \max \int_0^T \sum_1^N \pi_i(x, E_i)\,dt \qquad (17)$$

denote the optimized seasonal net revenue, corresponding to a given recruitment R_k and escapement S_k. Then the interseasonal optimization problem is

$$\max \sum_{k=0}^{\infty} \alpha^k W(R_k, S_k)$$

subject to eq. (1), where α is the periodic rate of discount ($0 < \alpha < 1$). This problem has an optimal equilibrium escapement population $S_k = S^*$ determined by the equations

$$F'(S) \cdot \frac{\partial W/\partial R + \partial W/\partial S}{\partial W/\partial S} = \frac{1}{\alpha},$$

$$R = F(S) \qquad (18)$$

(see Clark, 1976, p. 253). The optimal approach to this equilibrium can be obtained via dynamic programming. Our fishery model is thus amenable to routine optimization analysis (but severe difficulties arise if capital costs are introduced and vessel capital is assumed to be nonmalleable – see Clark et al., 1979).

It is clear from the above analysis that the unregulated, open-access fishery achieves a suboptimal result, both intraseasonally (too many vessels, and too much effort per vessel) and interseasonally (depletion of the fish population). The specific externality producing this result is the "stock externality" (see eq. (3)), whereby the catch taken from the common stock by any individual vessel reduces the subsequent catch rates of all vessels,

---

[5] These statements need to be modified in the case that vessel capital is costly and nonmalleable; see Clark et al. (1979).

and also affects the future productivity of the population. Any effective regulation program must in some way compensate for this externality.[6]

5. Total catch quotas

We next use our basic model to predict the response of the fishery to the traditional forms of regulation based on the fish population itself. We shall suppose that the management authority sets a total seasonal catch quota Q, and closes the fishery when the total catch reaches that level. Since our model is deterministic, this amounts to the same thing as managing in terms of a set escapement level S.

With escapement fixed at S, then, our model becomes:

$$\frac{\mathrm{d}x}{\mathrm{d}t} = -qx\sum_{1}^{N} E_i \qquad (0 \leqslant t \leqslant t_f), \tag{20}$$

$$x(0) = F(S), \qquad x(t_f) = S, \tag{21}$$

$$c_i'(E_i) = pqx \qquad (i = 1, 2, \ldots, N), \tag{22}$$

where t_f denotes the closing date. Assuming that $S > \bar{S}$, for the unregulated bionomic equilibrium (otherwise the regulation has no effect), we see that, for fixed N, every vessel exerts more effort, catches more fish, and earns a greater net revenue than before.[7] If access is not restricted, as we are supposing, it follows that additional vessels will then enter the fishery. The overall effect will generally be a *shortening* of the fishing season, a process that will continue until net revenue of the marginal vessels again falls to zero. This tendency towards progressive expansion of fleet capacity and shortening of the fishing season has been observed in many quota-regulated fisheries, including tuna, salmon, halibut, herring, and anchoveta fisheries.

In a sense, total quota regulation (or a similar biologically based policy) leads to an intensification of the economic problem of the fishery, even though *temporary* gains (increased catches and revenues) may result if additional entry does not occur immediately. But over the long run, a new equilibrium is established with more excess capacity than prior to the regulation.[8]

[6] In theory, the externality would be internalized if fishing rights were vested in a "sole owner" (Scott, 1955). This case, which is seldom feasible, needs no further analysis.

[7] This refers to the long run; over the short run catches may be temporarily reduced (even to zero) in order to allow the depleted stock to become rehabilitated (i.e. as long as $R_k < S$).

[8] The quota regulation will nevertheless produce *some* long-term benefits, in this case an increase in producers' surplus earned by the more efficient vessels. If demand is not perfectly elastic there will also be an increase in consumers' surplus.

6. Restricted access (vessel licenses)

Next we suppose that a fixed number N_0 of vessels are licensed to catch fish. The total annual catch may also be regulated. Since the licensed vessels still compete for the catch, their effort levels will continue to satisfy

$$c_i'(E_i) = pqx \qquad (i=1,2,\ldots,N_0). \tag{23}$$

Thus, the vessel licensing policy remains suboptimal: vessels continue to exert excessive levels of effort, especially at the beginning of each fishing season. How serious this will be depends, among other things, on the shape of the cost curves $c_i(E_i)$.

Our present model assumes, unrealistically, that the effort–cost functions $c_i(E_i)$ are permanently fixed. Thus, technological innovations that reduce the cost of generating a given level of standardized effort (i.e. of fishing mortality) are ignored. In a limited-entry fishery, however, large potential revenues will generate a strong incentive for introducing such innovations. Indeed, game-theoretic considerations (Clark, 1979) suggest that individual vessel owners will be motivated to adopt additional capital-intensive innovations, provided net revenues are sufficiently large. Whether this tendency could be effectively countered by regulation of vessel size, horsepower, gear, and so on, remains controversial (cf. Munro, 1977; Crutchfield, 1979).

7. Taxes

Suppose a tax τ must be paid by fishermen, for each unit of fish landed and sold.[9] Then the perceived net revenue for the ith vessel becomes

$$\pi_i(x, E_i) - \tau h_i = (p - \tau)qxE_i - c_i(E_i), \tag{24}$$

and the profit-maximizing hypothesis now implies

$$c_i'(E_i) = (p - \tau)qx \quad (\text{or else } E_i = 0). \tag{25}$$

Comparing this with eq. (15) we see that the optimal exploitation rate will result if

$$\tau = \lambda(t),$$

i.e. if the tax is equal to the shadow price of the resource stock. This is of

---

[9]An effort tax $\tau_E = qx\tau$ would obviously have the same effect as a landings tax τ. In practice, however, taxation of effort requires accurate measurement of effort levels of each vessel – a notoriously tricky problem.

course a standard result. Note, however, that the theoretically optimal landings tax τ must vary (in fact, decrease) over the fishing season,[10] as well as from one season to the next.

It is noteworthy that a single tax $\tau = \lambda(t)$ on catch serves (in our model) to optimize effort, vessel numbers, and the fish biomass. This is a consequence of having assumed a single source of externality, namely the stock x itself. It there are other externalities, such as congestion of vessels, then a more complex tax scheme becomes necessary (Clark, 1980, sec. 6). Of course, a tax on effort must be vessel-specific (see footnote 9).

8. Allocated catch quotas

We imagine next that each vessel has a seasonal catch quota Q_i which it cannot exceed. For the moment, assume that transfers of quotas are not allowed; this assumption will be dropped later.

Let $y_i(t)$ denote the cumulative catch of vessel i during a given season. Our quota constraint is then

$$y_i(T) \leqslant Q_i. \tag{26}$$

How does this constraint affect the vessel owner's profit maximizing behavior? We now assume that the ith vessel maximizes its net seasonal revenue:

$$\max \int_0^{t_f} \left(pqxE_i - c_i(E_i) \right) dt \tag{27}$$

subject to

$$\frac{dy_i}{dt} = qxE_i, \qquad y_i(0) = 0, \qquad y_i(t_f) = Q_i, \tag{28}$$

$$t_f \leqslant T. \tag{29}$$

(Eq. (28) assumes that the quota constraint (26) is actually binding; the opposite case is trivial.) We also suppose that, in choosing $E_i = E_i(t)$ to maximize (27), the vessel owner *assumes* that $x(t)$ will follow a given path resulting from the cumulative catches of all vessels. We also suppose that this expectation is rational, i.e. correct.[11]

---

[10] That $\lambda(t)$ decreases with t follows from eq. (17), which incidentally also shows that $\tau_E(t) = qx\lambda(t)$ *increases* with t!

[11] An alternative approach would treat the problem as a competitive game; see Clark (1979) for a related model.

A routine application of the maximum principle leads to the results:

$$c_i'(E_i) = (p - \lambda_i)qx \tag{30}$$

where

$$\lambda_i = \text{constant}$$

and

$$E_i(t_f) = E_i^r(\text{if } t_f < T). \tag{32}$$

These conditions determine a unique solution for λ_i, t_f, and $E_i(t)$. Thus, given a fixed quota Q_i, the vessel will employ a decreasing level of effort $E_i(t)$ over the season, and will stop fishing at some time $t_f \leq T$. This solution is suboptimal (since $E_i(t)$ should remain constant), but is an improvement over the case of total catch quotas (see eq. (22)). The fact that each vessel is guaranteed the right to a quota Q_i *reduces* the incentive for a competitive "scramble" for the total catch, but some externalities remain, owing to the benefits obtained from fishing when the population abundance x is high.

Whereas some fish stocks are in fact heavily fished down every season (e.g. prawns; see Clark and Kirkwood, 1979), this case is probably exceptional. Otherwise, where catch per unit effort does not show a marked seasonal decline, a fixed catch tax $\tau = \bar{\tau}$ would produce a nearly optimal result.[12] Alternatively, the quotas Q_i can be determined so that $\lambda_i = \bar{\tau}$ for all i, and such quota allocations will lead to the same effort levels $E_i(t)$ as the tax $\bar{\tau}$. In other words, the efficiency implications of vessel quotas and catch taxes are identical – provided quotas are optimally allocated.[13]

What happens if the management authority allocates quotas improperly? If the quotas are nontransferable, it is clear that the fishery could become locked into a grossly inefficient pattern. If quotas are freely transferable (in whole or in part), however, it can be shown that, under suitable assumptions, quotas will in fact be transferred so as to achieve an optimal reallocation. To see this, assume that quotas are bought and sold on a quota market (assumed perfect), and let m denote the market clearing price. Then m represents an opportunity cost to each quota holder, whose perceived net revenue flow thus becomes

$$\pi_i(x, E_i) - mh_i = (p - m)qxE_i - c_i(E_i). \tag{33}$$

---

[12] In cases where the stock is greatly reduced each season, taxes or quotas could be set for shorter time periods; for example, vessels could have monthly quotas instead of annual quotas.
[13] The distributional implications of taxes and quotas are obviously quite different.

Thus, m plays the same role as a catch tax – see eq. (24). If the total quota $Q = \Sigma Q_i$ is equal to the optimum total catch, it is easy to see that the price m will be equal to the optimal tax τ (more precisely, the suboptimal constant tax $\bar{\tau}$); see Clark (1980) for details. Hence, the ultimate quota reallocation will be the optimal one.[14]

This completes our review of the simple (deterministic, lumped-biomass model) theory of fishery regulation. The results can be summarized briefly as follows: total catch quotas do not work at all, limited entry (licenses) works poorly if at all, both taxes and transferable allocated quotas work and are equivalent – all this in terms of achieving economic efficiency. Note, moreover, that taxes and allocated quotas can be used in combination, in which case the market clearing quota price m will simply equal the difference $\tau - \tau_0$ between the full optimal tax τ and the imposed tax τ_0. This means that the management authority can simultaneously achieve economic efficiency and any desired level of sharing of economic rent between fishermen (i.e. the original quota recipients) and the government.

Further research is required to extend our analysis to more realistic models, particularly involving greater biological complexity, as well as uncertainty. We conclude the present paper with a suggestion for modelling one important aspect of the multi-species fishery.

9. Multi-species fisheries

There may be no fishing vessel on earth that actually catches only a single species of fish, although some vessels (such as tuna purse seiners[15]) are highly specialized. In many areas, the fishery exploits a wide variety of species at several trophic levels. The management of such fisheries is obviously difficult and complex (May et al., 1979). The present practice is mainly to set total catch quotas for each species. presumably with the purpose of maximizing the overall "total catch", but the objectives of management are seldom clearly stated. It seems clear from our single-species model that (nonallocated) total catch quotas can be expected to lead to severe economic distortions in a multi-species fishery. The current situation in the fisheries of New England seems to bear this out.

---

[14]According to Scott (1979, p. 734): "at the level of formal analysis, price restriction is the dual of quantity restriction".

[15]Tuna boats in the Eastern Tropical Pacific catch two main species of tuna (not to mention some seven species of porpoise caught incidentally with yellowfin tuna schools).

10. The bicatch problem

One problem that has proved particularly troublesome is the "bicatch" problem. Roughly speaking, a bicatch is the incidental catch of some species other than the species sought after ("targeted") by the fisherman. This definition, however, is rather unsatisfactory since it depends upon a knowledge of the fisherman's motives. Let us agree here that bicatches simply refer to any species caught in conjunction with other species.

Two basic problems associated with bicatches can be identified: (a) the depletion problem, whereby species A becomes depleted primarily because it occurs as the bicatch of a targeted species (examples: halibut in the Northwest Atlantic; porpoises in the Eastern Tropical Pacific); and (b) the discard problem: marketable species are discarded at sea in order to accommodate more valuable species in the vessel's hold. For a discussion of the depletion problem, see Clark (1976, pp. 303–311); here we briefly describe a model pertaining to the discard problem.

Let $x_1, \ldots, x_m$ denote the biomass levels of m species. Assume the following catch relationships for a typical vessel:

$$h_j = q_j x_j E, \qquad j = 1, 2, \ldots, m, \tag{34}$$

where E denotes the vessel's fishing effort. Note that we are supposing here that fishing is completely *nonselective* – the mix of species caught at any given time cannot be influenced by the fisherman.[16] However, the proportion θ_j of each species *retained* can be selected, subject to

$$0 \leqslant \theta_j \leqslant 1. \tag{35}$$

As noted above, the fisherman would tend to discard fish of low value if his hold capacity were limited. We model this somewhat abstractly by means of the constraint

$$\sum_{j=1}^{m} \theta_j h_j \leqslant \overline{H}, \tag{36}$$

where $\overline{H}$ represents the hold capacity of the vessel.[17]

---

[16] For a fishery model pertaining to targeting of vessels on alternative species, see Anderson (1979).

[17] A more realistic model would concern itself with a vessel's operation during each fishing *trip*. Our simplified capacity constraint (36) seems to capture the main feature of the discard problem, however.

The profit maximization hypothesis for the unregulated vessel now becomes

$$\max\left\{ \sum_i p_j\theta_j h_j - c(E) \right\}$$

or

$$\max_{\theta_j, E}\left\{ \left(\sum_j \theta_j p_j q_j x_j \right) E - c(E) \right\} \tag{37}$$

subject to the constraints (35) and (36), where the p_j's denote the dockside prices of the m species. Consider first the discard aspect, i.e. treat E as a parameter and maximize (37) with respect to the θ_j's. We obtain the simple linear programming problem

$$\max_{0 \le \theta_j \le 1} \sum_{j=1}^{m} p_j q_j x_j \theta_j$$

subject to

$$\sum_{j=1}^{m} q_j x_j \theta_j E \le \overline{H}. \tag{38}$$

The solution is obvious: retain the most valuable species, up to hold capacity. Specifically, assume that

$$p_1 \ge p_2 \ge \cdots \ge p_m$$

and let $k(1 \le k \le m)$ be such that

$$\sum_{j=1}^{k} q_j x_j \le \overline{H}/E, \quad \text{but} \quad \sum_{j=1}^{k+1} q_j x_j > \overline{H}/E. \tag{39}$$

Then

$$\theta_1^* = \cdots = \theta_k^* = 1; \qquad \theta_{k+1}^* \in [0,1); \qquad \theta_{k+2}^* = \cdots = \theta_m^* = 0. \tag{40}$$

In short, the fisherman will simply discard "trash fish", i.e. the less valuable species. Which species are in fact "trash" depends on the total catch rate relative to capacity. In particular, this depends upon E.

Having determined $\theta_j^* = \theta_j^*(E)$, the profit-maximizing effort E is then obtained from

$$\max_{E}\left\{ \sum_{j=1}^{m} p_j q_j x_j \theta_j^*(E) E - c(E) \right\}. \tag{41}$$

We can now go ahead, in principle, to analyze the behavior of the fishery under alternative regulatory schemes. The details, which promise to be distinctly nontrivial, will be left to a future publication. Let us just note that, by taxing some species and (perhaps) subsidizing others, the management authority can in principle control discarding in any desired manner. The effects of quota regulation (allocated or otherwise) are less obvious; clearly quotas on valuable species might lead to their being discarded (or passed off as other species).

11. Conclusion

The business of catching fish in the sea is really a dynamic, competitive game, the outcome of which obviously depends very much on the rules under which it is played – that is, on the underlying *property rights* configurations (Cheung, 1970). It also depends on the extent to which these rules are adhered to. Like any common-property situation, the fishing game has the basic structure of the prisoner's dilemma – all fishermen (hence society) can come out better if they cooperate, but each individual competitor has an incentive not to cooperate.[18] The basic problem of fishery management, it would seem, is to devise a system of regulations (property rights) that will effectively resolve the common-property dilemma. Obviously no single approach is appropriate for all fisheries.

Currently quite a few fisheries are in the throes of having regulations introduced with the *intent*, at least, of improving economic performance. It is unfortunate that the recommendations proffered by professional economists have often had to rely upon seriously deficient models of the fishery. A cynic might say that it would require a miracle for the recommended regulations to have the desired effects.

The analysis offered in this chapter is still deficient, of course, but I have attempted to indicate that predictive models of fishery regulation are both essential and possible. Perhaps, with the need so great, other workers will be able to refine and generalize the model described here. Case studies, based on actual fishery data (biological and economic), would be most useful at this stage – provided that the models employed have some resemblance to the real world!

---

[18] This is more than the "free rider" phenomenon, although it is obviously closely related.

References

Anderson, L.G. (1977) *The Economics of Fisheries Management* (The Johns Hopkins University Press, Baltimore).

Anderson, L.G. (1979) "The Economics of Multipurpose Fleet Behavior", chapter 11 of this volume.

Cheung, S.N.S. (1970) "The Structure of a Contract and the Theory of a Non-exclusive Resource", *Journal of Law Economics*, 13, 49–70.

Clark, C.W. (1976) *Mathematical Bioeconomics: The Optimal Management of Renewable Resources* (Wiley-Interscience, New York)

Clark, C.W. (1979) "Restricted Access to Common-Property Fishery Resources: A Game-theoretic Analysis", in: P.-T. Liu, ed., *Dynamic Optimization and Mathematical Economics* (Plenum, New York) pp. 117–132.

Clark, C.W. (1980) "Towards a Predictive Model for the Economic Regulation of Commercial Fisheries", Canadian Journal of Fisheries and Aquatic Sciences, 37, 1111–1129.

Clark, C.W. and G.P. Kirkwood (1979) "Bioeconomic Model of the Gulf of Carpentaria Prawn Fishery", *Journal of the Fisheries Research Board of Canada*, 37, 11, 1304–1312.

Clark, C.W., F.H. Clarke and G.R. Munro (1979) "The Optimal Exploitation of Renewable Resource Stocks: Problems of Irreversible Investment", *Econometrica*, 47, 1, 25–47.

Clark, C.W. and G.R. Munro (1975) "The Economics of Fishing and Modern Capital Theory: A Simplified Approach", *Journal of Environmental Economic Management*, 2, 92–106.

Crutchfield, J.A. (1979) "Economic and Social Implications of the Main Policy Alternatives for Controlling Fishing Effort", *Journal of the Fisheries Research Board of Canada*, 36, 7, 742–752.

Crutchfield, J.A. and A. Zellner (1962) "Economic Aspects of the Pacific Halibut Fishery", *Fishing Industry Research*, 1, 1.

Gordon, H.S. (1954) "The Economic Theory of a Common-property Resource: The Fishery", *Journal of Political Economy*, 62, 124–142.

May, R.M., J.R. Beddington, C.W. Clark, S.J. Holt and R.M. Laws (1979) "The management of Multispecies Fisheries", *Science*, 205, 267—277.

Mendelssohn, R. and M.J. Sobel (1980) "Capital Accumulation and the Optimization of Renewable Resource Models", *Journal of Economic Theory*, 23, 243–260.

Munro, G.R. (1977) "Canada and Fisheries Management with Extended Jurisdiction: A Preliminary View," in: L.G. Anderson, Ed., *Economic Aspects of Extended Fisheries Jurisdiction* (Ann Arbor Science) pp. 29–50.

Reed, W.J. (1975) "A Stochastic Model for the Economic Management of a Renewable Animal Resource", *Mathematical Biosciences*, 22, 313–337.

Ricker, W.E. (1954) "Stock and Recruitment", *Journal of the Fisheries Research Board of Canada*, 11, 559–623.

Scott, A.D. (1955) "The Fishery: The Objectives of Sole Ownership", *Journal of Political Economy*, 63, 116–124.

Scott, A.D. (ed.) (1970) *Economics of Fisheries Management – A Symposium* (University of B.C., Institute of Animal Resource Ecology, Vancouver).

Scott, A.D. (1979) "Development of Economic Theory on Fisheres Regulation", *Journal of the Fisheries Research Board of Canada*, 36, 7, 725–741.

Smith, V.L. (1969) "On Models of Commercial Fishing", *Journal Political Economy*, 77, 181–198.